CRISIS, INEQUALITIES AND POVERTY

Studies in Critical Social Sciences Book Series

Haymarket Books is proud to be working with Brill Academic Publishers (www.brill.nl) to republish the *Studies in Critical Social Sciences* book series in paperback editions. This peer-reviewed book series offers insights into our current reality by exploring the content and consequences of power relationships under capitalism, and by considering the spaces of opposition and resistance to these changes that have been defining our new age. Our full catalog of *SCSS* volumes can be viewed at https://www.haymarketbooks .org/series_collections/4-studies-in-critical-social-sciences.

CRISIS, INEQUALITIES AND POVERTY

The Structural Inequities of Capitalism, from Lehman Brothers to Covid-19

FRANCESCO SCHETTINO
AND FABIO CLEMENTI

TRANSLATED BY
BETHAN BOWETT

Haymarket Books
Chicago, IL

First published in 2022 by Brill Academic Publishers, The Netherlands
© 2022 Koninklijke Brill NV, Leiden, The Netherlands

Published in paperback in 2023 by
Haymarket Books
P.O. Box 180165
Chicago, IL 60618
773-583-7884
www.haymarketbooks.org

ISBN: 979-8-88890-011-6

Distributed to the trade in the US through Consortium Book Sales and
Distribution (www.cbsd.com) and internationally through Ingram Publisher
Services International (www.ingramcontent.com).

This book was published with the generous support of Lannan Foundation,
Wallace Action Fund, and the Marguerite Casey Foundation.

Special discounts are available for bulk purchases by organizations and
institutions. Please call 773-583-7884 or email info@haymarketbooks.org for more
information.

Cover design by Jamie Kerry and Ragina Johnson.

Printed in the United States.

Library of Congress Cataloging-in-Publication data is available.

This book is dedicated to Giulio, Leon, and Noel

∵

Contents

Foreword

Almost two years since the outbreak of the Covid-19 pandemic, it is now overwhelmingly clear that it has had significant economic consequences and that the most economically vulnerable have been affected the most: the unemployed, low-wage workers, those on fixed-term contracts or working informally, and families and individuals with precarious incomes.

This asymmetric impact of the pandemic has spurred renewed interest on inequalities. In the wake of the 2008 global financial crisis, the issue of inequality made a sensational comeback in political and academic discussion. The Covid 19 crisis has furthered this interest and placed inequality firmly back at the centre of the economic policy debate. This book on crisis, inequality, and poverty is therefore very timely.

The first central theme of the book is the financial crisis, approached in a manner that differs significantly to the mainstream. We have become accustomed to thinking of the crisis as the unexpected breakdown in a supposedly 'natural' equilibrium. Market forces, as the economics establishment has been teaching for the last half century, if left to operate freely will lead to a natural equilibrium. Of course, the path towards equilibrium may have its bumps and glitches, but to paraphrase Keynes, *in the long run we will survive,* and the equilibrium will be reached. And in those cases where this does not seem to have happened, as with the 2008-2009 crisis, this can simply be put down to exogenous forces/agents that have failed to comply with the 'appropriate' market functioning.

This book, heir to a long-standing heterodox tradition that understands crises as inherent to the capitalist economy, provides us with an entirely opposing interpretation. For Schettino and Clementi, the crisis is both endogenous to and a direct consequence of the *modus operandi of* the capitalist mode of production. Capitalist production is not primarily oriented towards satisfying needs, but towards generating profits and continuing the process of capital accumulation ad infinitum. Goods and services are produced without the guarantee that they will be consumed, and thus their value realized. Therefore, not only does supply not generate its own demand (in contradiction to Say's law), but as the book explains, the increased competition typical of this *global* phase of capitalism increases the risk of more frequent and intense *overproduction crises*. This heightened global competition translates into both an ever-greater investment in capital aimed at increasing productivity and a series of measures aimed at reducing the cost of labour; the ultimate effect is – and herein lies the great contradiction – that these interventions lead to a reduction in the purchasing power of wages. As such, when goods and services reach the market, they run the risk of not finding adequate *effective demand.*

Overproduction and underconsumption therefore coexist but are considered by *mainstream* economic theory to be frictional and solvable through basic adjustments to prices (if the price of goods is lowered, consumption increases). However, such phenomena are structural, and so require intensive external intervention. Yet even where such interventions are carried out, the relief will only be short term, as the experience of 2008–2009 demonstrated to full effect. Indeed, in the long run they exacerbate the problem. Measures like the ones taken in 2008 quickly transform a local crisis (the American real estate sector) into a global financial crisis capable of putting at risk the solvency of entire states (Greece) and the very existence of a currency (the Euro).

Crisis and inequality, the second key theme of the book, are inextricably linked. The growing loss of purchasing power among the American and European working classes observed after the fall of the Berlin Wall translated into growing indebtedness. The problem of debt, particularly in the United States, was further aggravated by the introduction of new forms of credit and particularly low interest rates. The mere desire to have a roof over one's head or to guarantee a better future for one's children through access to higher education now requires families to accumulate more and more debt; households are spending more than they earn because they no longer earn enough to maintain a standard of living that had previously been the norm. Incomes therefore lost purchasing power and real household wealth declined, but only for the poorest 90%. In the United States, the income share of the poorest 90% was about 66% in 1970; within 40 years it had fallen to about 52%. Looking at financial and real estate wealth over the same period, this fell from 40% to about 25% (Piketty, 2014).

Inequality and income distribution have returned to the centre of the economic debate after having essentially been entirely absent during in the 1980s and 1990s, despite the fact that for the fathers of classical economics like Adam Smith, David Ricardo and John Start Mill, inequality was central. Leaving aside the reasons for the return of inequality (and poverty) to the limelight, I believe it is far more interesting to reflect on current trends. Today, thanks to research of authors like Piketty, Milanović and Zucman based on extensive analysis of data, we have a range of irrefutable evidence on global trends in inequality. Inequality is increasing in all countries, developed and under-developed. If we use accumulated wealth instead of income as a metric of inequality, the gap is even greater. Finally, in addition to the data on income surveys and tax records, we now also have access to information regarding the wealth hidden in tax havens (which forms the basis of Zucman's work). When all of this is taken together, we are confronted with a truly astonishing picture.

Lastly, it should be emphasized that the book is based on extensive and reliable elaboration of data. It would seem a paradox to reiterate the importance of data and correct data analysis at a time when we are effectively overwhelmed by statistics. However, the current crisis has made it clearer than ever that the supposed neutrality of numbers is a fallacy. Presentation of facts and figures is always underpinned by precise ideological assumptions, and even the constant bombardment of numbers can be understood as an attempt to muddy the waters rather than clarify the situation. Every day, for example, we are inundated with data on the progress of the pandemic, on the number of dead and infected, with a myriad of newspapers and websites making comparisons between different countries. Does all this data really help us to get an idea of the whole picture, and can we extrapolate from it, e.g., information that allows us to understand the economic impact of Covid-19?

Unfortunately, confusion abounds. There are a few reasons for this. Firstly, counting deaths, which historically was one of the first tasks that the administrative systems of modern states assigned themselves, is proving to be a rather arduous exercise and is subject to a great deal of manipulation. So much so that today, for example, despite the enormous effort to standardize statistics and administrative data at the European level, it is very difficult to compare deaths from Covid-19 in Italy, Belgium, the Netherlands or Spain, let alone make valid comparisons between European countries and other continents.

If, therefore, such 'visible' statistics as mortality rates are incomparable or even inaccurate, one wonders how precise projections on the economic impact of the crisis can be, especially as economic estimates are, by definition, (predicting the uncertain future) characterised by uncertainty. Yet such predictions are too often taken for granted, not only by the general public, but also by entrepreneurs, financial investors and governments, who make policy on the basis of estimates which, as discussed at length in the book, are often then subject to drastic revisions. Therefore, predictions that may turn out to be wrong immediately condition trends in the real economy, influencing, e.g., the investment decisions of an entrepreneur (the *animal spirits* of Keynesian memory), but even triggering dizzying speculation on financial markets to the point of jeopardising the financial solvency of a state.

The facts (and well-documented data) are stubborn, and this book demonstrates that very clearly. A series of concrete hypotheses are expressed and are supported by scrupulous use of available information. The reader is led through indicators and often complex numerical calculations, whose methodological assumptions and economic and social significance are explained in a comprehensive manner. While maintaining a rigorous scientific approach to the handling of data, the book succeeds in explaining in accessible terms what has happened to the world economy over the last ten years and how the crisis has had serious repercussions on the everyday lives of people across the globe. In other words, it presents us with a truth in sharp contrast to what we too often read in academic texts or the specialised economics press.

Rome, 15th November 2021
Vasco Molini
World Bank Economist, Washington DC, USA

Acknowledgments

This book is rooted in more than a decade of research on the subject, and in discussions we have had over recent years with colleagues, students, workers, and activists. Everyone we have been in contact with over the years, in their own different ways, has contributed, even unconsciously, to the preparation of this book. Among them, we cannot fail to mention Carla Filosa and Gianfranco Pala, together with the entire editorial staff of the Marxist journal La Contraddizione, which for three decades has provided an authentically class-based interpretation of the development of the current mode of production. In addition, the contribution of all those who participated in our first presentations – in particular Salvatore D'Acunto, Stefano Lucarelli and Domenico Suppa – was crucial in refining the entire work. Special thanks also go to the publisher of the first Italian edition, Giordano Manes, as well as to the translator Bethan Bowett and to Vasco Molini and Haider Khan who wrote the preface and the afterword respectively.

Finally, we are grateful for the extraordinary support and patience of our families without whom this book would never have seen the light of day.

Figures and Tables

Figures

Tables

CHAPTER 1

The Nature of the Crisis

1   Underconsumption, Prices and Profits

Since at least as far back as the post-war era the economics professors, pundits and professionals have had, among their various tasks, one of particular clarity of purpose. Their job is to construct an ideological denial of the both very evident and entirely scientific conflict between capital and labour, which in the wage/profit contradiction finds the means for the monetary transformation of the relation of exploitation.

This capitalist apologetics – uncritically espoused from the lectern and across the pages of textbooks – legitimises profit as the duly earned remuneration of the capitalist, with no mention at all of wages as the monetary form of the exploitation of human labour. On top of this, the supposed risks borne by capital – yet more justification for its right to profit – is given far greater prominence than the very apparent and all too material risk of actual death borne by workers or wage-labourers. Indeed, each year, more than around 2.3 million people die as a result of work-related incidents, amounting to an incredible 6,000 per day, with an additional 160 million work-related illnesses being reported in the same period (ILO, 2020c).

In April 2008, only months before the global crisis hit, the esteemed Bank of International Settlements published some uncomfortable data, that seemed to bring into question the supposed compatibility between the two forms of earnings (wages and profits). In technical terms it showed without a doubt that when the global total of wages paid to workers decreases, capital's profits increase. At the same time however, there was nothing in the numbers to suggest a general increase in the rate of accumulation. Consequently, what this data showed is that if there is a reduction in the share of the working day during which the worker sells *her* commodity (her labour-power) in order to reproduce herself, measured against an equal number of hours worked and level of productivity under previous conditions, the share appropriated by capital automatically increases, thus resulting in a higher rate of exploitation. By way of example, if we look at objective data for Italy, we see that in the two decades preceding the crisis, the so-called profit share grew in comparison to the wage share, resulting in a roughly 20% increase in the rate of exploitation of Italian workers. However, while such manoeuvres may have provided capital with some respite, they could essentially only act as a palliative against a crisis that had been looming on the horizon for many decades, since the end of the Bretton Woods era.

Both the academy and the media has worked hard to obscure the glaring fact that for many years, since at least the 1970s, labour incomes globally have been falling in both relative and absolute terms (see also ILO/OECD, 2015). Nevertheless, the materiality of the wage means that those who depend on it for survival are well aware that their living conditions have been progressively deteriorating, and that their future prospects will fall far short of their expectations. The proliferation of precarious contracts, and a generalised rise in prices that is clearly much higher than official statistics for developed economies would have us believe, has significantly undermined the living conditions of workers, to the embarrassment of those columnists, professors, and policy makers who post-2008 were falling over themselves to champion the importance of household 'purchasing power,' claiming to oppose increasing living costs.

However, purchasing power is not a hidden virtue or an occult entity but rather a concept very close to that of wages, which needs to be understood as quite distinct from the actual paycheck.

> The value of labour-power is determined, as in the case of every other commodity, by the labour-time necessary for the production, and consequently also the reproduction, of this specific article [...]
>
> MARX, 1867: 274

> Some of the means of subsistence, such as food and fuel, are consumed every day, and must therefore be replaced every day. Others, such as clothes and furniture, last for longer periods and need to be replaced only at longer intervals.
>
> MARX, 1867: 276

In other words, wages represent none other than the worker's potential to purchase the commodities needed to subsist and so to reproduce her commodity (labour-power), which, expressed through the course of the working day, allows for the functioning of capital through the mechanism of exploitation.

Wages and purchasing power are therefore conceptually one and the same:

> It is an extraordinarily cheap kind of sentimentality which declares that this method of determining the value of labour-power, a method prescribed by the very nature of the case, is brutal, and which laments with Rossi in this matter: 'To conceive capacity for labour (*puissance de*

travail) in abstraction from the workers' means of subsistence during the production process is to conceive a phantom (*être de raison*). When we speak of labour, or capacity for labour, we speak at the same time of the worker and his means of subsistence, of the worker and his wages.'
MARX, 1867: 277

As such, it is scientifically implausible to defend the purchasing power of workers whilst also hoping for a recovery in productivity that would restart the economy (i.e. boost capital accumulation), as this recovery would necessarily be premised on greater exploitation of labour-power and so on wage restraint.

Indeed, suffice a quick calculation to debunk the assertions to the contrary, which are based on inconsistent evidence and are used purely to create confusion. If we take into account the fact that capital accumulation is almost stagnant (GDP growth has for many years not exceeded 1–2% yearly), where the common objective is a growth in productivity this in fact means aiming for a growth in profits. Since the proverbial pie (i.e. total capital) remains essentially the same, the only means of realising greater profits is through a reduction in workers' wages (or rather by a 'freeing up' of wages from the more expendable portions, i.e. less qualified and more easily substituted, sections of labour). In a scenario such as this, it is in fact not impossible that workers will see a slight increase in their take-home pay, but we must remember that take-home pay represents only a part of workers' wages. In order to guarantee a rise in profits, it is possible to reduce the residual portion of the value of labour-power through, for example, cutting back on public services, or using inflation to reduce the quantity of commodities a worker can buy, bringing down the value of her labour-power.

This use of inflation to decrease the value of labour-power, in particular, has become widespread in recent years, accompanied by a mystifying narrative that serves to mask the real intent. An example of this is the way the euro has been singled out as the principal enemy of the Italian public's pockets, despite the change being purely formal, concerning essentially only the outward metal, paper, and electronic expression. This perception is born out of the fact that the introduction of the euro had a dramatic impact on many Italians (namely, wage earners) yet was a nice earner for the ruling classes (on top of allowing Italian capital to attach itself to a more stable currency bloc), who to an extent are able to set the cost of living themselves, securing their share of profits in the manner explained above.

A generalised increase in prices – affecting all but the more high-tech commodities – has also had an effect on the public finances. In this respect, the case of Italy is exemplary. Excepting basic necessities, for every purchase a

22% tax is taken by the state in the form of VAT. Impacting only indirectly on income, VAT is a deeply regressive form of taxation, essentially resulting in a transfer of resources from the poorest to the richest. It thus works in the opposite direction to the stated aims of the tax system. Observing Italian data from the last few years we see how revenue generated from VAT has sharply increased, driven, of course, by inflation. Indeed, since the introduction of the euro, VAT has come to represent more than half of the Italian state's revenue from indirect taxation and more than a quarter of its total tax income. Yet VAT is by nature less visible than other forms of direct taxation, meaning that in spite of Italy's dramatic public debt situation, it was possible to make commitments on pay rises and tax cuts while also promising profit increases. This use of indirect taxation as tool of deception is of course nothing new. Hobson, for example, in his study on imperialism observed that "to support Imperialism by direct taxation of incomes or property would be impossible [...] not chiefly on grounds of convenience, but for purposes of concealment" (Hobson, 1902: 104).

2   Excess Commodities, Excess Needs

An endemic characteristic of capitalism is its voracious appetite for profit; without this characteristic it would probably never have become the dominant mode of production. And it is precisely in the continual satisfaction of this insatiable need that the capitalist organism gets the sustenance to continue its frenetic course towards ineluctable death. Yet in its worst moments of suffering, the sick organism that is capitalism becomes more and more dependent on its substance of choice, which for its part becomes ever scarcer. Descending deeper into schizophrenia, it seeks out even more ruthless and efficient stratagems to guarantee its next hit. The assimilation of surplus-value – i.e. unpaid labour – is only the first part of the process, taking place at the point of immediate production: it is necessary but not sufficient. Indeed, as long as the extraction of surplus-value does not translate into profit, there is no accumulation of capital, and as such the purpose of production is still to be realised. Or in other words, if the commodity produced (whose value is composed of constant and variable capital as well as surplus-value) is not sold, the monetary transformation of unpaid labour has not yet taken place. The voracious appetite therefore remains unsatisfied, and capital is one step closer to its demise. In the case of a single capitalist, this means bankruptcy, in the case of capital as dialectical unit it means the end of its dominance as a mode of production.

To elaborate:

> The conditions for immediate exploitation and for the realization of that exploitation are not identical. Not only are they separate in time and space, they are also separate in theory. The former is restricted only by the society's productive forces, the latter by the proportionality between the different branches of production and by the society's power of consumption. And this is determined neither by the absolute power of production nor by the absolute power of consumption but rather by the power of consumption within a given framework of antagonistic conditions of distribution, which reduce the consumption of the vast majority of society to a minimum level, only capable of varying within more or less narrow limits.
>
> MARX, 1894: 325

For more than five decades, capital has been experiencing a crisis that materialises itself primarily as a generalised contraction in the profit margin, resulting mainly from an increase in the deployment of constant capital (machines and technical instruments) in relation to variable capital (labour). The attempts to resolve this contradiction – which remain futile insomuch as it is a contradiction immanent to the capitalist mode of production – appear in the 'first act' of our hypothetical drama in the form of a reduction in wages and the appropriation of unpaid labour during the process of immediate production, as we have seen. However, this method assumes that the mass of surplus-value (and value) can be inflated potentially ad infinitum. It also fails to provide any guarantee that in the 'second act' – the act of sale, or circulation stage – this surplus-value will indeed be realised, allowing for an adequate level of accumulation.

And the problem does not end here. In the suffocating climate resulting from the endemic crisis of a falling rate of profit, there exist the germs of another contradiction equally unsolvable and of equal gravity: a crisis of overproduction of capital and so also of commodities. In a historical period in which hunger and poverty are a daily reality for a significant part of the global population, a crisis of overproduction would seem paradoxical. Absent serious analysis, this contradiction is misperceived, provoking handwringing over the 'waste produced by consumerist culture.' In actual fact, it is precisely due to the nature of the capitalist mode of production that such a crisis occurs, especially when – the case since at least the fall of the Soviet bloc – the capitalist system has subsumed the entire planet, realising a global market that is now close to the point of saturation. The objective of capital is not the satisfaction of needs but the production of profit; the purpose of the production of commodities is their exchange not their use. It therefore follows that capital's anarchic *natural* tendency towards immense accumulation of commodities stands in scientific contrast to any type of social planning.

Thus, overproduction, during the 'first act,' becomes excessive where the value and surplus-value produced is not realised at the second stage, in other words, when commodities, goods or services, are produced but not sold. The reason for this can be related to the fact that

> the whole capitalist mode of production is precisely [...] a relative mode of productive, whose barriers are not absolute, but only absolute for it, on its basis. How else could there be a lack of demand for those very goods that the mass of people are short of [...] It is because it is only in this specific, capitalist context that the surplus product receives a form in which its proprietor can make it available for consumption as soon as it has been transformed back into capital for himself.
>
> MARX, 1894: 366

With the purpose of extracting the maximum surplus-value from labour-power, capital, contradictorily, is forever seeking to reduce labour power's exchange-value (i.e. wages, or also purchasing power). This then comes back to bite at the point when capital brings its commodities to market to find there is no *effectual demand*, due to the unequal distribution of resources it itself has established.

3   Pressure to Purchase, Debt and Speculation

Accordingly, the reduction of wages (and therefore of workers' purchasing capacity) is (paradoxically) what impedes the realisation of previously produced value and surplus-value, worsening the already critical situation resulting from the excess production of commodities. This dynamic – which originates in the production stage but becomes manifest in that of circulation – can claim a significant number of victims on both sides of the workers/capital binary, especially in acute periods of generalised crisis, and can send serious shockwaves through the capitalist system more broadly.

For its part, capital is very aware of this widespread purchasing incapacity among workers, the mantra of consumer sovereignty notwithstanding. Consequently, it has for some years been attempting to resolve the unresolvable, seeking to institute a way of life that (indirectly) induces populations to buy as much as possible, even where the material conditions are lacking. In

other words, even people without the sufficient wages must be constantly persuaded to buy an appropriate number of goods and services (why else would
we need the marketing industry?) As a result, by 2005, we were already seeing
a negative propensity to save, real consumption rising at more than 3% a year,
debts rising with a trend of over 11%, and a debt-to-available-income ratio of
126% (up 31% in 2011 from 2001 which had been thought of as a critical year).
In the US, for at least the last few decades, families have been spending more
than they earn, and the trend is only growing.

And these statistics are not confined to the US. Levels of debt have been rising all over the globe (starting well before the Covid-19 pandemic): households
in advanced economies like Japan, Australia and the United Kingdom have a
debt-to-income ratio of around 150%, while those in in northern Europe are
sometimes over 200%, meaning that the value of their purchases is double
their actual earnings. This strategy makes use above all of the instrument of
commodity fetishism, which, like a form of religiosity, offers the consumer a
path to spiritual elevation. Exploiting a state of generalised ideological confusion and cultural decline, it has been relatively easy to impose this type of
lifestyle, a lifestyle that, for as much as its real material conditions are effectively obscured, is based on possession and property. The mechanisms that
persuade the masses to make their way every weekend to the shopping centres
are countless and highly effective.[1] Expertly-designed visual and auditory stim-
uli attack the senses, driving consumers to spend without even considering the
use-value of the commodity they are buying; the only thing that matters is how
it looks and what it represents. Consequently, shop displays are always full of
discounted items, something that on first reflection would seem paradoxical.
And this is also why new forms of finance are being offered to cover truly paltry
sums, something that only a few years ago would have seemed bizarre.

Yet even this strategy has its limits and obstacles, which become particularly
apparent when there is a need to sell commodities subject to speculation by
financial capital, as we saw in the first decade of the 21st century.

Hence at the beginning of the new millennium when it was evident that
a large part of US workers no longer had the ability to keep on purchasing,
so-called financial operators, tasked with selling artificially over-valued real
estate, began offering finance to people that were clearly insolvent. The need
to unlock sources of money to be used as capital on the one hand, and to realise surplus-value on the other, were the root causes of the subprime crisis (and
not its effects).

---

1   The number of visitors to one of the biggest shopping centre in Rome is around ten times
    higher than the number of visitors to the Colosseum.

Again, the motivations of this seemingly so irrational speculative behaviour lie in the saturation of the global market, which has pushed transnational capital to the limits in its attempts to resolve the irresolvable crisis towards which it is precipitating. The overproduction of capital and commodities has given rise to the formation of an excess of money capital (though such excesses can also occur as a result of a momentaneous lack of investment outlets). Being capital and not wages, and having thus the objective of producing profit, this money capital is invested where there exists scope for self-valorisation. However, here profit is made not through production of new value but by detracting surplus-value from other capitalists. This movement of money capital thus renders itself entirely autonomous from the phase of immediate production. The first period of the current crisis (the early 70s) was emblematic in this regard. Here we saw how, through the so-called adjustment plans that redesigned sovereign institutions (many years later, the Greek case attests to the current state of the same project), and above all through the creation of ad hoc military dictatorships, excess money capital was put to use in speculation on the national bonds of poorer countries (in particular in Latin America). It was this speculation on public debt that contributed significantly to the formation of the vast sums of foreign debt that still today represents one of the main causes of widespread global poverty (Schettino, 2002).

However, our contemporary conditions are even more complex. Today, the general rate of profit is in free fall, ironically sustained by the only large power that identifies as socialist: China (Schettino et al., 2021). As a result, the risks involved in speculation have increased, as profit tied to speculative activity has been limited by the contraction of real accumulation. Faced with an outlook of this nature, it should not be surprising therefore that capital has turned to speculating on real estate and then on basic necessities, starving and killing millions of people in the process. While very conscious of the general lack of effectual demand, capital nevertheless understands that food and housing, being essential for living, are among its last few refuges. Where making profit from the immediate production of commodities is becoming a struggle, basic necessities remain free of the risks that can be associated with other types of commodities, with a guarantee of at least a base rate of profit. Many decry the immorality of this behaviour, but we must remember that capital, after all, was born "dripping from head to toe, from every pore, with blood and dirt" (Marx, 1867: 926). The aim of capital is to make profit; philanthropy does not come into this at all.

In 2007/2008 the subprime bubble burst to devastating effect. A decade and a half later, however, the intricate system of hedging created by dollar capital, through the invention of derivatives of derivatives (known as 'structured finance') that obscure the real nature of the securities being sold, has simply displaced the worst outcomes of this crisis (the precise means of this will be the subject of subsequent chapters). These complex forms of finance are not a solution to the crisis, which on the contrary seems to be deteriorating, and in many ways they have only made its effects more unpredictable.

4   Financial Speculation and the Ratings Agencies

[The speculator] does not hold securities in the hope of sharing in the higher profit – as an investor does – but seeks to gain by buying and selling his securities. [...] If all speculators played the same side of the market, that is, if they all simultaneously placed the same higher or lower value on securities[3]' there would not be any speculative gains at all. [...] The different valuations made by buyers and sellers, at a particular time, result in losses for some speculators and gains for others.

> HILFERDING, 1910: Chapter 8

Vulgar economics actually does nothing more than interpret, systematize and turn into apologetics the notions of agents trapped within bourgeois relations of production.

> MARX, 1894: 956

In the months immediately following the financial crisis of September 2008, we became used to seeing unthinkable, seemingly apocalyptic sums flashing across our screens, each day worse than the one before. The situation seemed so out of control that the international agencies were forced to regularly update, or rather downgrade, assessments they had made only the week before. Even the IMF had to rewrite its *World Economic Outlook,* as the forecasts for global recession made in October 2008 (IMF, 2008) were already seeming too hopeful. Finally, the necessary courage was found to admit that 2009 would be a devastating year to say the least, and that greener pastures may not have appeared for much time to come (though in hindsight, even those predictions were too optimistic). The image of 'no light at the end of the tunnel' became a commentators' staple, as all the global indexes for industrial production were in free fall. Emblematic was Japan's 12.8% reduction in production, and a similar two-digit reduction was registered by all advanced economies. What this demonstrated was that at the global level – China and a few other Asian economies aside – the capitalist class was responding to the effects of the crisis with a dramatic cutback in the use of industrial capital. This resulted in the destruction of large parts of variable capital, perhaps capital's last available resort in terms of kick-starting accumulation, at least in the short- to mid-term. Or to put it in far simpler terms, masses of workers were being laid off across the globe. The ILO estimated in 2009 that around 50 million men and women would be laid off from jobs in production that year, creating a pool of 200 million 'newly-liberated' workers (in Marx's terms) to add to the vast number (around 1 billion) of people who have yet to ever access the job market (ILO, 2009).

Capital's inability to make use of the abundance of money capital that has been accumulating since the 1970s, coupled with the contradictory impossibility of realising as profit all the previously-produced surplus-value, has as a matter of course led its agents to make widespread use of speculative instruments – i.e. financial markets – in order to scrape together as much indirectly produced surplus-value as possible. In the process, they have pushed up the rate of global accumulation, causing misery to the working class and some fellow capitalists as well (who become thus 'hostile brothers'[2]).

However, this reality is hidden from us, turned on its head through a mechanism of conscious deception. The move to place the blame for our current conditions on the financial system is in fact fruit of a precise strategy designed to mask a *real* systemic crisis of the capitalist mode of production. Still today, we are led by the media and the economics establishment to believe that the 2008 crisis was simply the result of speculative activity on the part of certain unscrupulous individuals, whose irresponsible behaviour infected sectors of the economy that were otherwise perfectly good and healthy.

The deregulation of the financial markets – a process which, uncoincidentally, began at the end of the 1970s – is presented as the cause of all our current and future woes, and not, as it should correctly be understood, as the instrument required by global capital as a system to combat a crisis that had been dragging on for more than half a century. The capitalist system was, to put it bluntly, well and truly addicted to those 'toxic' securities. This is how we should interpret the events of recent decades that have gradually revealed to us the mountainous quantities of derivatives and junk securities in circulation, an enormity directly proportional to the capitalism's growing incapacity to accumulate capitalism.

Nevertheless, new means are always being found to obscure the real causes of these dramatic circumstances. The very framing of the question is a distortion of reality, conforming instead to a desire to propagandise on the part

2 "The capitalists, like hostile brothers, divide among themselves the loot of other people's labour which they have appropriated so that on an average one receives the same amount of unpaid labour as another." (Marx, 1861–3: vol. 31: 264).

of the various agents of capital, ubiquitous across our media under the guise of 'the expert.' It would be entirely contrary to their mission to admit that engendering crises is part and parcel of the dominant mode of production's natural development, or, in other words, to admit that what we are currently experiencing is not the exception but the rule. The explanation for the crisis that attributes it to exogenous causes is instrumental to preserving the mainstream's myth of capitalism's capacity for perfect equilibrium when freed from all interference. To these ends - and not because they were genuinely seeking the truth - as a response to the crisis, the dominant class began a hunt to root out the 'rotten' elements of the system, singling out a few dozen supposed causes with great rapidity, though of course all was quietly forgotten about some time after. The only party whose guilt was universally acknowledged and maintained were the ratings agencies, which are still seen by many today as the principal, if not only, real authors of the crisis.

Yet if speculation became the scapegoat for a crisis of which it was in fact effect or mere manifestation, the rating agencies nevertheless did have much to answer for. That the crisis had far deeper structural roots does not absolve them of their share of responsibility.

To determine what part they played, it is important to lay out exactly how the 'trinity' (Moody's, Standard & Poor's, and Fitch Ratings) of international ratings agencies operate. The history of the ratings agencies begins in the US at the beginning of the 20th century, following the development in the rail sector of bond issuance as a financing tool. It was precisely the high rate of insolvency associated with these bonds in the run up to the first great crisis of capitalism[3] that led John Moody to publish the first assessment of the creditworthiness of a bond issuance. Sometime later, Standard Statistics – which went on to merge with the publishing house Poor's Publishing to become Standard and Poor's – and Fitch Ratings began to offer the same services, continuing to do so until 1975 when they were granted the status of "nationally recognized statistical rating organisation" by the United States government.

A century later and the activity carried out by the ratings agencies, now a global operation, has grown to impressive proportions. Coming into the second decade of the 21st century, Moody's has branches in 17 states (with a 40% share of the market); Standard and Poor's publishes 23,000 ratings of private and public companies, as well as sovereign states (with a 39% share of the market); while Fitch Ratings, currently the smallest of the agencies (16% of the

---

3   We refer here to the crisis which began around 1870.

total market), operates across almost all continents, though with more limited activities.

To give an idea of the weight the ratings agencies have within the current hierarchy of global capital, suffice to note that as early as the turn of the new millennium at least half of all businesses with a turnover of more than $500 million received either a Moody's rating, an S&P's rating, or both. In Europe this number was less, just under 15% in the Netherlands and the UK for the same period, 5% in France and just over 2% in Italy and Germany. Over a decade later, it is very possible to imagine that the number of European private and public entities soliciting ratings will have grown significantly. What is important to note is that until the 1980s the work of these agencies was carried out for free, as the agencies were able to fund themselves through the sales of the physical copies of their reports. As technology has evolved, however, and as electronic documentation has become commonplace, it is the companies being assessed that pay, raising suspicions of potential corruption, especially as there are known to be cases where the rating was less than objective.

Over time, with the process of financial disintermediation – i.e. with the creation of new forms of liquidity (money capital) through the issuance of debt securities, made all the more necessary by the steady progression of the crisis whose worst consequences we are now experiencing – the importance of the ratings agencies has increased significantly, conferring on the 'Big Three' a delicate and decisive role in the current inter-capitalist struggle.

The infamous rating itself essentially consists of an alphabetical scale (from AAA to D) with an additional +/- and then an outlook report. This symbology is the synthesis of all the different kinds of information the agencies collect, analyse, elaborate and then communicate in their final assessment, expressed by that alpha-numerical code that represents an evaluation of a debt issuer's creditworthiness, i.e. their ability to pay back both the sum owed and the interest accrued in a timely and correct manner.

The determination of the rating (and the associated outlook) is based on an analysis of a set of indicators detailing the characteristics of the company or state being rated. Without going into too much detail, this analysis – which looks at both quantitative and qualitative elements – encompasses a survey of the sector, of the company's competitive position, and its economic/financial situation (especially in the case of a sovereign bond rating). Supplementary documentation, e.g. a document on the state of the country's economy and finances for government paper, or a business plan in the case of a private business, can also be taken into account. Following this inspection, financial projections are drawn up producing an evaluation of the company's (or state's) debt capacity (its ability to repay the money it has borrowed), and then finally,

using highly sophisticated (so we are told) methods of quantitative data processing, an analysis of the company's risk sensitivity is produced, focusing on
the potential for stability in scenarios of particular difficulty. Once this proce-
dure has been completed, the final judgement can be pronounced, expressing not the absolute probability of default but rather the company's relative
ranking within a defined category. Importantly, the 'Big Three' keep their statistical and econometric models entirely secret. This lack of transparency is
something that certainly contributes to the suspicions of manipulation in the
ratings process, as the agencies are essentially not subject to any form of third-
party oversight.

The rating can be an assessment of either an issuer's solvency in general,
without reference to any specific debt issuance, or the solvency of a particular
offering. In the case of sovereign bonds – the centre of much debate in Europe
over recent decades – the rating is extended to cover the different classes or
series of securities (e.g. BTPs, CCTs, BOTs etc. for Italy). Given the scarcity
of information on the market – a golden rule in the inter-capitalist struggle,
dressed-up by the media as 'healthy competition' – investors use the ratings,
theoretically a 'technical' instrument, when making decisions about which
securities to purchase (or rather to whom to offer credit). Portfolio decisions
are thus made by weighing alternatives against each other in an objective manner, and then against the individual investors' subjective propensity to risk.
Such choices take on particular significance in a crucial period such as our
current crisis – characterised by a paradoxical difficulty in accessing credit in
concurrence with an excess of money capital – as the assessments made by
the Big Three have significant influence over the how investment capitalists
will behave, directing them towards those companies with a more favourable
rating, which for the creditor means a greater probability of having the capital
and interest returned as per the contract.

Aside from this main function, their *raison d'être*, in 2003 the Securities
Exchange Commission identified other services the ratings agencies could
offer, both for those that use the ratings to make investment decisions and for
the companies rated. Among these many extra functions are services relating
to containing the cost of capital, simplifying private placements and negoti-
ated transactions, and boosting investor confidence in financial management.
In addition to this, ratings are frequently used as input by businesses in their
investigations into possible price misalignments in purchases and sales of
securities (their own and others); by brokers to persuade the middle-classes
to buy glossed-up share packages; and in the negotiation of private contracts,
where a future declassification of a company's creditworthiness can imply certain consequences as per special clauses. On top of this, when we consider

the fact that the ratings of government bonds have taken on such importance that they could arguably even have the potential to be the cause of the fall of the eurozone – much as that remains unlikely – it becomes clear how the ratings agencies have come to play such a central role in the current phase of capitalism.

So, while the ratings system has the appearance of functioning according to rigid procedures, in reality no one can say how reliable they really are. Indeed, the agencies themselves maintain that their assessments must be understood as opinions regarding the general creditworthiness of an issuer or of a particular security based on the main risk factors, and are not intended as recommendations to buy, sell or negotiate. Therefore, as the Big Three claims (we refer to an S&P disclaimer but the other two use a similar formula), beyond identifying obvious risks, the ratings are not a failsafe representation of reality. It is undeniable that in general, or at least in around 80–90% of cases, they provide a fairly accurate description of a (private or public) entity's solvency, as many studies have confirmed. Nevertheless, there remains a margin of error that cannot be ignored, and which has at times produced some highly unpredictable outcomes.

In all the major catastrophes in capitalism's recent history, in fact, the Big Three have had a hand, falling spectacularly short in their task by failing to identify crucial bankruptcies. The first major 'error' of this kind was Enron, which despite sizeable losses as early as 2000 was still rated by S&P in November 2001 (a month before the collapse) as BBB. Only slightly less disastrous was the case of WorldCom which was rated as a modest BB just two months before revelations of serious accounting fraud brought the company to its knees. The same thing happened again with the Italian company Parmalat, which maintained its BBB rating right up to two weeks prior to default. However, the agencies' shining moment came with the subprime crisis. Less than sixty days before it went bankrupt, Lehman Brothers was rated A, A2 and A+ by S&P's, Moody's, and Fitch Ratings respectively. The same went for AIG, Bear Stearns, Freddie Mac and even Fannie Mae, which boasted a propitious triple A only seven months before it had to be bailed out by the US government. On top of this were the consistently misleading findings on those collateralised debt obligations (CDO) that were in reality packed full of toxic mortgage-backed securities, which thanks to their good rating made their way onto the balance sheets of investors everywhere, including in Asia and Europe, definitively compromising the entire global financial system.

As much, then, as the agencies are at pains to stress that their ratings are the result of an objective analysis of quantitative and qualitative data, their involvement in the cases mentioned above raises many questions. Even if it

remains true that their judgement has for the most part been sound, the excep-
tions represent a glitch truly difficult to ignore. However, the essential point
to understand is that the handing out of 'inaccurate' ratings during the global
economy's most critical moments, as least as far as the last half century is concerned, has negatively impacted many market actors, but, crucially, favoured
others. To put it bluntly, the effect of the so-called subprime crisis has been to
destroy any façade of independence the ratings agencies might have retained
up to that point. Subsequently, where any semblance of reliability persists, it is
taken with far more precaution.

Yet as we have argued, blaming inaccurate ratings for halting the accumulation of global capital and so for a crisis that dates back to at least the 1970s
is the product of a twisted logic. The ratings agencies, like the financial/spec-
ulative system as a whole, are an integral part of the current capitalist formation, and their importance grew precisely because of a general worsening in
conditions for global capital. The crisis of overproduction, making it necessary
to invest as fictious capital, has inevitably valorised the role of the Big Three,
which took on an ever more central position. The rapidity of the expansion
of so-called mobile capital (i.e. fictitious or speculative capital), an effect of
the crisis, means that speculators need to have ready access to information
regarding the creditworthiness of a security. Determinations of a company's
or a state's solvency have thus taken on a value that over a century ago, when
Moody first decided to rate US railway bonds, would have been unimaginable.

So if it is an error of logic to attribute causal responsibility to credit ratings, a
far more accurate narrative is one which places the Big Three within a context
of inter-capitalist struggle, viewing them not as third parties or external enti-
ties but as capital proper. These very powerful businesses, as capital, behave as
such, in a competitive struggle that in times of crisis becomes ever more acute.
Indeed, to understand this we need only look at the agencies' owners: the largest shareholders of Moody's are Warren Buffet (via Berkshire Hathaway Inc.),
The Vanguard Group, and to a lesser extent, BlackRock.

The presence of Warren Buffet, among the top 10 richest people in the world,
is indicative of the real nature of the Big Three. Berkshire Hathaway, aside
from its involvement in Moody's, holds significant (often controlling) stakes
in many important dollar firms. This includes banking (American Express,
US Bancorp), foodstuffs (Coca Cola), pharmaceuticals (Johnson & Johnson,
Procter & Gamble) as well as traditional industrial sectors such as PetroChina,
and even large retail chains including Wal-Mart. The largest shareholder of
a rating agency is also, therefore, the owner of some of the most important
dollar companies, business which themselves make use of the ratings of their
securities. As such, it is not at all misplaced to view this as a potential conflict

of interest. We can also take Capital World Investors, a subsidiary of the Capital Group, which manages thousands of investment funds, including hedge funds, overseeing around $1,000 billion in securities. It is only natural that a company involved in activity so sensitive to the effects of ratings would be a majority shareholder in McGraw-Hill, the giant publishing empire that owns Standard and Poor's. Ownership of Fitch Ratings is slightly more complex: 60% of the shares are held by the French finance company FIMALAC, hence by capital that is presumably euro capital, with 40% held by the media giant Hearst Corporation which owns hundreds of newspapers and magazines in the US, as well as TV and radio operations.

With the emergence of the crisis of 2008–2012, the media attention given to the credit ratings agencies exploded. It has become commonly accepted that the negative ratings given to Greek sovereign bonds, as well as to other EU states excepting Germany and very few others, conditioned the development of the eurozone sovereign debt crisis, pushing euro capital into a tight corner and even bringing the existence of the single currency into question (this will be covered in greater detail in subsequent chapters).

The groundwork for the attack on the Greek public debt, as will later be explained in more depth, was laid by US fictitious capital (headed by George Soros), which had identified in sovereign debt the Achilles heel of its principal antagonist: the euro. It is therefore precisely as part of a conflict among factions of capital associated with different currencies, that we should understand the (often deliberately irresponsible) activities of the ratings agencies. The continual declassification of the sovereign bonds of eurozone states, on top of the heavy-handed austerity measures that placed further burdens on production especially in the so-called PIIGS (Portugal, Italy, Ireland, Greece and Spain), inevitably persuaded many short- and long-term investors (most of them Chinese) to move their liquidity across the Atlantic. At a time when credit was hard to come by (this was, after all, the period known as the credit crunch), this arrival of liquidity was a godsend for dollar capital. Due to the action taken by the ECB in response, this phenomenon went relatively unobserved, however. Faced with this large-scale withdrawal of investment, the ECB was forced to act like the Federal Reserve and implement a form of quantitative easing, flooding the European market with liquidity so as to avoid potential blockages in the circulation and production of European capital. As such, the eurozone markets continued functioning, but the consequences this had for the value of the euro were all too predictable. In this climate of widespread instability, it lost much of the attractiveness it had had prior to 2008. So much so that the general trend towards the euro substituting the dollar as the currency of international reserves, dating back to the early 2000s, was stalled and even reversed; the decisions, e.g., of the Chinese government are indicative in this respect.

The political and economic implications of decisions made by the ratings agencies were therefore substantial. Their ability to influence the choices and therefore the movements of capital, movements that in today's world can occur in the space of seconds, confers on them great power. Today, the governments of those states that found themselves in the most difficulty, principally euro-zone states, seem less concerned to comment on the frequent downgrading of private or public securities. More than a mere distrust of the ratings system, however, this attempt to discredit its value is arguably a strategic response, which should be framed within a context of intense inter-capitalist conflict.

So, while their methodologies are kept secret, the work of the ratings services can, broadly speaking, be considered technically valid. However, as a faction of capital themselves and being owned by some of the same monopolies they rate and which are the principal agents in the current currency conflict, it is only natural that their modus operandi will be less than transparent. This is entirely in keeping, after all, with the logic of capitalist competition, especially where what they are rating is essentially an enemy company or state. To consider these agencies as the root of the crisis is a serious misreading of reality. Nevertheless, it is important to recognise the role they have played in determining the direction of development of the global crisis.

5   Currency Conflict

What we see emerging through the events described above is a conflict between the dollar and the euro which since the single currency's introduction has brought about a qualitative shift in the nature of inter-capitalist competition. In order to correctly comprehend how the concept of currency areas functions in the current phase of capitalism, it is necessary to define the role played by money within the capitalist mode of production. This theoretical clarification – by no means exhaustive – becomes even more important when we consider the uses and abuses of the concept of money, which distort and obscure the true essence of the current currency conflict. Indeed, we should remember that economics as a discipline is based on an assumption that money is a merely a veil; an inessential element in the production of commodities and so, in our terms, in value and surplus-value. In actual fact, nothing could be further from the truth.

"The riddle of the money fetish," to use Marx's terms, is so "dazzling to our eyes" (Marx, 1867:187) that the "dominion of the accursed metal [...] appears as sheer insanity," an insanity that emerges from the economic process itself. Yet this madness is what really "appears," in all its inadequacy, to the popular consciousness, which "therefore perceives money in its determinations of measure and coin as arbitrary, as inventions conventionally introduced for the sake of convenience [...]" (Marx, 1858: 486) It is unsurprising, then, that according to the *common sense* (but not *good sense!*):

> the consciousness of men, especially in social orders declining because of a deeper development of exchange-value relations, rebels against the power which a physical matter, a thing, acquires with respect to men, *against the domination of the accursed metal which appears as sheer insanity.*
>
> MARX, 1858: 487, emphasis added

This is the illusion of an epoch, the mere appearance of a reality whose laws of movement are elsewhere, lying in the production and circulation of capital, commodities and surplus value.

Ours is a period in which the alarmist cries of monetary 'storms' and unending currency wars are detached in the minds of the general public from the real crisis, which it is claimed can be exorcised or shut off into discrete domains. In other words, the public imaginary is missing Marx's far more powerful conception of the 'storm' he warned those 'monetarists' of his day about, theorists who were unable to see the specificity of the function of money capital, or rather of the money-form of capital.

> It was no longer a matter of single economic phenomena – such as the depreciation of precious metals in the sixteenth and seventeenth centuries confronting Hume, or the depreciation of paper currency during the eighteenth century and the beginning of the nineteenth confronting Ricardo – but of big storms on the world market, in which the antagonism of all elements in the bourgeois process of production explodes [...]"
>
> MARX, 1859: 412

The scientific and ideological errors and limits of the monetarists of Marx's time – though even today the situation is not much different – consisted in an inability to identify the cause of crisis in the conflict between the different elements of capitalist production. Instead, they sought both its origins and its solution in the "the sphere of currency, the most superficial and abstract sphere of this process" (Marx, 1894: 681), extending the dogmas of bourgeois political economy from the laws of the circulation of metal to those of paper and credit. The bourgeois economists' theory of money is "singularly apposite since it gave to a tautology the semblance of a causal relationship" (Marx, 1894: 681).

The transnational concatenation that changed the configuration of inter-imperialist struggle so that it was no longer cleanly divided along nation-state lines, has resulted in capital seeking greater penetration into the global market. As such, the predetermination of an investment's association with a currency area has come to override its mere geography, something that would also explain why some financial centres develop at the expense of others.

In this way, today more than ever we see how these developments have to do with much more than the geographical circulation of actual money. It would be a grave mistake therefore to view money and currency as simply a superfetation, as something separate from industrial strategy, as is still commonly the case. On the one hand are grouped the characteristics of a desperate pursuit of the 'real economy' within the current international division of labour: production chains; dislocations; outsourcing, subcontracting on a global scale; Euro-Asian corridors and other transport infrastructure; talk of 'competitive advantage'; centralisation and transformation in international ownership structures; the upending of the relationship between supra-state organisms and nation states; privatisations (where they are seen to be more efficient); the list could go on. On the other are the features of a 'monetary economy' where the struggle is for a hegemonic redefinition of the currency areas towards a 'unified' global market.

The issue of currency areas comes to the fore when we look at which cost components are expressed in which currencies, and then in which currency the future sales price is presented. From this we can deduce some key arguments. The current structure of the production costs (and to a lesser extent circulation costs) of the various chains or sub supply chains in the different currency areas, rather than within the spheres of influence of the opposing geographical poles, includes the impact of exchange-rate fluctuations on invoicing. It also implies the reorganisation – centralisation plus decentralisation – of the whole system of industrial production on a global scale, with a consequent international re-composition of dependent labour. In this way, neo-corporatist ideology confirms itself as the supreme form of global control and conflict repression.

In other words, if we continue to refer to separate and contrasting imperial 'poles' we risk getting the wrong end of the stick. Currency areas, in contrast, – while operating from clearly identifiable geographic centres with their corresponding political and economic strategies for global hegemony, meaning they are by no means de-territorialised – cut through the entire global market.

In today's world, a large transnational company operating across the three imperialist continents, perhaps following a merger, is still free to decide to use the currency most attractive to it. In this sense, the concept of transnational imperialism – seeing as it concerns companies' mergers, acquisitions and foreign investments – would seem more appropriate to describe something that retains roots within the existing productive structures of the various locations, yet at the same time moves its centre of gravity to the given currency area (the set currency for its costs and prices), regardless of its geographical location.

The currency areas therefore have nothing to do with revenue expenditure (as enormous as this may be) but rather relate to capital payments (i.e. investments used as a tool for world domination). In other words, they operate on a plane quite distinct to that of aggregate demand.

Production on a global scale implies both a logical and real sublation on the part of the largest sections of capital above all. It also corresponds that the circulation of the commodities produced must satisfy effectual demand (investment plus consumption), i.e., the whims or necessities of those who have enough of the chosen currency to pay for it. Therefore, when we take into account the totality of the many similar transnational circumstances, we see that effective control of capital (operative but also speculative) no longer depends on the place in which that particular capital resides – or from which it emerges to then expand into other nations (multi-nations), as was the case in the classic nation-state phase of imperialism – but rather, dominant states are now forced to direct all their real power towards establishing the supremacy of a certain currency over others through currency conflict. Consequently, each currency area is, in the last instance, in the control of the central banks, the stock markets, and the governments of those imperialist nation-states who are able to redefine their role as such. The attention given to exchange-rate fluctuations in terms of possible price and cost differences is such that this has direct effects on the rate of profit (not on the surplus-value produced). For this reason, it concerns circulation and production equally, though in such a way that the reduction in circulation costs (fake production expenses – *faux frais*) becomes indirectly determinate even in production strategies.

Hence why capital has turned its fleeting attention to the economy created in the sphere of circulation. This means both the economy created through what can be defined as 'ordinary' circulation, and through what we can call 'forced' circulation (in reality production proper as it includes subcontracting), which is centred on unequal exchange with dominated countries (by means of an oppressive redistribution – i.e. plunder or robbery – of the global surplus-value, which has become essentially static, or at least is insufficiently dynamic).

Thus, a cost advantage is achieved through a reduction of (true or 'false') production costs, i.e. through reducing both the costs inherent to (sub) production in the strictest sense and those arising from circulation. So where capital broadens the scale of its activities, this influences not only the costs of circulation in a strict sense but extends to the economy of all business costs (costs relating to subcontracting and outsourcing, which, in the early days of capitalism, in all the different parts of the world being progressively conquered by the new mode of production, coincided with the actions of the so-called compradors). A currency's capacity to influence the transnational economy (the dollar currently being the most powerful) is therefore tied to its ability to control the currency area. Wealth produced elsewhere is transferred by paying lower production costs, in a local currency for example, and selling at a higher price (something which has in fact happened regularly over the course of capitalism's history).

If this reduction in overall costs occurs solely in the sphere of circulation, then it represents simply a transfer of wealth, and does not generate a net increase in value and surplus-value. In other words – looking solely at the rate of profit, whose cyclical collapse is what capitalists' aim to counter – there is no effect on the numerator (surplus-value) of the ratio that defines the rate of profit, as it can only a reduce the amount of advance capital required, i.e. act only on the denominator, through an indiscriminate reduction in all costs. There is therefore a 'negative' limit, which can be significantly relaxed through compression of the costs that contain it, but which nevertheless will be reached. As such, unless the numerator (surplus-value) is increased – i.e., unless the accumulation of capital on a global scale can be resumed – this tinkering around with prices is really only palliative.

In this sense, the big financial holding companies' production plans for each sector, or rather supply chain, has great strategic importance. This strategy is inherent both to the choice to relocate costs (production costs, subcontracting most of all, but also circulation costs in the strict sense) to the various dominated countries, and to sales prices, depending on which currency area the different countries have as their main reference point. As such, if we examine these holding companies' balance sheets, it is important to pay particular attention to the composition of costs and the definition of prices (the 'value chain' as Harvard Business School professor and Institute for Strategy and Competitiveness director Michael Porter would say), in order to evaluate their activities as a whole. It is here, therefore, that the question of costs arises. Where costs are paid in less valuable local currencies, in comparison to the final sales prices which are still mostly invoiced in dollars, the difference arising from the bearing of one currency area on the other translates into greater (or smaller) profit.

The media depiction of currency conflict as a simple question of the prices of different currencies – resulting from mere exploitation of the exchange rate – is useful for the ruling classes because it obscures the fierce conflict between 'hostile brothers' (factions of capital), which in the current phase has developed into a struggle to subsume the largest number of dominated countries within a currency area, in the hope of countering the natural compression of the rate of profit. This is done by working to lower the cost structures of financial holding companies in the dominant countries in relation to the final sales prices. However, as this can only incidentally alter the mass of new value produced, especially in a phase of acute crisis such as that which we are currently living through, its effect is to damage in inverse proportion other capitals' capacity to accumulate in an already sluggish environment.

CHAPTER 2

Dollar vs. Euro

From the 2010 Attack to the 2015 Surrender

1   An Evening in Manhattan

2010 was one of the coldest winters of recent decades. Manhattan was no longer the land of plastic smiles and exclusive parties in fancy apartments: even in this glittering city the devastating effects of the crisis that followed the collapse of Lehman Brothers were beginning to be felt. Rough sleepers and beggars were no longer confined to the usual pockets of deprivation but had begun to haunt the realms of prosperity; the crude reality of the capitalist mode of production manifested in flesh.

Yet the familiar smoke and smells remained. And it is precisely an Allenesque dinner of roasted lemon chicken and prime-cut fillets that we can imagine was taking place at the house of a small broker (of Monness, Crespi, Hardt & Co.) on the night of February 8th, 2010. Gathered there that night were various American finance gurus, some of the global working-class's most ferocious enemies, including representatives of the Soros Group, SAC Capital Advisors, Greenlight Capital, Brigade Capital and Paulson and Co. (not the same Paulson who resigned as CEO of Goldman Sachs to serve as Bush's Treasury Secretary, who was said to have opposed the plan masterminded at the dinner). Though these somewhat unremarkable names may belie their avaricious potential, each of their meetings would represent a serious threat to the lives of millions of workers everywhere. As the managers of the some of the weightiest hedge funds in the world, the converging of their interests was sure to create a financial storm reaching to every corner of the globe.

The crisis of the late 90s (Mexico, the Asian tigers, Russia, Brazil) had already demonstrated the destruction these hedge funds were capable of causing when they moved their fictitious capital *en bloc*, fictitious capital referring to a peculiar form of capital's (non) existence. What is important to bear in mind however is that it is not merely the most 'evil' or parasitic sections of capital that perpetrate this kind of speculative activity – a phenomena that corresponds to the most acute phase of the crisis cycle driven by overproduction – but rather the entire capitalist class. The financial derivatives that have formed the basis of all the stock market meltdowns of modern times are precisely this capital in fictitious form. They represent bets on the fluctuations of the markets and on future valuations (futures and options contracts that allow investors to profit from the change in an asset's price over time, futures and options based on indexes rather than individual assets, short selling, etc.), almost always undertaken without material possession of the sums involved. This is therefore what leads to the production of speculative bubbles.

On that cold February Monday, as the Wall Street Journal would later chronicle (Pulliam et al., 26th February 2010), the men gathered for dinner decided that the time had come to launch an attack. However, there was a novelty in this new enterprise, as this time their target was not an Asian or Latin American developing economy but the weakest appendages of the euro area. A conflict that had been brewing for almost a decade between euro capital and dollar capital – characteristic of the current phase of capitalist imperialism – had reached boiling point. Using credit default swaps as their weapon (one of the most common financial derivatives), capital's hit squad moved on the economies of the peripheral European countries that have come to be known as the PI(I)GS: Portugal, Ireland, Italy, Greece and Spain.

The plan that emerged from the Manhattan "idea dinner" (Pulliam et al., *Wall Street Journal*, 26th February 2010), seems to have consisted in investing heavily in the depreciation of the euro, which from the high of $1.50 reached in 2009, according to the speculators' forecasts, had the potential to be forced down to $1 through an orchestrated effort targeting the eurozone's most obvious contradiction: the sovereign debt of southern Europe. According to an account of events, it was the head of Brigade Capital, Donald Morgan, who first identified Greek debt as the opening through which to stick the knife, to create a domino effect that would bring about the desired result. The idea must have been very convincing to all present, as within the same week the number of bets being made on the fall of the euro reached its highest point of around 60,000 futures contracted, according to the admission of Morgan Stanley. Unsurprisingly, only days after February 8th, the dollar/euro exchange rate reached a minimum of €1.35, a drop evidently driven by a series of planned and coordinated actions. It was an expertly crafted venture, to be expected given the involvement of people like Soros, who in the 90s had been involved in a similar speculative operation against the pound, pocketing around a billion dollars of profits as a result and forcing the UK to leave the European Exchange Rate Mechanism, with disastrous consequences for British workers. Indeed, some time before February 2010 Soros had been on record stating he believed the euro "may fall apart" (Pulliam et al., *Wall Street Journal*, 26th February 2010).

Though it may not always have been so obvious, it is not a stretch to conclude that the root of the Greek crisis, or of the European crisis, is essentially the same as that of the 2008 crash that shook the entire capitalist mode of production. Even Jean-Claude Trichet in his official capacity (as governor of the ECB), on May 8th 2011, described the situation as a systemic crisis. What underlies all these shocks of recent years, therefore, is the same crisis of over-production, tied to the falling rate of accumulation, which both encourages the proliferation of speculative activity and heightens the conflict between capitals belonging to imperialistically opposed production chains. Without going into a detailed analysis of the current general crisis of capital (which dates back to the end of the Bretton Woods system), a crisis consisting in alter-nating phases of ever stronger expansion and recession with a general down-ward trend (see Pala, 1981), it is nevertheless important to remember that it is this same general crisis that bears the main responsibility for the financial collapse of the southern European states. All too often, when confronted with shocks like the eurozone crisis, many so-called experts are at pains to point the finger and pick out a scapegoat, just as happened with the ratings agencies, believing it is possible to isolate the hypothetical rotten apples (in this case the speculators) that are poisoning an otherwise healthy whole.

As such the 'unscrupulous speculators' (more correctly termed fictitious capital) were held up as the culprits of the euro disaster, as if such a thing as a 'scrupulous speculator' could exist, or as if it made any sense to distinguish between 'good' and 'bad' capital. This kind of division is highly misleading: it is based on a non-sensical accusation of 'unbridled' free-marketism (can we firmly 'bridle' the 'free' market?) and on the resulting hypothesis of *ad hoc* economic policy-making and 'market regulation' (of financial markets, labour markets, etc.) it is believed will contain and prevent this phenomenon. Such a perspective therefore excludes any understanding of the contradictory unique-ness and multiplicity of the capitalist mode of production, or of its general, and particular, functioning. Capital's objective is to accumulate, and this can take place with or without the production of value. And since capitalist pro-duction is distinguished from previous modes of production precisely because it has the goal of commodity exchange and not use in its very foundations, "the original starting-point of capital, money in the formula $M - C - M'$" can be "reduced to the two extremes $M - M'$", or rather "money that creates more money" (Marx, 1894: 515).

One of main factors that deter small capitalists, only apparently closer to working-class living conditions and interests, from engaging in speculation is that playing the markets in this way is a zero-sum game (it is not at all because small businesses are more 'ethical'). In other words, without the capacity to detract shares of surplus-value from other capitalists, it is impossible to stay afloat. It is precisely this zero-sum nature that it is important to clarify. After every particularly disastrous trading session, it is generally reported that billions

or millions of euros or dollars are 'burnt' (or earned in the opposite case) as if
what was being dealt with was real wealth, or rather already-produced value.
The reality of it is, however, that these stock market fluctuations concern something entirely immaterial, something that is already entirely alien to tangible
wealth. Marx's remark of more than a century and a half ago that "With the
development of trade and the capitalist mode of production, which produces
only for circulation, this spontaneous basis for the credit system is expanded,
generalized, and elaborated" (Marx, 1894: 525).

What we find here, then, is that

> The complete *objectification, inversion* and *derangement* of capital as
> interest-bearing capital – in which, however, the inner nature of capital-
> ist production, [its] derangement, merely appears in its most palpable
> form – is capital which yields 'compound interest.'
> MARX, 1861–3: vol 32, 453, emphasis in the original

The concept of appearance or simulation is already intrinsic to the etymol-
ogy of the word *fictitious*. If the performance of securities on the markets are
for the most part based on bets made concerning their prices, it is clear that
the whole edifice is really entirely detached from any previously produced and
existing value, especially in the most acute phases of crisis. Furthermore, it
does not determine the creation of new value, as it makes use of wealth that is
only apparently new. As Marx observed,

> In so far as the rise or fall in value of these securities is independent of
> the movement in the value of the real capital that they represent, the
> wealth of a nation is just as great afterwards as before [...] As long as their
> depreciation was not the expression of any standstill in production [...]
> the nation was not a penny poorer by the bursting of these soap bubbles
> of nominal money capital.
> MARX, 1894: 599

What we are dealing with therefore, is a complex system based on the interaction between the different operators' valuations and the effect of this on prices.
These prices are thus entirely – or almost entirely – distinct from the production base (value), which as a result remains unaltered by the operations. As
such, the rule of the game is to maintain confidence; the gamblers potential
to make a winning (or a loss) lies solely in the relative erroneousness (or cor-
rectness) of the predictions of their competitors. In synthesis, leaving aside
for the moment general or artificial increases in shares (so-called bubbles), a

speculator's winnings are equal to the sum of the losses of the other players. And this is where the ratings agencies have a role to play. The ratings agencies allowed the market dealers and bankers to manipulate the prices of securities that were in fact highly risky (containing junk bonds), meaning they could be passed off as premium products. However, the obvious dishonesty aside, it was not the agencies themselves who bore responsibility, as we have argued. Holding them responsible would be like blaming a murder on the knife and not the murderer: it means confusing the agent with the weapon.

Having determined the irreproachable 'capitalist morality' of the New York diners, it is nevertheless important to reflect on the motivations that led them to attempt such an ambitious operation, intended to strike at the heart of one of global capitalism's dominant production chains: euro capital. Much noise was made about the accounting fraud committed by the Karamanlis government,[1] which declared a deficit of far less than the 12.7% the Pasok Papandreou government later discovered had been the case (a figure three times higher than the eurozone limit imposed by the Stability and Growth Pact). However, these misdeeds in reality represented nothing more than the product of a generalised situation of crisis in the Greek economy, around a third of which (a third of Greek GDP) was estimated to be constituted by illegal activity (the informal economy).

It was this potential insolvency of the Greek state (some rightly spoke of technical default) that became the pretext for an inevitable downgrading of Greek bonds to junk status, immediately provoking a collapse in their value. This then led to a drastic reduction in the fictitious wealth of the bond owners – principally European banks (see, among others, Barclays Capital, 2011; Zettelmeyer et al., 2013) – and the sparking of a wave of panic across stock markets everywhere. Indeed, an important point to underline is that a large part of this credit, which in recent times had come to lift a significant weight off the Greek state, came from German banks tied to local government, and were essentially 'guaranteed' by the Merkel-Karamanlis political axis. It therefore makes sense to speak of the first package of loans given to Greece by the EU as a means of ensuring 'allied' creditors were paid at least some of their due. And if we look closer at the functioning of this mechanism for guaranteeing precarious sovereign debt, we see how those early steps began to spin a web from which it would become difficult to break free. When, following the Lehman Brothers collapse, the US and many states in Europe bailed out their banks, the finance for those measures (as absurd as it sounds) came mainly from those

---

1 Costas Karamanlis was head of the Greek government on and off from 2004 to 2009.

same banks that were facing bankruptcy. Between the end of 2008 and the beginning of 2009, European banks bought up €357 billion in sovereign bonds, raising their combined ownership to €1,552 billion. If we take into account the fact that this is essentially equivalent to Italy's entire GDP for 2009, it seems a truly incredible figure.

It would therefore be fair to ask why these banks facing collapse were able to acquire such exorbitant numbers of eurozone member states' sovereign bonds. The response, which at first appears ludicrous but is in fact entirely in keeping with the logic of rescuing a mode of production at the limits of failure, can be found in the generous loan (with a nominal 1% interest rate) that the ECB conceded without conditions to the ailing banks. This on the one hand meant that the ECB was able to secure its own debt, as it was essentially buying the debts of its debtors (a conceptual contortion that would seem to make little sense), but it also meant the banks pocketed millions of euros in interest on the sovereign bonds, essentially a transfer of indirect wages (taxation) into the hands of the banks.

Yet it is important to keep in mind that the problem was far broader than the precarious debts of one or more states. Even at a time when the Greek catastrophe was still unfolding, it was a crisis that already involved the entire capitalist mode of production. According to a study carried out by the Italian financial broadsheet *Il Sole 24 Ore* (Lops, 9th November 2012), the cumulative debts (private and public) of the USA, the UK, Japan and Canada amounted to $130 trillion. To better understand the scale of this, $130 trillion was at the time twice the production value of all the commodities in the world. The USA accounted for around half of this, while total European debt was around 40 trillion. Greece's $300 billion of debt therefore appears paltry in comparison, demonstrating yet again that the Greek crisis did not in itself represent an insurmountable problem, especially for the eurozone as a whole, even considering the issues mentioned above.

The real problem lies in the fact that, though for some decades the capitalist market has been sustaining rates of accumulation that its finitude is unable to guarantee (a finitude that jars with capitalist production's dangerous propensity towards limitlessness), the agents of capital have inflated, or artificially altered, the global fictitious wealth to phenomenal proportions through mechanisms based purely on trust, through gambling on a knife edge. If one competitor (opportunistically tied to a consortium) decides to attack another, aiming for the weak link in the chain, the whole pyramid will come crashing down like a Ponzi scheme, and the owners of those securities will find themselves with a balance full of junk (e.g. the sovereign bonds of PIIGS states), putting them at risk of collapse. In this way the capitalist economy is like walking a tightrope: with the right conditions the walker can go for miles but at the slightest hesitation or gust of wind he trips and falls, never to regain his former momentum.

From 2008 onwards global capitalism has been precipitating towards the critical condition whereby it must contend with both an evident contraction in real global production and an increase, in absolute terms but even more so in relative terms (through financial leveraging), in fictitious assets across the board, belonging to capitalists but also to households (see e.g. the use of pension funds). The whole thing is kept afloat solely thanks to a precarious climate of mutual trust that could break down at any moment. The mechanisms for 'bailing-out,' as we will look at later, frequently involve a simple transfer of debt (termed 'refinancing') from one ailing entity to another that itself is also heavily indebted but which is just that bit more creditworthy than the first. The entire situation has become so contorted that a more trustworthy debtor only has to assume the debts of a fellow-debtor in danger to stabilise the mood of the markets. In these conditions of generalised crisis all strategizing is thrown to the wind and the dominant approach becomes simply to hit and run (with the money). At the same time, these operations are complemented with a politics of austerity that consists in drastically reducing the exchange-value of labour-power (both indirectly and directly in terms of wages), thus allowing for a further transfer of surplus-value from the subordinate classes to the dominant class. Yet as consultancy firm McKinsey & Co. (2018) estimated, the operations aimed at reducing debts are not without costs even for capital as a whole. In the majority of cases where such interventions have been carried out (roughly 45 since 1930), they have provoked a recession of two or three years on average. And, in a phase such as the one we are currently living through, the next time round could be much worse.

As was also broadly asserted at the time, more than economic stability, the Greek collapse represented a litmus test for the political stability of the euro. Many were quick to accuse Germany and Angela Merkel, in particular, of equivocating for too long, of losing precious time to intervene. All sorts of nightmare scenarios were being imagined, including a return to the drachma and a default on Greek debt, as maturity dates loomed large. Whether intervention came too slowly or not it is difficult to judge, but what is sure is that the impact of the 2010 speculative attack was so extensive it made any decisions on how to confront it incredibly complex, even for the most long-sighted of politicians. Many called for immediate and broad-ranging action on the part of the IMF and the ECB to calm the storm, that from end of April to the beginning of May 2012 began to blow across large parts of Europe. However, Article 123 of the Lisbon Treaty limits the ECB's scope for action (something which is still true today, though this is being tested post-pandemic), prohibiting it from buying up sovereign or public sector bonds directly. At the same time, Article 123 does not prohibit purchasing through certain operations on the open market. This means that the ECB, according to prevailing interpretations, can buy the sovereign bonds of EU states on condition that it act like a normal private investor. What this requires, however, is that it comes up with large sums of euros, which can then be immediately poured back into the bond market.

On the night between the 9th and 10th of May, while it was waiting to announce its most significant response to the 2010 speculative attack (a programme of quantitative easing, which we will look at in further in subsequent chapters), the ECB put together an emergency rescue package of 750 billion composed of a complex variety of different financial instruments, with the objective of stabilising the financial markets and guaranteeing a much-hungered-for release of liquidity. Indeed, this lack of liquidity had brought back memories of the deadlock on Wall Street in the weeks immediately following the collapse of Lehmann Brothers, though beyond their common cause there is in fact little similarity in the way the two crises unfolded.

The response of the markets only hours after the plan was announced was seemingly enthusiastic, and the financial reporters rushed to laud the skill of its developers. After weeks of blood, sweat and tears the European stock market indexes climbed to double percentage points, especially in those cities that had been in the eye of the storm (Madrid + 14.43%, Milan +11.28%, Athens + 9.13%). The bond market reacted similarly, bringing down the spread between the yields of Portuguese, Greek, Irish, Spanish and UK bonds on the one hand, and German bonds on the other, to much lower levels than the week before. Unfortunately, however, these initially positive appearances would prove to be deceiving.

Indeed, while the stock markets remained positive, the bond and currency markets in a broader sense – essentially the crux of the matter – did not see the same sustained improvement. And even where the stock markets were registering optimal performances, they were undoubtably still being weighed down by the hedging operations of bearish speculators using techniques like short selling. Short selling, or shorting, effectively means borrowing rather than buying securities to sell on (leaving the investor 'short' of the security), with the expectation that when the time comes to return the borrowed securities they can be bought back on the market for a cheaper price (and then returned). This is a bearish strategy because the expectation is that the security's price will fall: the earning is made through the difference in the security's price from when the short seller sold it to when they bought it back on the market to return it to the lender. However, if the downward trend predicted is suddenly bucked, the short seller must buy immediately, before prices rise even further meaning increased losses. Such gains and losses can be vast and immediate, with trading happening even after hours or overnight, as stock markets can be highly volatile (registering waves of panic or euphoria). With this in mind it, is difficult to imagine that in the midst of the turmoil that hit the European markets on that May Monday, the speculators would just sit back and watch.

2   The Spectre of Speculation

US public debt – a double debt as it has both a domestic and foreign component – has for a long time been at extraordinary levels. As such, the mega-loans given out in the decade following the Lehmann Brothers collapse had the effect of compromising the entire structure of the USA's accounts. The US deficit for the year 2021 is around 13% of GDP and its debt situation is even worse. Post-(or rather 'mid-') pandemic, before the Biden stimulus, the value of public debt as declared by the Federal Reserve in 2021 (Federal Reserve Bank of St. Louis, 2021) was 135% of GDP. On the face of it, this could perhaps be worse, but to arrive at a value comparable to the measurement used in Europe, we should include in the calculation the potential losses on government-sponsored mortgage enterprises (i.e. Freddie Mac and Fannie Mae), which is in the hundred billions; the gains made in terms of rights to future social provisions; and local government debt. Using these parameters, the total is significantly larger, perhaps even well above that of the most indebted European countries.

This imposing debt is the result of the fact that over recent decades the USA has been hit worse than anyone else by the crisis. It has also without doubt been impacted by the rise of euro capital, from the start of the century onwards, and by the strengthening of the Asian economies centred around the irresistible ascent of China. More recently, the various Wall Street collapses also complicated the situation considerably. To address the severe disruptions in production that took place following 2008, the US government has been forced to 'stimulate' the economy by leveraging (private and public) debt. However, aside from adding yet more to their dues, the most tangible result of this has been the use of these loans or hand-outs for speculation rather than for the production of commodities, as the saturation of the markets does not allow for genuine investment solutions (see our concluding chapter for a more in-depth look at this). As such, the real estate market has not seen substantial change, unemployment remains stagnant, and the wages of both the working-classes and the middle-classes have been falling. The hoped-for recovery (as if crisis were a fleeting phenomenon) has continued to elude, and various US governments have been unable to enjoy the fiscal advantages that would be derived from a growth in accumulation and wages, despite significant spending. As a result, the debt just keeps piling up, as spending is not being compensated for through revenue. And for the same reason, despite its arrogance, the Trump administration's attempts to rein in the US economy through tariffs only temporarily boosted some of the structural indicators.

At a distance of more than a decade, it seems safe to say that the crusade launched against the 'unscrupulous speculators' has been unable to generate any positive effects in terms of stability, global growth, or unemployment. Indeed, the same financial instruments (the MBS backed by subprime mortgages, the Ponzi-scheme like structures, and so on) that were singled out as scapegoats for a crisis which is in fact immanent to the capitalist mode of production, initially curtailed through basic ad hoc regulation, were rapidly replaced by something far more complex. This is precisely because capital in its imperialist phase cannot go without them. As we have argued, the use of financial instruments unrelated to production, and so to the production and accumulation of surplus-value, is not a deviation from the capitalist system produced by the manipulation of reckless agents, but rather the logical and immediate consequence of the real crisis.

Yet just a few years after 2008 many supposed experts were again falling into the same trap and accusing a new generation of speculators of jeopardising the precarious progress made since the crisis by the supposed 'good' capitalists. The declarations made by the Financial Stability Board at the end of 2011 on the 'potential vulnerability' of a set of new financial products that were becoming fashionable, pejoratively termed 'synthetic' (synthetic ETFs), set alarm bells ringing, bringing back memories of the MBS or CDOs full of junk bonds and subprime-backed securities that spread across markets everywhere in the years prior to 2008. In other words, everything was changed so that everything could stay the same. Capitalism's critical phase has continued to race full steam ahead, much to the detriment of workers and the unemployed. Or, as Italy's financial broadsheet *Il Sole 24 Ore* put it 'the music has restarted, with the same orchestra and the same conductors as before.' Through a sleight of hand, the subprime securities, having been sacrificed at the altar, were immediately replaced by equally complex and dubious products – ETFs, cov-lite loans and ABS in particular – carrying incredibly high risks and having no anchorage in a material value. Of these three financial products, those which caused the most concern were the ETFs, and the newer developments in 'synthetic' EFTs, in particular. Mario Draghi, then president of the FSB, defined them as "unsettling", warning that their innocuous appearance was deceiving. ETFs are an index fund similar to mutual funds, meaning that they are managed passively by replicating the performance of a basket of underlying securities that mirror a market index (we will look in further depth at the potentials of indexes later on). Unlike mutual funds, however, ETFs have limited fees and restrictions on entry and exit (e.g., no minimum holding period), allowing them to be traded throughout the day and out of hours, and allowing for shorting. For this reason, they are used in bearish speculation, a practice which, as was demonstrated in the eurozone crisis, can cause notable damage. Finally, the 'untrustworthy' nature of the more recent iterations of the EFT is related to the fact that they are tied to asset classes where liquidity and transparency are, by definition, scarce. And when we consider events that took place at the end of 2019, the subject of our final chapter, these concerns appear all the more well-founded.

Alarm bells were already ringing in 2011, when the volume of these securities reached the astronomical sum of $1,300 billion globally, of which $1,000 billion were owned in the US. Aside from the FSB, other so-called market analysts were also flagging potential dangers, albeit in a less diplomatic manner, including the president of Harch Capital Management and the head of research for Morningstar's European ETFs, who thought it improbable that sufficient assets existed for all the ETF derivatives in circulation at the time. In short, many analysts were being forced to admit that a complex house-of-cards structure was being created that closely resembled that edifice whose collapse between 2007 and 2008 brought down so many US financial institutions and businesses. The fear was that there would be a second collapse, the consequences of which – for workers first and foremost, as it is of course workers who always bear the brunt – would be far more painful than in 2008.

In addition to the 'suspicious' dealings of the synthetic ETFs, it was around the same time that so-called cov-lite loans began to emerge – loans granted without any limitations or guarantees to protect lenders. In the first quarter of 2011, these loans were worth $25 billion, 24% of the total of all loans, with an absolute value five times that calculated during the same period of the previous year. Finally, there were the asset-backed securities (ABS), structured financial instruments with a high risk-factor tied to low-quality debt categories (i.e., debt contracted by individuals or entities whose solvency is highly precarious). ABS are different from MBS only in that the underlying assets are not mortgages but other assets like auto loans. In the first quarter of 2011 the total value of existing ABS was $18 billion, though Ally Bank and Santander went on to announce the creation of a further $2.9 billion and $784 million respectively. On top of this, as Hedge Fund Research (HFR) calculated, the funds being managed by hedge funds had surpassed the peak of June 2008, arriving at an astronomical $2,000 billion in the US alone.

It was in this context of a seriously compromised global economy that one of the defining events of the post-crisis period took place. After a couple of years of upheaval that in the global North had affected mainly the US, or more accurately, dollar capital, in the second half of 2010 the epicentre began to shift to Europe, at least phenomenologically speaking. It was at this point that the question of eurozone debt (specifically eurozone member states' sovereign debt) – an issue that for some time had been left to simply bubble below the surface – reached a boiling point. In the ensuing drama, it was the so-called PIIGS that took on a central role, albeit against their own will.

> The national debt, i.e., the alienation [Veräusserung] of the state – whether that state is despotic, constitutional, or republican – marked the capitalist era with its stamp. The only part of the so-called national wealth that actually enters into the collective possession of a modern nation is – the national debt.
>
> Hence, quite consistently with this, the modern doctrine that a nation becomes the richer the more deeply it is in debt. Public credit becomes the *credo* of capital. And with the rise of national debt-making, lack of faith in the national debt takes the place of the sin against the Holy Ghost, for which there is no forgiveness.
>
> The public debt becomes one of the most powerful levers of primitive accumulation. As with the stroke of an enchanter's wand, it endows unproductive money with the power of creation and thus turns it into capital, without forcing it to expose itself to the troubles and risks inseparable from its employment in industry or even in usury. The state's creditors actually give nothing away, for the sum lent is transformed into public bonds, easily negotiable, which go on functioning in their hands just as so much hard cash would. But furthermore, and quite apart from the class of idle *rentiers* thus created, the improvised wealth of the financiers who play the role of the middlemen between the government and the nation, and the tax-farmers, merchants and private manufacturers, for whom a good part of every national loan performs the service of a capital fallen from heaven, apart from all these people, the national debt has given rise to joint-stock companies, to dealings in negotiable effects of all kinds, and to speculation: in a word, it has given rise to stock-exchange gambling and the modern bankocracy.
>
> MARX, 1867: 919

Though we can say with certainty that from 2010 onwards the heart of the storm passed from the USA to Europe (via means explained previously), it is also important to stress that it was a mistake to class the 2008 crisis as a uniquely North American crisis. And by the same token, viewing the post-2010 turmoil as a European event, and more specifically a 'sovereign debt' crisis, is equally imprecise. As we have emphasised, both phases were consequences of the downward tendency in accumulation that began to take hold at a global level from the early 70s onwards – specifically following the unilateral decision taken by the US government to unbind the dollar from convertibility into gold – which has impacted capital in its entirety, or rather in its natural essence, which is its global form. Between 2008 and 2012, capital's typical systemic tendencies exploded in spectacular form, the pressure having built up over decades. This was, in spite of the numerous interventions, intended to smooth them over or postpone their eruption. For many reasons, and not least because it has significant political value, it is important to frame the problem within these terms, without assigning sole responsibility to any particular behaviour or policy.

Indeed, when it came to the 2010 crisis, the media expended much energy in side-lining any analysis of this kind and in upholding the view that the roots of the problem lay in the fact that the populations of developed economies were living to excess (the abuses of the term 'austerity' are in this sense not unintentional). The idea was that debt was the result of a desire on the part of populations to access more resources than should be considered normal and correct, shifting onto the working classes the blame for a situation that was engendered within the very heart of global capitalism, by its innermost essence. This interpretation serves to keep at bay the ever more frequent outbreaks of desperation and dissent: it seeks to subdue any opposition to policies that keep the subordinate classes (from the destitute to the lower middle classes) forever impoverished. Yet at the same time, shifting the blame onto overconsumption or 'consumerism' (whatever the term) also masks the true extent of the debt problem, paradoxically helping to maintain the artificial demand needed to absorb the overproduction of commodities and capital. As such, in the absence of a solid scientific framework and of a class consciousness among the working classes, the issue is successfully transformed into a question of morals.

However, in spite of these ideological contrivances and the various policies put in place, the health of euro capital remained critical throughout 2012 and 2013. This was particularly true from the perspective of public and private debt, and even more so if debt is considered the Achilles heel of European capital in the context of an ongoing battle against dollar capital. While the misfortunes facing Greece and the other PII(G)s were already known to all, the innovation of 2012/2013 was the apparent precarity of the world's fifth largest economy: France, second only to Germany in the continent (which was itself risking contagion).

Rumours concerning a possible downgrade of France's bonds began to circulate at the beginning of 2012, rigorously rebutted by the then President Nicholas Sarközy. S&P did indeed make its announcement however, provoking yet another crash in markets across a lot of Europe. Ten months later, on November 19th, 2012, Moody's, the most influential of the Big Three, followed suit, demoting French paper from AAA to AA1, confirming and even inflaming a perception within the finance sector of a certain level of instability in the French economy. Though the governing logic of the ratings agencies often overrides their institutive functions, as we described in the previous chapter, we must nevertheless be careful not to neglect the significance of these events, whose effects on fictitious and speculative capital flows – incoming and outgoing – can be considerable, impacting thus interests rates and bond spreads, elements which condition the development of the conflict among the various factions of capital.

Two days prior to the downgrading, the *Economist* ran an editorial describing France as a 'time-bomb at the heart of Europe,' accompanied by a cover photo depicting a bundle of baguettes tied together with a fuse. According to the magazine, this somewhat provocative move was motivated by very serious concerns. In the *Economist*'s view, France was headed towards disaster, on the basis that "wealth, profits and high incomes are heavily taxed, the rich are routinely abused, and people are instinctively hostile to capitalism. Everything from the labour market to pharmacies to taxis is heavily regulated: no wonder would-be entrepreneurs feel discouraged [...] trade unions and protesters tend to take to the streets at the first hint of reform. It adds up to a deeply anti-business culture." (Peet, 2012) If *The Economist*'s rhetoric was somewhat heavy-handed, the question was understood in far less ideological terms by Moody's, which attributed the downgrade to weak competitivity, weak growth, and a rapidly growing debt, part of Sarközy's legacy, a view that Hollande's Finance Minister, Pierre Moscovici, was keen to propagate.

For the most part, however, it was Hollande's government that was accused of being too 'socialist'; of refusing to pursue the consensus on austerity as laid down by the EU institutions – synthetised in the Fiscal Compact – and of using an excessive quantity of public resources for consumption or investment of various types. In other words, even France's primary balance – the difference between tax revenue and spending on goods or services and investment minus interest on government debt – was negative by around 2% of GDP. As the primary balance is one of the components of total debt, a primary deficit would put France's debt in danger and cause great distress to the advocates of a restrictive fiscal policy, Merkel above all. Nevertheless, France was in a far better situation than the PIIGS, in terms of the 120% threshold considered a red line (at the end of 2019 France's debt to GDP ratio was still around 100%). In fact, it is entirely coherent to the capitalist mode of production, even in terms of state accounting, that in a phase of prolonged crisis – where private capital is unable to maintain the necessary levels of profitability or does not have the means to help itself (insufficient accumulation) – the state, acting as public *capital*, functions as an investor, so as to be able to then hand over to the private sector the capital it has accumulated. *The Economist's* imagined 'socialism' could therefore not be further off the mark.

While France was showing some signs of distress, the PIIGS continued to teeter on the brink. In terms of sovereign debt – which aside from the accumulation of the deficits of past years, also encompasses interest payments – at the end of 2012, only Spain had a debt to GDP ratio of under 100%, and even then only by a whisker. Greece's debt to GDP ratio stood at 175%. The so-called politics of austerity – meaning austerity for workers and not for capital (of course) – were effective enough to produce the desired effect in terms of the public finances. They also brought about a reduction in GDP, with a consequent lowering of the tax revenue (directly connected to wages and to production and demand). Yet, the variable that France was being attacked for, the primary balance, in fact had Italy at the top of the eurozone class. The cuts to public spending (so to schools, hospitals, public sector wages, etc), and the cuts to capital account outgoings above all, together with rises in both direct and indirect taxes (VAT, property taxes, etc), were so extreme that in spite of the reduction in production, Italy's finances, on these terms, became the most 'virtuous' in the continent (though it came with incalculable social cost).

After 2012 the Italian state had even overtaken Germany by this measure, due to an excess of income in comparison with outgoings, just under 3% of GDP, or around €39.5 billion. Nevertheless, with its colossal spending on interest, at the time around €80 billion, its debt continued to grow, to the point of surpassing the €2,000 billion mark according to the Banca d'Italia, amounting to 126% of GDP. And the total has only continued to increase. To guarantee this gargantuan debt – owed principally to private capital – the institutional expressions of the ruling class (government and parliament) have no choice but to bleed the working classes dry by any means at their disposal. And looking at the numbers, they have been very successful in this respect. When this is taken into account, therefore, the crusade against the public debt waged by certain sectors of the political class seems particularly irrational. Motivated by what would appear to be a mix of voluntarism and moralism, its proponents are either unable or unwilling to understand that the creditors they are so concerned about, and which parliaments are so servile to, are actually mon-strously large capital funds.

As we have stated, the burden of financing the public debt repayment plans – and more broadly of the attempted (and so far, unrealised) restructur-ing of global capital – has fallen on the working classes. The fact that hundreds of thousands of pensioners are being forced to survive on poverty incomes (see our subsequent chapters); that unemployment in southern Europe is around 20/30% for the whole adult population and in many cases above 50% among young people; that the new jobs being created are overwhelmingly precarious; and more generally that the *social* wage – i.e. the income of the working classes both in and out of employment – has been reduced to levels that would have been unimaginable for the post-war generation, is all part of capital's attempt to reboot accumulation.

The all-too-predictable scenario that began to manifest itself during the eurozone crisis saw a local bourgeoisie attempting to break out of the malaise into which it had been dragged by the struggle against dollar capital. The methods used in Italy – though not as severe as those used in Greece and par-ticularly Spain, where the accumulation crisis was worse – still had the same objective of *naturally* reducing the value of labour-power (wages) and of liber-alising its use, forcing labour to become more 'adapted' to the current phase of crisis (meaning longer working days, more flexible hours, zero-hours contracts, etc.). A new international division of labour was taking shape, with the effect that significant sections of the working classes in the peripheral European states (the PIIGS) – potentially excepting a few of the more industrial areas like Catalonia, the Basque country, or some parts of northern Italy – were mov-ing towards wages (exchange-value) and working conditions (use-value) that were not too dissimilar from those existing in parts of the world like the former Yugoslavia. The idea being that this would encourage foreign investment.

Consequently, from 2012 to 2014, the crisis of the PIIGS became more and more dramatic, seemingly ever further from resolution. In September 2012, the German constitutional court approved of the European Stability Mechanism, something many believed would help to keep the speculators at bay. However, the ESM, essentially a bank financed by all the EU economies and governed by their finance ministers, was created with the sole purpose of overcoming the issue of the ECB's statutory inability to buy eurozone members' debt on the primary market, i.e. at issuance. In contrast to the Federal Reserve, which is able to print money as and when Washington deems necessary, the ECB is restricted from aiding eurozone states in a liquidity crisis, making them easy prey for the bond vigilantes. As such, the creation of the ESM merely created a more even playing field, and even at the time the granting of this new role of

'lender of last resort' to the ECB seemed insufficient to protect from speculative attacks of the likes that hit Greece, Spain and later Italy, serving more as a
flimsy deterrent than a real solution.

3   The Final Surrender: The Greek Clinamen[2]

The end of June and beginning of July 2015 made for without doubt the most
dramatic, but also the most interesting, period of recent EU history. If for nothing else because of the unpredictability with which events unfolded to reach
the climax of July 5th, the EU's most fateful day to date, the day when the Greek
people went to the polls to decide whether to accept the terms of the Troika
bailout.

It was over that summer that the conditions were created that would
precipitate a rupture in the negotiations between the Troika (the European
Commission, the ECB and the IMF, referred to here as 'the institutions') and
the Greek government, represented by the Prime Minister Alexis Tsipras and
his finance minister Yanis Varoufakis. This rupture then prompted Tsipras to
turn to the Greek people, putting the choice of whether negotiations should
continue or not to a referendum. The situation in short was that the Greek government's response to the institutions' request that Greece bring its debt under
control consisted in a proposal to clamp down on tax evasion and increase
taxes for the very wealthy and the capitalists. This proposal however stood in
sharp contrast to the demands of the Troika that Greece continue to place the
burden of debt repayment on Greek workers through indirect taxation, including on basic necessities, as well as cuts to pensions and to public sector wages,
and an immediate increase in state retirement age.

For her part, the then president of the IMF, Cristine Lagarde (now governor
of the ECB), insisted that an increase in direct taxes on big capital would have
an unpredictable impact on the country's finances, whereas greater taxation
of workers would bring more stable results. It was a view that on the surface
would seem to be common sense: an increase in taxes on workers provides a

---

2 In Epicurean physics, clinamen was the name given to the spontaneous swerve of atoms
   that occurs when they drop straight into a void. The entirely unpredictable movement, in
   terms of both time and space, allows atoms to bump into each other. The concept was introduced by Epicurus using the Greek word parénklisis (παρέγκλισισ) and was later developed
   by Democritus and then by Lucretius who gave it the Latin name clinamen. Marx discussed
   the topic in his *The Difference Between the Democritean and Epicurean Philosophy of Nature*
   (1841).

guaranteed income for the state, whereas taxing wealth and capital is less reliable. Yet the rigidity with which the ECB stuck to its guns betrayed the ferocity of an agenda motivated by class interests. If Tsipras was shocked by this inflexibility, decrying a difference in treatment for Greece and other EU members like Portugal and Ireland, the attitudes of Junker & co. had been entirely explicit throughout: when it comes to credit, no one gets a special deal. The fact that large parts of the Greek workforce would be condemned to live in conditions of absolute poverty for years to come, that Greek hospitals could not provide basic care and supermarkets food, and that there was now a whole sub-population of people living on the streets or in their cars (all while the big shots of international finance were free to enjoy the Aegean Islands on their yachts), was not considered by the institutions to be an immediate problem, or in any case a priority.

The Greek government, elected at the beginning of 2015, was undoubtably burdened by a number of political contradictions, from Varoufakis's self-styled 'Marxian eccentricity' to the alliance with a right-wing grouping in the parliament that guaranteed it its majority, not to mention the heterogenous nature of Syriza as a political force. Turning back the clock to the beginning of 2015, when the results of the Greek general election were announced, there were many who saw the timidity of the newly established government's attempts to break free of the grasp of international capital as a sign that the Troika would make quick work of any resistance. Others still pointed out that their electoral programme would be unimplementable. Considering that the Tsipras government was forged within a balance of power relations steeply tilted against it, such concerns were not unreasonable. Yet as it turned out, month after month, meeting after meeting, Syriza's wait-and-see approach began to pay off, tipping the balance in favour of the Greek government which had initially appeared objectively weak and incapable of dictating terms (the rise of Podemos in Spain, Syriza's political allies, also helped in this regard). We can speculate that Varoufakis's familiarity with game theory also helped. In any case, only months from the Syriza government's swearing in, a situation was created whereby the entire global economy (and not only Greece's creditors, as we will see) came to depend on the outcome of the Greek referendum, as evidenced by the dramatic stock market crashes in all parts of the globe following the breakdown of negotiations. Perhaps underestimating characteristic Greek pride, the institutions had convinced themselves that sooner or later Tsipras would have to back down, knowing also that he was plagued by infighting within his party. Things did not turn out that way, or at least, if there was ultimately a surrender of some sorts, it did not produce the desired results.

The greatest paradox of the Greek case is that, for two main reasons, it could have had a very different outcome. Firstly, it could have been handled very differently by the institutions. Greece is not a particularly important economy (in terms of wealth produced), and its collapse would not be of grave concern to the global economy or even the EU. Its GDP is less than that of Lombardy, a single region of Italy, and its public debt is in absolute terms was not excessively large (around €300 billion in 2020, little more than 10% of that of Italy). The other reason is that, as of September 2009, Greece's unattractive bonds had effectively been entirely removed from the balance sheets of private capital, as they were bought up by the public sector. In other words, the institutions (the Troika) had themselves allowed the majority of Greece's bad debt to be acquired by the public sectors of EU member states, in order to relieve the private banks of the burden. Prior to 2009, those most exposed to Greek debt were, as was well-known, French (€79 billion) and German (€45 billion) capital, followed far behind by the Dutch (€12 billion) and Italian (€7 billion euros) private sectors. In the space of a few years, following an exceptionally foul operation from the perspective of labour, these bonds were redistributed among the public balance sheets of the four EU countries with the highest GDPs, so that by the end of 2015, while Germany was still ahead in its share, this time it was its public sector with the greater proportion (€62 billion in the public sector and €14 billion private), followed by France (€47 billion only in the public sector), Italy (€41 billion, public sector) and then Spain (€27 billion, public sector). In short, the law of 'privatise profits, socialise losses' was shown once again to be a guiding imperative, especially in times of crisis. The ESM, which provided the basis for the manoeuvre, had successfully facilitated the offloading of a large portion of Greece's junk bonds onto the two most important 'PIIGS' (Italy and Spain), dramatically aggravating their already compromised public sector finances.

When we consider these two points together – the relative insignificance of the Greek economy and its debt, and the fact that this debt had in any case been transferred from the private to the public sector – there seems no reason why European capital should have taken such a hard line. The inoculation of private capital against the worst effects of bad Greek paper, in theory should have provided the institutions with reason to adopt a less rigid and more collaborative approach. On the contrary, the absolute intransigence of the ECB, IMF and European Commission – as much as the Greek government was culpable at times of a lack of clarity in its proposals – seems to have been inspired by an excessive dogmatism that in fact fits ill with the interests of European capital, especially where, as was the case here, it does not actually stand to lose much. Moreover, the unsightly spectacle of a country experiencing a long-term humanitarian crisis being bullied by institutions lead by the continent's richest states was becoming increasingly difficult to justify.

Such seemingly illogical behaviour would seem to support the hypothesis of an indirect strategy on the part of the institutions. What would appear to be an entirely counterproductive approach given the circumstances had in reality the underlying primary objective of sending a clear message to those members states at risk of becoming the next Greece, especially in the PIIGS group. This flexing of muscles was thus meant to act as a deterrent against any support for what is crudely defined as 'anti-austerity politics,' deployed by so-called 'sovereigntist' governments.

Yet it was not only European capital that involved itself in the Greek tragedy. Since the inauguration of the Tsipras government, Russian capital, represented by Putin, had had its eye on Greece, putting itself forward as the credible alternative to the iron fist of the Troika. During Greece's most dramatic months, relations between the two countries became closer, with Russia particularly keen to bring Greece into the fold due to its strategic position in relation to the Turkish Stream gas project, initially presented as a valid alternative to the conditional aid proposed by the EU institutions/IMF. China too declared itself ready to play an active role, as the repercussions of a possible Grexit would have been felt across the globe and not only in Europe. For its part, however, China had an interest in ensuring that Greece remain in the eurozone: since the eurozone was one of China's key trading partners, a euro-wide crisis would not be good news. Finally, there is the question of Piraeus, the Mediterranean's most important port. China had been eyeing the port for years and eventually bought up a major part of it,[3] creating a fair number of problems for the parties involved in trying to negotiate TTIP (we will look at this in more depth in the last part of this chapter).

The Greek case was therefore permeated by the inter-imperialist conflicts that characterise capitalism's present stage of development, of which the many recent outbreaks of physical conflict (in the Middle East, Ukraine, etc.) are only the external manifestation of what is a far more complex economic phenomenon, characterised by the confrontation between dollar/euro capital and the members of the Shanghai Pact, Russia and China first and foremost. It was for this reason – to avoid a situation where a country of such symbolic important for Europe became entangled in the sphere of influence of hostile powers – that Obama understood the moment had come to intervene, putting great pressure on Junker to do all he could to avoid either a default or a Greek

---

3   In 2010, Cosco Shipping took over management of the harbor's container terminal.

exit from the eurozone. Losing even a single component of TTIP, as insignificant as Greece was, would have risked destabilising what for US capital was a key element in its strategy to contrast Asian capital, and which was intended to mark the victory of dollar capital over its 'hostile brother,' euro capital, following its initial speculative attack on Greek debt in 2010.

The outcome of the Greek tragedy is well-known. The unexpected victory of the no vote in the referendum (the *Oxi* vote – Greek for no), representing the refusal of the Greek people to accept the conditions put to Greece by the institutions, sparked a political earthquake that ended in a split in the Syriza government. The minority of hardliners calling for the referendum to be respected, led by Varoufakis, were eventually side-lined by Tsipras and his allies who then took it upon themselves to overturn the referendum result and accept the harsh bailout agreement. In hindsight, it is safe to say that the Troika programme was unable to generate any tangible results for Greece. Still today the country is plagued by a generalised deterioration of its economy, and the restructuring of both its economy and its debt is far from being realised.

4   TTIP, TPP and Global Conflict

If the US had therefore been relatively successful in offloading onto the EU the worst effects of the crisis generated by dollar capital, aided also by the EU's dogmatic adherence to austerity, the prospects for recovery were not great even for North America. In a context of persistent crisis, global capital was initially slow to gather the strength to overcome its significant accumulation issues, despite its heavy-handed attacks on the use of labour-power, including in relation to its value (direct and indirect wages).

In exactly the same way that the crisis of the close of the 19th century – the first typical to the capitalist mode of production – was only partially resolved with the First World War, when the 2008 crisis manifested itself in all its specificity, inter-capitalist conflict was accordingly intensified. For decades wars have been fought at the level of 'low intensity' or through proxies (Ukraine, Syria, Libya, Iraq, Afghanistan), partly due to the presence of nuclear weapons acting as a deterrent. However, this dislocation should not be read as a sign of constraint on the part of powers who for centuries have sought out "profitable business and lucrative employment from the expansion of military and civil services" as Hobson noted in 1902 (Hobson, 1902: 68).

Militarily, the inter-imperialist struggle has become polarised over the last few years over the questions of Ukraine and the war against Isis in Syria and Iraq (with the recent insertion of the Iran issue), conflicts that have seen dollar/

euro capital pitted against rouble capital (and renminbi capital). However, while all this is taking place, not a day goes past that these same rival states are not meeting and signing new free trade agreements.

Before we look at the evolution of the TTIP and TPP negotiations, it is worth taking a minute to clarify conceptually what is meant by the term free trade and by its opposite, protectionism, in order to avoid the conceptual traps of the discussions around the global market and globalisation that were dominate in the 90s and early 2000s.

> To sum up, what is Free Trade under the present conditions of society? Freedom of Capital. When you have torn down the few national barriers which still restrict the free development3 of capital, you will merely have given it complete freedom of action. So long as you let the relation of wages-labor to capital exist, no matter how favorable the conditions under which you accomplish the exchange of commodities, there will always be a class which exploits and a class which is exploited [...] (Moreover, the Protective system is nothing but a means of establishing manufacture upon a large scale in any given country, that is to say, of making it dependent upon the market of the world; and from the moment that dependence upon the market of the world is established, there is more or less dependence upon Free Trade too. [...] But, generally speaking, the Protective system in these days is conservative, while the Free Trade system works destructively. It breaks up old nationalities and carries antagonism of proletariat and bourgeoisie to the uttermost point. In a word, the Free Trade system hastens the Social Revolution.
>
> MARX, 1848: 463–465

In July of 2013, on the shores of Lough Erne, the G8 began a round of talks. These negotiations were to become the basis of what would go on to become a historic trade agreement. The name this agreement would take was TTIP: the Transatlantic Trade and Investment Partnership. TTIP's importance to the continued functioning of the capitalist system means that for the most part the records of these negotiations remain classified, to keep them from falling into the hands of dollar/euro capital's global competitors, Asian capital for the most part. Nevertheless, what is known is that this opening up of free trade in goods and capital between the USA (which still maintains significant tariffs on certain key goods) and the EU, would have in effect created a single market composed of the world's two largest economies, and, more importantly, its two strongest currency areas, the dollar and the euro, at a time when euro capital was experiencing serious difficulties.

Attesting to its importance to dollar capital, a series of studies were commissioned during the last part of the Obama administration to give greater ideological impetus to the TTIP accord. Carried out by generously subsidised universities and research centres, the studies spoke of the enormous benefits that TTIP would have produced in terms of well-being for citizens on both sides of the Atlantic (though obviously only in the northern hemisphere, and even then, in just a small part of it), even claiming it would have a positive knock-on effect for the rest of the globe. In short, it seemed to be of great benefit to all (or at least, all involved). According to the findings of the Centre for Economic Policy Research, if fully implemented, the growth in exports and imports of goods and capital TTIP would have guaranteed GDP growth of around €119 billion for the EU and €95 billion for the USA, translating into an increase in wealth of €545 for a family of four each year, or ten euros pro capita each month (gross). In addition, it would have generated an increase of close to €100 billion for the rest of the world. As far as the labour market was concerned, the European Commission's summary on the progress of negotiations made the highly superficial remark that the increase in productivity and output that would have resulted from labour market liberalisation would have pushed up wages and created new opportunities for both skilled and non-skilled workers. How this result would fit with the sums mentioned above, of a ten-euro monthly increase in pro capita income, remains a mystery, however.

At the end of October 2014, a documentary on TTIP was broadcast on Italian TV (Pozzan, 2014). The documentary focused on the question of the food supply which, as important as this is, was only one of the central aspects of the agreement. Of all the information relayed, something that stood out was a quote from Lori Wallach of Public Citizen's Global Trade Watch. Commenting on the TTIP lobby he said "I know many of these lobbyists. I've heard them say 'it's fantastic that the crisis has hit Europe hard, they're desperate. They are in such need of growth that they'll accept conditions they would never have accepted in 1998, in 2000 or in 2005.'" What these remarks made clear therefore, was that the TTIP negotiations were taking place at a moment when euro capital was experiencing a major weakness. In other words, it seemed that following its decades-long conflict with the dollar, euro capital was now ready to raise the white flag.

However, while the pro-government think tanks lauded the development of TTIP, a more independent study by J. Capaldo of Tufts University (2014) came to some very different conclusions. Taking the CEPR report to task, Capaldo asserted that the proposals contained in the TTIP drafts represented a seriously bad deal for European workers and even for some parts of European capital. The real risk was that a regulatory framework similar to that which exists in the US would be gradually implemented in the European labour market, with the aim of creating system that is as far as possible homogenous, levelling downwards both the conditions for the use of labour-power and its exchange-value (wages).

In sharp contradiction to the CEPR report, and to the claims of other TTIP supporters, it would seem that in the long term, 600,000 jobs would be 'freed up,' mostly in the north of the continent and in the more fragile and less protected sectors that are easy prey to centralisation by larger and more expert foreign capital. Reductions in yearly wages for European workers could amount to €3,000 per worker, rising to over €5,000 in France. If this were to materialise, the impact on euro capital accumulation and on EU public finances would be similarly negative. Finally, there is the thorny question of genetically modified foods, and the food supply more generally. In terms of food and agriculture, the regulatory frameworks in the EU and the US differ hugely, risking again a situation where a levelling downwards (towards the US) would allow for the introduction of directly or indirectly genetically modified food (seeds or animal feed), likely leading to a pushing out of non-GM products that would see even the most minimum protections for human health and the environment destroyed.

And there were other even more complex elements to TTIP, that again gave the impression that the balance of forces was firmly in the US's favour. These include the plan to harmonise intellectual property rights in the pharmaceutical and chemical sectors (and there are also key differences in web user data management and web access). The liberalisation of such rights would allow American Big Pharma to gobble up major shares of the European market. Then there were the questions of how to regulate speculative capital, and of how to conduct international arbitration, with the proposal that a third-party institution (e.g. the World Bank or the IMF) would be called upon to intervene in the case of a dispute between a transnational corporation and any of the states signatory to TTIP.

However, even with the balance of power firmly in the US's favour, the TTIP negotiations met with many obstacles. During his election campaign, Trump had promised an 'America First' approach, and explicitly stated he would withdraw from TTIP. Appearing to hold true to his word, Trump publicly abandoned negotiations once he took office, though talks continued in some form. Even the Biden administration currently seems reluctant to return to TTIP. And if the possibility remains that negotiations will be revived, it is likely this would not be until long after the dust of the pandemic had settled.

Yet while the Transatlantic Partnership was faltering, the US's negotiations with its Pacific neighbours were not showing much promise either. The Pacific

equivalent to TTIP was TPP (Trans-Pacific Partnership) and involved (aside
from the USA) Canada, Peru, Chile, Australia, Vietnam and most importantly
Japan (as well as other smaller nations). TPP can be seen as the mirror-image
of TTIP: the attempt by a part of US capital to extend its sphere of influence
towards Asia, though importantly by bypassing China and Russia, suggesting
the underlying motivations are strategic and not strictly economic. As was the
case with TTIP, the contents of agreements were classified, though the central
themes were known, and were essentially very similar to TTIP. While Wikileaks
was able to obtain some documentation, most importantly concerning negotiations over intellectual property, we cannot know the finer details. However,
what concerns us is showing how these negotiations over free trade served as
an important instrument in the fight between competing capitals.

Indeed, TPP was clearly intended to counter the Shanghai Pact (the
Shanghai Cooperation Organisation) whose members include, aside from
China and Russia, the ex-Soviet republics rich in prime materials, India,
Pakistan, Afghanistan and Iran, uniting as such many states that, in spite of
the crisis, had experienced significant growth over recent years. Yet the most
important takeaway from the experience of the TTIP and TPP negotiations, is
that the global crisis, which emerged with full force in the US, paradoxically
turned out to be an ideal moment for dollar capital, allowing it to undermine
support for euro capital and liberating enough resources to permit an advance
on another enemy capital. That new and highly competitive enemy capital is
renminbi capital, capital based in China, supported by Russian capital, or rouble capital. However, with the election of Trump in 2016, expression of a very
different part of American capital to that which supported Obama, all of this
was overturned. Elected with significant popular support consolidated around
the slogan of 'America First,' one of his first acts in January 2017 was to withdraw from TPP, as had been promised during the election campaign. In place
of TPP the Trump administration sought a return to the strategy that had been
in vogue in the 90s, consisting of forming similar accords bilaterally, in order to
monetise America's military and economic strength.

As such, the US has proceeded to sign bilateral agreements with all the same
TPP member states, while the Shanghai Pact continues to bind China, Russia,
India and Iran (and others), both in terms of economic policy and in terms of
military or foreign policy. It would seem, therefore, that capital, in its highly
advanced stage of imperialism,

> shows us that certain relations are established between capitalist alli-
> ances, *based* on the economic division of the world; while parallel with
> this fact and in connection with it, certain relations are established

between political alliances, between states, on the basis of the territorial division of the world, of the struggle for colonies, of the 'struggle for economic territory.'

LENIN, 1917a: 92

Yet at the same time we have seen over the last few years a qualitative shift, representing a discontinuity with the past. With the Chinese economy in continual expansion, despite its rivals' attempt at sabotage, Chinese capital has attracted admiration even from the prestigious publications of the high capitalist class. The People's Republic has made agreements to hand over extraordinary sums of money (surpassing thousands of billions of dollars) to countries across Asia (Russia in particular) for the construction of infrastructure and energy supply, and has proposed a free trade area to explicitly counter TPP, prompting talk of a 'Chinese century' or a 'changing global equilibrium.' The conflict between factions of global capital is thus intensifying, now between a different set of rivals. The crisis of capital as system, though having initially emerged in the USA, later hit hardest those European states that were entirely unprepared for the speculative attacks beginning in 2010, with the excessive bureaucracy that had built up in Europe over time adding to the eurozone's woes. As a result, it seems that euro capital is momentarily on the side-lines of the imperialist contest, relegated to cheerleading its counterpart from across the Atlantic. In the meantime, while Japan's economy conspicuously deteriorates, Chinese capital, allied with Russian capital, has the upper hand in the current state of play, with dollar capital continuing to play a major role despite its ailing health. An agreement between the two countries – which could entail what would essentially be symbiotic economic ties between China and Russia, as well as the use of renminbi and roubles as payment for raw materials to the exclusion of dollar capital – could bring about a serious shift in the global balance of powers, economically speaking but also in terms of political and military power. Indeed, this seems ever more likely. And to give an idea of the possible consequences, the last person to propose a currency change for the pricing of oil (from dollars to euros) was Saddam Hussein. How that ended is well known, and this time the stakes are even higher.

CHAPTER 3

A Flood of Liquidity

From QE *towards a New Despotic Management of Capitalism*

> But if this new accumulation comes up against difficulties of appli-
> cation, against a lack of spheres of investment, i.e. if branches of
> production are saturated and loan capital is over-supplied, this
> plethora of loanable money capital proves nothing more than the
> barriers of *capitalist* production. The resulting credit swindling
> demonstrates that there is no positive obstacle to the use of this
> excess capital.
>
> MARX, 1894: 639, emphasis added

∴

1 'Hostile Brothers' and Fictitious Capital

So far we have referred only in passing to the monetary policies put in place
by the Federal Reserve and other central banks (the Bank of Japan *in primis*)
in the post-2008 period, looking for their possible positive effects in terms of
recovering dollar capital's capacity to accumulate. However, it is important
that we make sense of the role monetary policy plays within a context of overproduction and ever-intensifying interclass conflict, in a stage of imperialism
defined by competition between rival currency areas.

In the years following the shock that rocked the entire global capitalist system – product of the uncontrollable emergence of a forty-year long global crisis of capital accumulation – the fight between euro capital and dollar capital
escalated to dramatic proportions. The most alarming moment by some measure was the US-based speculative attack on Southern European public debt
that took place almost ten years before the outbreak of the Covid-19 pandemic
(see subsequent chapters for more on this). Since then, with the stalling of the
TTIP negotiations, there has been a relative lull, seemingly due to a current
balance of forces favourable enough to warrant a let up on the part of the USA.

In the face with this ferocious attack, euro capital found itself somewhat
unprepared. And something that made things more difficult was the fact that

the ECB is legally constrained from buying up euro member bonds directly on the primary market, action that could potentially mitigate a surge in eurozone periphery sovereign bond yields and spreads. As it was, the speculators found they were able to work unhindered.

For Europe, this relative lack of options meant creative solutions needed to be produced. Some called for the most debt-burdened states to leave the eurozone, others for a two-track eurozone to adapt to economic differences. What none of these well-meaning proposals considered, however, was the fact that the scenario Europe was facing was the result of a conflict between capitals that saw a well-armed attacker on one side and a vulnerable and relatively defenceless victim on the other. In circles where this was more correctly understood, the focus of debates turned to removing some of the constitutional constraints placed on the ECB, both to aid the current crisis and to show its 'hostile brothers' that next time round the eurozone would find itself better prepared. While the anti-EU front was growing louder, in the first few months of 2012 it was already clear that the ECB was ready to step up to the challenge and set a new precedent, sidestepping, or radically reinterpreting its constitutional limitations in order to protect German capital above all and, by knock-on effect, the rest of the eurozone.

The result of this, in July of the same year, was Draghi's now famous "whatever it takes" speech. With just these three simple words, the President of the ECB sent an unequivocal message to US capital that euro capital was ready and willing to defend its interests. The plan that had been decided on went by the name of the Outright Monetary Transactions programme (OMT) and would form part of the European Stability Mechanism (ESM), an apparatus created to stabilise the common currency by providing financial aid to member states. Though it was limited to the modest sum of €650 billion, the ESM at least served as a deterrent for future speculative onslaughts (indeed, the programme came to be known as Draghi's 'bazooka,' the bellicose connotations clearly intended).

While the package of measures served more as a mere inhibitor than a lasting solution, limited in quantitative and qualitative terms as it was, its announcement nevertheless coincided with a slow but steady rebalancing. By the end of 2012, from a financial perspective at least, the worst of the shock could be said to have been absorbed (or at least the risks of a new speculative attack had been curtailed, as confirmed by the progressive reduction in Greek and other spreads). However, this 'sterilisation' – managed by and for capital – was carried out principally through the implementation of austerity regimes, i.e. through the contraction of a quantitatively significant section of the working class's (indirect) wages in the form of public services such as healthcare, education, and so on, and even through the imposition of constitutional requirements on balanced budgets. As such, even while euro capital suffered at the hands of its rival currency – its hostile brother – it still sought to seize the opportunity to tighten the screws on its own local working class. Indeed, it went above and beyond in pursuing the most effective of the crisis-fighting tactics: bringing down the value of labour-power and concurrently 'liberating' large numbers of workers, called upon by the ruling class's powerful propaganda machine to sacrifice themselves for the sake of the 'homeland.'

2   Quantitative Easing (QE)

In material terms, over the course of 2012–1016, the ECB's QE programme delivered €1,140 billion in liquidity, a total that was divided into weekly issuances of around €60 billion each. This new money was granted to the national central banks under the condition that they use it to buy sovereign bonds on the secondary market, i.e. not at issuance, allowing the principle of central bank independence from government to remain unviolated, a principle that since the 90s has been central to the European project. Greece was initially excluded from the programme as, having 'suspended' its austerity measures, it essentially renounced its right to be exempt from the rules that barred a state with highly insolvent bonds from accessing ECB liquidity. Most of the bonds that were bought (around 80–90%) were supposed to stay on the books of the individual central banks, leaving the rest to the ECB, which would therefore be kept from exposure even where one of the states involved defaulted (as unlikely as that would have been). This seemingly unimportant detail in fact prompts two very significant considerations. Firstly, as the bonds bought were basically bad debt, it meant that once again that the public sector (or parastatal sector, as we could consider the 'independent' central banks) was acting like a bad bank on behalf of the private sector, hoovering up junk securities in exchange for liquidity. Moreover, in order to circumvent the regulatory obstacles described above, the ECB took from each state only 20% of this mass of bonds, requiring the local central banks to shoulder the rest. In this way the ECB was able to shift much of the responsibility for the operation's success. Secondly, a key reason for choosing to carry out the programme in this manner was the fact that the eurozone's strong economies (Germany *in primis*) were unwilling to let their central banks, or the ECB, take on an oversized share of the burden, preferring instead to see the unreliable foreign bonds (essentially Greek, Spanish, Portuguese, Italian or Irish bonds) distributed across the eurozone.

Many so-called experts were deceived by the launch of the QE programme. While they recognised that the ECB's inability to act as 'lender of last resort' represented a key weakness of the founding treaties, they also incorrectly assumed that this flood of money would automatically translate into increases in production and employment, leading the EU economy out of the woods. But if it were that simple, why had this principal element of the ECB's constitution not been questioned before? Had the alterations been made before the 2010 speculative attack, surely the whole catastrophe could have been averted. And if these monetary policies were so beneficial, why did the EU leadership dig in its heels in defence of the diktat of the 'institutions,' continuing with austerity and the gospel of balanced budgets, remaining essentially unmoved in the face of the collapse of half of Europe's economies?

The reasons, still today skilfully obscured, lie in the fact that the authors of the ECB's constitution were driven by a worldview, ostensibly scientific though in reality deeply reactionary, that held that so-called expansionary monetary policies only ever lead to inflation. Following the marginalist line, the theory is that variations in the quantity of money in circulation have no relation whatsoever to the production of commodities, or even less on employment, as fluctuations in the money supply can only influence prices, and as such inflation. Therefore, the ECB's cardinal objective was not boosting employment but keeping inflation low, with a precise 2% mark as its target. Any other kind of intervention was outlawed. Indeed, even before the announcement of the OMTs programme (the original 'bazooka'), the central bankers had been forced to wait for the German constitutional court to determine if such action was compliant with German law, such was the fear of the ECB overstepping its narrow remit.

What changed to make QE seen as permissible, then, especially from 2015 onwards, was not the legal framework that regulates the ECB's actions but rather developments in the economies that make up the eurozone. Indeed, at the time of the "whatever it takes speech" the trend in some countries in the consumer price index was negative (i.e. deflationary), something which could potentially repeat itself. It was for this reason, therefore, that the injection of liquidity in the form of QE could be considered consistent with the eurozone's constitutional framework: where the objective was to maintain a pre-established level of inflation, and where expansive monetary policy is able to raise general price levels, in a deflationary (or low-inflationary) situation it made sense to allow QE. In other words, what changed was prices, not the ideology.

From the very beginnings of the 2008 crisis, only shortly after the Lehman collapse, the US monetary authorities had followed a very different approach.

Taking advantage of the absence of the kind of rigid dogma that plagued the European institutions, Ben Bernanke – under explicit instruction from Obama, a far cry from the doctrine of central bank 'independence' – very quickly abandoned the idea that monetary policy was purely a vehicle for controlling inflation. Instead, he invested in monetary policy the potential for development in terms of accumulation, and for reducing unemployment, which was rising at alarming rates.

Indeed, as it was dollar capital that was in fact in the most trouble, it was the Federal Reserve that had begun the (potentially lethal) cycle of liquidity injections. In 2009, well before the 2010 speculative attack on the PIIGS, the Fed had magicked $1,700 billion (QE I) out of thin air, with the aim of cushioning the dramatic effects on the US economy, but also of creating the conditions that would allow the epicentre of the crisis to be shifted onto euro capital, a manoeuvre which took only two years to materialise. However, despite the enormity of the sums being created within the US economy, it took some time for any effects to show. The Fed was therefore forced to launch a second tranche, amounting to $600 billion (QE II), matched by a similar though much smaller programme on the British side announced by the Bank of England.

And in 2012, just as euro capital was going through its worst months and was tearing itself apart through internal conflict, the Fed launched QE III, safe in the knowledge that its main rival had for the moment been incapacitated. Dubbed 'QE-infinity' this new programme saw new liquidity being created on a weekly basis, with the idea that this would continue until of a set of macroeconomic objectives (job creation above all) had been reached. By the time this third 'mandate' was wound up, over the end of 2013 and the beginning of 2014, it had pumped another $2,000 billion into the system. Yet the results were not much of an improvement on the previous two rounds. Once again, while market indexes markedly improved, the impact on capital accumulation was generally negative. From 2013 onwards, while the markets continued to behave as if the crisis had ended, both production and the circulation of commodities effectively remained stagnant. So, while an accumulation crisis rumbled on under the surface, just five years on from 2008, the synthetic Dow Jones index, like its Japanese counterpart, had already surpassed its pre-crisis values.

3   The Effects of Quantitative Easing

Considering how events unfolded, if we take a step back and look at the whole picture there are two things that stand out. First and foremost, investing the Fed's manoeuvres with the responsibility to resolve the US's weak accumulation problem was even at that time an operation not without caveats. Though the bulk of the liquidity created – effectively gifted to the private sector and in exchange for debt of dubious quality – ended up being used for speculation, it is not difficult to believe there was some trickle-down, some respite provided for a few small capitalists of limited importance (after all we are speaking about a total sum of $4.5 trillion, which with the current exchange rate would equal twice Italy's public debt). It is not unlikely, therefore, that a portion, however small, was used by dollar capital to produce new commodities and new value. However, it was a truly small proportion in relation to the whole, especially when we consider the fact that the liquidity created was so vast it represented 30% of US GDP. A scheme of such magnitude, or even a more cautious programme, should have created far more value and surplus value, as well as extra jobs.[1] Add to this the fact that the Japanese QE programme was similarly ineffectual, and one starts to have real doubts about the usefulness of such measures.

So how are we to make sense of the failings of expansionary monetary policy? The answer is by looking at it from a different perspective. If we try to judge the effectiveness of the ECB's flood of liquidity according to the tired old paradigms inherited from marginalism and Keynesianism we end up in a conceptual blind alley. Where the latter sees in monetary policy the possibility for expansion in production and employment (which we can term Keynesianism, though this is somewhat simplified), the former stresses the 'neutrality of money' (rejecting any notion that monetary policy can affect real variables). But what both frameworks have in common is the assumption that economic relations are immutable and minimally bound to the course of history.

In other words, what we need to understand is that an 'injection' of liquidity may have very different effects depending on the contemporary stage of accumulation. Presumably, during a favourable period for capital accumulation, greater access to liquidity can indeed serve as an accelerator in the production of commodities and value. But the opposite is also true. In a phase of sluggish accumulation due to overproduction, meaning reduced profit rates and an excess of money capital:

> *Over-production* is specifically conditioned by the general law of the production of capital: to produce to the limit set by the productive forces (that is to say, to exploit the maximum amount of labour with the given

---

1   In our final chapter we will calculate the precise scale of the different expansive policies put in place following the crisis and will discuss the results in terms of job creation and economic growth.

amount of capital), without any consideration for the actual limits of the market or the needs backed by the ability to pay; and this is carried out through continuous expansion of reproduction and accumulation [...]

MARX, 1861–3: vol 32. 163–164, emphasis in the original

Once the existing 'limits of the market' have been reached, new liquidity – or rather new, essentially free credit – can no longer guarantee a recovery in accumulation.

And in both of these cases credit is still denied to many who need it (small and very small businesses *in primis*), meaning projects for increased production meet with no corresponding effectual demand, as markets simply do not have the purchasing power. In the same way, conditions do not change for the workers applying for credit to buy cars, appliances, or houses, as their credit-worthiness (on which basis the bank decides to grant or deny application) is determined by the stability of their employment or by other asset guarantees, and so is entirely unaffected by the presence of greater liquidity in the economic system. Furthermore, as we have come to understand over the years, the contemporary collapse of interest rates makes lending itself unprofitable for banks. As a result, the bulk of the liquidity is gobbled up by financial capital, which is easily able to make use of it, both by clearing any bad debt off its books in exchange for cash (passing the bonds onto the local central bank), and then by transforming it into fictitious capital, which, paradoxically, only serves to further inflate the speculative bubble that since 2020 has been expanding to alarming proportions.

For these reasons, those who once saw in credit facilitation the panacea of all economic ills, now have found themselves entirely disappointed by reality. While there are some signs of recovery, these are mostly side-effects, and more likely the result of other forces unleashed by capital to counteract the crisis (e.g. downward restructuring of the labour market). What we can be sure of, however, is that these vast amounts of liquidity have added to the bubble stuffed full of derivatives that has been snowballing over the years, reinforced again in 2014 by the Bank of Japan's QE programme (once again referred to as a financial 'bazooka') and by many other subsequent programmes by central banks across the globe.

4   Capitalism's Addiction Problem

The devastating effects of heroin are well-known, whether through cultural representation or from direct experience, especially for those growing up in the late 70s and early 80s. Indeed, its effects are known too by the ruling classes, who, by allowing the markets to flood with heroin in the place of softer drugs, found a successful way of killing off antagonistic social movements (see, e.g., D'Angelo and Virdis, 2013). It is also known that cocaine circulates in abondance on Wall Street, as the graphic details of the recent Scorsese (2015) film attest.

Drugs, dependency and addiction are therefore elements that in one way or another are inherent to the capitalist mode of production, since capitalism itself, being a social mechanism that functions as a biological organism, cannot avoid being attracted to addictive substances to help ease the pain of deep-rooted crisis.

In this case, however, the substance is something else. While it may not be a chemical, it is a substance that has nevertheless become a drug for much of global capitalism, generating dependency and the ensuing violent swings between depression and euphoria, a bipolarism that seems to have no other cure. One could easily think here that we are speaking about profit, the monetary form of exploitation, or, more astutely, surplus-value, with Marx's assertions about the 'voracity' of capital in mind. In reality, however, what we are referring to is something that has no beneficial effects on the accumulation cycle, but simply acts to numb the pain, a temporary lull inevitably followed by a destructive come down.

Trapped in a dangerous situation – in many ways more critical than that which followed the collapse of Lehman Bros., as we have shown – the fortunes of dollar and euro capital (and more broadly of capital globally, of their other hostile brothers) have over the last decade depended heavily on so-called liquidity injections (the metaphor makes itself as injection is in fact the technical term). In other words, the quantitative easing proposed by the Federal Reserve and then by central banks across the globe has kept alive a system that not only has spent the last ten years of crisis failing to solve its problems, but has even managed to exacerbate the situation, as we saw above.

It was in the first half of the 1970s that capitalist accumulation globally experienced its first major setbacks, due for the most part to the US dollar crisis that led to the unilateral decision to end the Bretton Woods accords. The same generation that had in the previous decades been at the fore of important social struggles – in the wake, paradoxically, of a recessive phase in capitalism – now seemed to have exhausted its revolutionary spirit, turning instead to drugs and rock and roll. This was after all the period in which the Rolling Stones were singing "please sister morphine, turn my nightmares into dreams."

The song (Jagger and Richards, 1971), in fact written by Mick Jagger's partner Marianne Faithful, met with the success it did because it interpreted a physical state common to many at the time, a set of intense emotions collectively felt by the generation born in the period between the end of the War and the reconstruction that followed. Serious drug addiction dragged people down into the underworld, from where only another injection could pull them out for just a brief moment before they would fall back even further, until eventually, as unfortunately happened all too often, they could never come back.

This feeling of desperately searching for the next hit cannot be far from what the representatives of fictitious capital were experiencing when in summer 2016, Mario Draghi convened his press conference to propose the continuation of the ECB's QE, marking the beginning of "phase two"; a second round of bazooka fire. The initial months of 2016 had been difficult for financial markets everywhere. In the first half of January alone, stock market values had plummeted by $5,600 billion (a deflation rather than a conflagration as was the metaphor used, seeing as there is nothing material involved, only fictitious gambles). The Shanghai stock market lost 15% and the Dow Jones and the Nasdaq about 10%, with the European and Japanese markets not far behind. In short, in fifteen days, the world's fictitious wealth was reduced by an amount equivalent to a third of US GDP. This generalised collapse, clearly a sign of systemic faults, sent stock market brokers and capitalists of various kinds running to the monetary authorities (the ECB and the Fed in particular), their dealers in liquidity, begging desperately for relief from withdrawal. However, though it was a severe case, manifestations of this dependency were not new, and nor was this episode even particularly visible. The only major difference was the unprecedented intensity with which it was confirmed that none of the issues plaguing the economy for more than a decade had been resolved.

Indeed, this time round the need was so acute that even bonds of the least stable African economies served to satiate it. When Rwanda issued a round of treasuries in 2016 the offer was significantly oversubscribed: demand for the securities was *eight* times greater than the supply, despite low yields and not insignificant risks. It is also important to note that the 10-year bonds were issued in dollars, a repeat on a smaller scale of an operation tried once before in Latin America (principally in Argentina) during the late 80s and early 90s, with disastrous consequences. In the Latin American case, as the debt was denominated in a currency stronger than their own, repayment became almost impossible, one of the main causes of Argentina's late 90s default.

5   When It Rains, It Pours

What all these figures and details add up to is a simple fact: during a phase
of crisis, where saturated markets mean capital cannot profit from production of commodities – i.e. through the production of value (the M-C-M'
formula) – capitalists must instead raid the stock markets in the hope of sub-
tracting value from their rivals (M-M'). What we are dealing with, therefore, is
the very opposite of what we were told by the stockbrokers and economists.
The 'credit crunch' was not due to a lack of liquidity, as liquidity was in fact
being made readily available. What happened instead was that the normal
channels through which credit flows from the banks to businesses and households broke down. This was because in times of crisis, like those we continue
to live through, both of these parties are unable to guarantee their debts. The
banks due to a glut in the market, and the borrowers due to the progressive
precaritisation of their employment and their lives in general. In other words,
there is not too little liquidity but *too much*. The real issue is that the prevailing
market conditions prevent a more efficient redistribution of the cashflow.

As such, if we were to consider the agents of capital as a monolithic unit,
or rather if we were to view the ruling class in its unity, it would make perfect
sense to conclude that flooding the global markets with liquidity is a point-
less exercise, something that can have little effect on material production or
on the existing power relations within the capitalist class. However, capital is
not a single whole. More than ever during periods of crisis the ruling class is
revealed to us in all its multiplicity, as internal conflict reaches new intensity.
Herein therefore, lies the real motivations for the various announcements of
QE: what was most significant was the timing of the different central banks'
interventions, each as expressions of a different capitalist class. Effective strategy allowed the economy suffering the most in 2008, the USA, to pick itself
up long before the rest, anticipating the moves of its 'hostile brothers' who
proved themselves to be much less agile and essentially incapable of resisting
the offensive. Draghi's reference to the ECB's monetary policy as a 'bazooka,'
is therefore far from accidental. The bellicose connotations conferred on the
'unusual' monetary manoeuvre are merely further proof of the ruling class's
awareness of the functioning of the system and class consciousness, infinitely
greater than that of labour.

If intra-capitalist conflict is key to understanding why seemingly useless
monetary policies, in terms of accumulation recovery, were pursued, there is
a further element we need to consider, which both confirms our findings and
brings into question how our present and future is commonly understood. It
is widely accepted that what happens in the Asian markets, at least since the

turn of the century, has a powerful impact on the capitalist system as a whole. The idea that 'communist' China has become the motor of 21st century capitalism is not unfounded. Neither is the notion, from a different perspective, that it is the world's only significant *socialist* economy that is keeping capitalism from an otherwise unavoidable ruin or has done so on at least on at least two important occasions. Since the second half of 2015, however, the West has begun to view China with suspicion and even fear, concerns that were strengthened in August 2016 when the Chinese authorities decided to devalue the yuan, giving a sizeable boost to the competitivity of Chinese exports (to the detriment of European and American trade). The immediate aftermath of this saw the collapse of markets across the globe as waves of panic spread to all corners. With a bit of time and effort (or rather a lot, we could say) calm was finally restored, but it was from this moment that the term 'currency war' returned to common usage, picking up on a theory developed in the US and relatively unknown in Europe (Rickards, 2011) that held (broadly summarising) that the focal point of capitalist conflict concerned the devaluation of currencies (principally the dollar, euro, yuan and yen) as an attempt to detract greater shares of the market from rival capitals.

On the surface this argument seems convincing. It applies the myth of 'competitive devaluation' to the world market, understanding competition on the global stage as playing out principally in the form of a propensity toward devaluation in order to make goods produced within a currency area more attractive to foreign buyers. The reality, however, is far more complex. Reducing the issue to a simple question of account imbalances, without consideration of the specificities of capital and its mode of production, means falling back on bourgeois ways of viewing the world, a view very similar in fact to that of the advocates for eurozone exit. This is not to say that the question of currency rivalry is unimportant. Indeed, as we have argued, the currency conflict is one of the most salient characteristics of the current stage of imperialism. But if we fail to contextualise currency conflict within the general laws of capitalist development, so within the production of value globally – which necessarily implies conflict between and within classes – it would seem to relate purely to accounting, seemingly of little interest. It is certainly true, though this is only one aspect of the issue, that pursuing currency depreciation is a reality for all the big central banks (EU, USA, China, Japan), especially in a context of generalised crisis, as they seek to give a gasp of oxygen to their choking local capitals. Yet as the financial press pointed out at the time (Longo, *Il Sole 24 Ore,* 24th October 2019), if everyone is resorting to the same 'unconventional' monetary measures and pumping the markets with liquidity on the basis of negative real interest rates – meaning effectively that interest rates are lower than inflation,

so borrowing costs nothing at all in real terms and is itself an investment –
then the effects are necessarily voided. In other words, if everyone does the
same thing, there is no 'competitive' advantage to be gained.

6   Capital's New Despotism

The 9th of November 2016 is a date that will not easily be forgotten in years to
come. It was this day that the world watched in astonishment as Donald Trump
was declared winner of the US presidential election. The fact that Trump held
extremist right-wing views, it turned out, was not enough to convince the
US electorate to make Hilary Clinton the first ever female leader of the USA.
Generally seen as the establishment candidate, with overwhelming support
from America's cultural elites, her defeat came as a shock, though she did in
fact win the popular vote by around two million.

In any case, the election of a new president in the US marked a considerable change of gear in the superstructural management of the crisis that had
peaked in 2008. With no opposition to speak of, except from within its own
ranks, the ruling class seemed to have revised some of the cardinal elements of
the system, erecting a power structure that was new in many respects, at least
in appearance, and which was certainly more adapted to the present stage of
capitalist development. One of the realities it was adapting to, perhaps one
of most dangerous phenomena for capital to have emerged over this last very
dramatic decade, was the depletion of the middle class[2] (which Marx referred
to as the 'lower middle class'), as its numbers returned to the ranks of the pro-
letariat. On the whole, and in most parts of the world, capital has so far handled this problem well. Indeed, it is a phenomenon very familiar to capital, not
dissimilar to that described by Marx and Engels in the Communist Manifesto:

> The lower strata of the middle class – the small tradespeople, shopkeep-
> ers, and retired tradesmen generally, the handicraftsmen and peasants
> – all these sink gradually into the proletariat, partly because their dimin-
> utive capital does not suffice for the scale on which Modern Industry is
> carried on, and is swamped in the competition with the large capitalists,
> partly because their specialised skill is rendered worthless by new meth-
> ods of production. Thus, the proletariat is recruited from all classes of the
> population.
>
> MARX AND ENGELS, 1847: 491–492

---

2   We will look at this in more detail in the subsequent chapters.

However, if for Marx and Engels this 'usurpation' of the labour aristocracy had revolutionary potential, history has shown this does not always play out. Indeed, in the absence of robust class organisation, it can result in a turn to extreme conservatism or reactionary politics; the shared genesis of fascism and Nazism, though both with their own particularities, is exemplary in this regard. As the general law of accumulation unfolds, especially in phases of crisis, it "makes an accumulation of misery a necessary condition, corresponding to the accumulation of wealth" (Marx, 1867: 799) (currently termed 'polarisation,' though this should be understood as a class polarisation and not just a polarisation in incomes), with considerable potential for destabilisation. The ruling class understands this well and seeks to manipulate it to its own advantage.

However, it is important here to make a conceptual clarification. Reference to rising inequality has become a recurring refrain even in traditionally reactionary circles such as the IMF, the World Bank, or the Vatican. With statistical data now widely available globally, it is difficult to deny that a process of extreme polarisation has taken place over the last few decades. Observation, though, is one thing; understanding this phenomenon for what it really is, is quite another. Far too often the issue is reduced to a question of income differences, of the gap between the 'rich' and the 'poor.' This incomplete analysis, which does not take account of property relations, is not the result of a mere terminological error but rather a distortion in the definition and comprehension of concepts. If the increase in equality is bracketed within the realm of income, wages and profits lose their class specificity and become mere numbers to be processed. In this way, the class struggle is obscured, replaced by the more innocuous notion of a struggle between income percentiles, as indeed Piketty (2014) and his followers have proposed (but also social movements such as Occupy Wall Street). This is a conceptual trap we must be careful to avoid.

It is commonly acknowledged that the progressive disappearance of the middle class – ideological (and material) cornerstone of modern capitalism – is a destabilising factor, potentially capable, we ourselves add, of revealing the true face of the capitalist mode of production. However, through skilful use of some powerful weapons – racism, terrorism, immigration, among others – the problem has for the moment been kept mostly under control. By exacerbating competition within the working class, guaranteed by the presence of an ever-growing industrial reserve army (i.e., the unemployed and the precariously employed), capital has favoured its further fragmentation and political disintegration.

The result of this has been a global wave of neo-fascist despotism, perfectly incarnated by Trump, Le Pen, Farage in the UK, the NPD in Germany, as well as Erdoğan, Orbán, Duda, Salvini, Bolsonaro, and in some respects Putin. Though

tempered in common parlance through terms like 'populism,' it seems fair
to say that the phenomenon has become so pervasive that there has been a
breakthrough in quality as well as quantity. Across the globe a clear pattern is
emerging, beginning with Brexit and then the startling election of Trump, but
also including Erdoğan's referendum (won by a whisker) and the inexorable
rise of the National Front in France. The bourgeois democratic model, based
on a bipartite system alternating between Left and Right, was able to survive
the period immediately following the collapse of the Soviet Union up to the
explosion of the crisis in 2008. Since then, however, it has not been providing
the same guarantees. The consistently high levels of unemployment – even
the OECD (2020) has admitted that the figure of around 10% usually reported
is likely underestimated – of poverty, and of inequality have exposed the illu-
sionary nature of so-called 'liberal democracy,' leading to a breakdown mis-
leadingly referred to as the collapse of the 'traditional parties.' Indeed, where
such processes were previously associated purely with the Global South, they
now affect the North. The imperialist democracies once held up as beacons of
stability, are now barely distinguishable from the rest.

What seems to be happening is that the capitalist system, as a result of
the ongoing accumulation crisis, is having to resort to a more authoritarian
management of the production and circulation of commodities. As the necessity of keeping potentially revolutionary classes under control becomes more
urgent than ever, the façade of bourgeois liberalism starts to crumble around
us. Indeed, this is the real purpose of the European constitutional reforms
being championed by JP Morgan (2013), or the repressive police reforms being
adopted in various European countries under the premise of anti-terrorism
and immigration control.[3] The production of value and surplus-value must
encounter no barriers and must continue to ensure capital is satiated. And so-
called labour market reforms are of course part and parcel. Yet this it is still a
process, and as such will continue to throw up contradictions, that manifest
themselves in the balance of power within the dominant class. As for the US
2016 elections, Trump and Clinton represented two factions of the same dollar
capitalist class, in many ways opposing but in others closely connected. In this
case, the contradictions between hostile brothers resolved themselves in the
victory of the faction that favoured greater protection of local markets over the
more extreme capitalist internationalism of Hillary Clinton.

---

3   In Italy this took the form of the security reforms passed by the Lega – Movimento 5 stelle
    coalition government.

The perspective of intra-class struggle and of the ruling class's necessity to adapt to the crises produced by the contradictions of capitalism helps us to read reality, but to provide a more solid theoretical underpinning, it is necessary to shift the discussion back onto the terrain of the material relations of production, or rather property relations. It would seem that what is taking place in the current mature phase of imperialism is the temporal inversion between formal and real subsumption, i.e., of the relation between base and superstructure. In general, in the more advanced stages of every mode of production,

> a 'breakthrough' to new social relations of production does not in fact occur – what we are dealing with is a sort of temporal inversion in the historical process: the old mode of production continues to lug around its carcass in a delirious torpor, in the midst of a throng of *zombies*, as they seek to prevail in the service of their masters. And where this quest produces any significant results, it is not only the processes specific to the mode of production that remain truly subservient, but also innovative processes that are unable to break out of the old *co-existing* system within whose confines they were contradictorily generated.
>
> PALA, 2019: 216–217

In other words, the historical reversal of base and superstructure dialectically generates a reality such as that which currently exists, whereby persistent and ferocious crisis is counterposed by an intensification in the ruling class's control and repression of the subordinated classes. What generates both extraordinary technological breakthroughs and a proportional undermining of the potential for accumulation, is the development of the capitalist mode of production itself. It is therefore only with a major change in the paradigm of political power (superstructure) that the ruling class can attempt to stem the rate of technological innovation and thus the development of new relations of production (base) that in the meantime tend to crystalise in the contemporary economic form.

So, beyond the single measures adopted, what interests us is attempting to determine the general direction of the management of dollar capital. Though Trump has not shown himself to be particularly politically astute, the straightforwardness of his language has worked in his favour (this was certainly something that appealed to his working classe voters). Trump was explicit in his desire to protect American industry (manufacturing and services) and to curb what he claimed were the effects of accelerated globalisation of the first part of the century: job losses for the white working class and factory closures due to the import of cheaper goods from Asia. The masses of red caps emblazoned with 'Make America Great Again' (ironically made in Vietnam[4]) were a celebration of protectionism – seasoned with a good helping of over-the-top nationalism – a guiding principle for the Trump administration. Trump's almost immediate withdrawal from TPP was thus a clear sign of the direction dollar capital was taking, preferring instead to seek out a head-on confrontation with Asian capital and China in particular. In 2017, the annual Davos conference presented the opportunity for a crystallisation of these two opposing positions. In the face of Trump's protectionist drift (crassly termed 'de-globalisation'), Xi Jinping put forward a very different vision in his speech, where he declared that

> It is true that economic globalization has created new problems, but this is no justification to write economic globalization off completely. Rather, we should adapt to and guide economic globalization, cushion its negative impact, and deliver its benefits to all countries and all nations [...] Whether you like it or not, the global economy is the big ocean that you cannot escape from.
>
> XI JINPING, 17th January 2017

It was within this context that the Covid-19 pandemic would hit, sharpening and redirecting these tensions that have been building up over years.

This dichotomy of 'protectionism' vs 'free market' has come to serve as a prism through which all public debate is distorted. We see this in political commentary that notes that whereas at the turn of the century 'globalisation' was all the rage among the political classes, today the preferred option is protectionism. What this highly superficial observation of course fails to understand is that this is fundamentally because we are living through a time of persistent crisis, and in a time of persistent crisis, a tendency to protect oneself is natural, however futile the attempt. And in this case it certainly is futile given the interconnectedness of global production chains. Protectionism is, put simply, merely the manifestation of the intensification of the intra-class conflict and its contradictions. This is also how we should view the UK's exit from the European Union. In the run up to the referendum, part of British (and international) capital used all manner of scare tactics to avoid an unwanted outcome, with tensions ramped up to such an extent that an anti-Brexit Labour MP was murdered in questionable circumstances. And in the aftermath, they did all

---

4 See, e.g., Fares and Volz (2017).

they could to overturn the result. Yet all failed, and now the UK outside the European Common Market is becoming a material reality.

The current despotic form of bourgeois power management should thus be understood through the contradictory process of the conceptual and temporal inversion (from a logical standpoint) of real subjugation with formal subjugation. 2019 has been the worst year since the beginning of the new millennium in terms of accumulation according to the IMF (2019), and none of the previous annual performances had been that much better. China's slowdown has had inevitable effects on the global economy. At the same time, since long before the Covid-19 pandemic, an immense speculative bubble has been looming ever larger above the heads of the ruling class, helped by the impact of the cryptocurrencies whose market value has risen by an incredible 100,000% in under ten years, and by the central banks' quantitative easing programmes. By the end of 2019, therefore, the stage was set for an epic disaster.

Income Distribution

Concepts, Analytical Tools and Empirical Evidence

1 Income Distribution

1.1 *Basic Concepts*

Income is generally considered an indicator of an individual or household's economic position and level of wellbeing, and income distribution refers to how much income is received by each unit of analysis (individual or household). Formally, income distribution consists in a collection of numbers with each figure representing the income of each unit that makes up the economy. According to requirements, the data can be analysed for a single moment in time or across different time periods – e.g., current income, or income across an individual's lifetime – and can be based on different units of analysis – e.g. individuals or families. It can also be relevant to look not just at how much people earn, i.e. *personal* income distribution, but also at the ways in which income is distributed among the factors of production – the *functional* distribution of income. The functional distribution of income describes the return received by the different factors of production – labour, capital and land – whereas personal income distribution refers to income flows to individuals or families. However, this chapter will look only at personal income distribution. We will discuss some approaches to analysing income distribution and look at income distribution in the world and then in Italy, which will be used as a single country example.[1]

1.2 *Representing Income Distribution*

There are many tools for representing income distribution. Some of these are specific to the topic (such as the Lorenz curve which we will look at in a subsequent section *Economic Inequality*), whereas others, such as frequency distribution, are basic statistical instruments for visually representing the patterns of an income distribution, allowing for comprehensive description of

---

[1] Analysis of the distribution of income is presented here in a statistical or quantitative rather than economic or qualitative manner. Issues around income distribution however are still relevant for the economics theory. For a comprehensive presentation of the main theories of income distribution see, e.g., Sandmo (2015).

the data and for easy comparison between different distributions. A frequency distribution describes the frequency with which the observations relating to a specific variable fall under pre-determined value brackets for that variable. In the case of income, these categories are income brackets (termed bins) of different ranges usually designed to be mutually exclusive. In terms of graphics, the distribution of income across different bins is usually represented by a *histogram*, a chart composed of rectangular columns whose widths represent the widths of the bins and heights the number (or percentage) of the income-receivers that fall into that bin. In this way, the height and area of each column represent, respectively, the density and number of income receivers in a given income bracket or bin. The total area of the columns put together is therefore equal to the total number of income-receivers (or to 1, if the number of income receivers belonging to the various brackets is expressed as a proportion rather than a number). Figure 1 is a histogram showing personal income distribution in Italy in 2016.[2] The source of the data is a survey carried out every two years by the Banca d'Italia (the Italian Central Bank) looking at household budgets in Italy.[3] The unit of analysis is the individual, with each person assigned the equivalised disposable income of the household they are part of.[4] The

---

2   The limits of the income intervals, or bins, defining the size of each bin, are based on deciles of the total, i.e., the range of income values divided into ten parts each containing the same number of observations. The area of each column therefore represents the same percentage of the total number of income receivers. In addition, to obtain more robust results, the income values of the poorest 1% and the richest 1% were fixed at the threshold values identifying these percentages.

3   The Banca d'Italia survey, used throughout this chapter can be found here (last accessed September 2021): https://www.bancaditalia.it/statistiche/tematiche/indagini-famiglie-impr ese/bilanci-famiglie/index.html?com.dotmarketing.htmlpage.language=1. One of the most reliable sources of statistical data on Italian income, the survery is ongoing since 1967, although data freely accessible for processing and research purposes have been available since 1977. For a description of how the survey came about and how it has changed over time, see Brandolini (1999).

4   Disposable income is the sum of all possible sources of income before tax. Equivalised disposable income is a way of measuring a household's income independently of its demographic characteristics. When an income distribution is based on households and not individuals, as in the Banca d'Italia survey, this creates obvious problems in terms of comparisons between households of different sizes, as households of different size and composition may enjoy very different levels of material well-being despite their total income being the same. In this case, a correction should be made to standardise these demographic heterogeneities to allow for meaningful comparison. This correction is called an 'equivalence scale', and 'equivalised income' is the level of income determined through application of a given equivalence scale. There is a wide range of equivalence scales in use in different countries. They all take household size into account: in many scales this is the only factor, while for those that take other demographic characteristics into account it is the factor with the

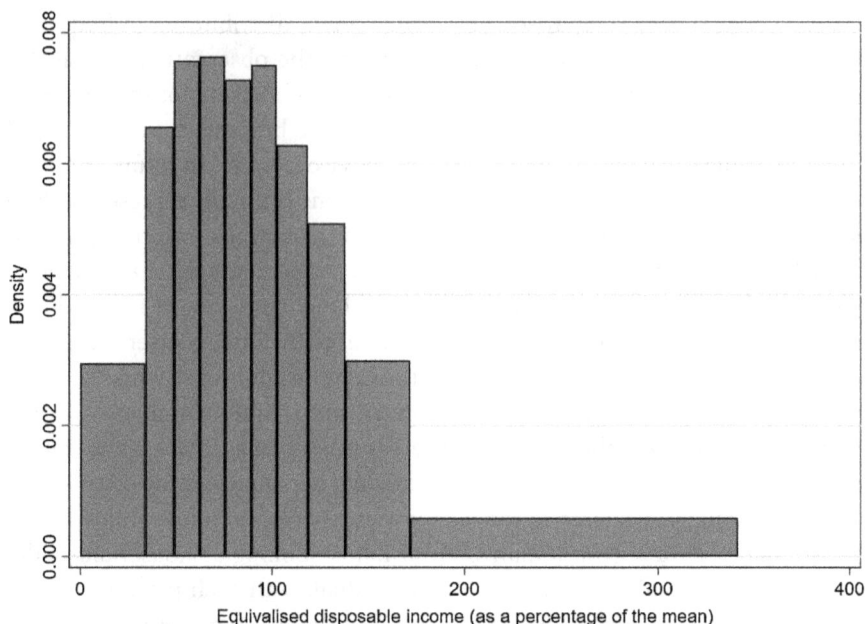

FIGURE 1   Representation by histogram of the distribution of equivalised household income
             in Italy in 2016
             SOURCE: AUTHORS' ELABORATION USING THE BANCA D'ITALIA
             INCOME SURVEY

distribution has the usual asymmetrical shape, with a relatively small proportion of people receiving very low incomes, a concentration around the lower
and middle incomes, and a progressively smaller share for higher incomes.

Despite its many advantages, however, some information is inevitably lost
through representation by histogram. For example, it is not possible to know
how income is distributed within each bracket or bin.[5] More information can
be represented by using income brackets or bins that are so small the height of
the column can be represented by short dashes that form a curve. This curve,
represented by the continuous line in Figure 2 is called the *frequency density*

---

greatest weight. The equivalence scale used for Figure 1 is the so-called 'modified OECD scale.'
This equivalence scale, recommended by the Organisation for Economic Co-operation and
Development (OECD), is currently used by Eurostat to calculate inequality and poverty indi-
cators used in the EU's official statistics.

5   A histogram can also be excessively sensitive to the widening or narrowing of bins, and
    so give a distorted idea of the overall pattern of income distribution. See, e.g., Cowell and
    Flachaire (2015).

function and expresses the proportion (or percentage) of income receivers corresponding to each income (in the same way the height of the columns do in a histogram), so that the area below the frequency density function is equal to 1 (or to 100%). Frequency density functions can have different patterns, but when referring to income distribution they typically display the form of the continuous curve of Figure 2, with the majority of observations concentrated on the left of the graph where the distribution reaches its highest point. The part of the distribution between the lowest income and the peak of the curve is called the *lower tail* of the distribution, and the part on the right, the *upper tail,* has a more gradual inclination and is longer than the lower tail. The typical form of income distribution is skewed right, with the right-hand tail tending to be the longer tail. The right-skewed asymmetry of the income density function is clearly shown in Figure 2, aided by comparison with a symmetrical bell curve (normal distribution) showing distribution balanced either side of a mean income value that is the same for both curves.[6]

It is possible to capture income data patterns by approximating the frequency density function with a non-parametric estimator (for more on estimating methods see Conti et al., 2006). Non-parametric estimating methods do not require an a priori hypothesis of the function's specific pattern – e.g., the normal density formula – to estimate distribution. Instead, a *kernel function* is used, which estimates the unknown density by 'regularising' the empirical income distribution. Rather than gathering observations into columns as with the histogram, the kernel estimator matches a small 'window' to each value along the income scale and calculates the density estimation for that value point based on the number of observations that fall within the window. More precisely, the estimated density in any one of the possible income values is obtained as such:

$$\widehat{f_h}(x) = \frac{1}{nh} \sum_{i=1}^{n} K\left(\frac{x - x_i}{h}\right).$$

---

6 Normal distribution is characterised by the following density function, often referred to as the Gauss or Gaussian curve:

$$f(x; \mu, \sigma) = \frac{1}{\sigma\sqrt{2\pi}} e^{-\frac{(x-\mu)^2}{2\sigma^2}}, x \in \mathbb{R}.$$

The curve is symmetrical in relation to the parameter μ, which represents the distribution mean and corresponds to the value where the curve reaches its highest point. When μ is varied, the curve shifts along the horizontal axis but its form remains the same. The parameter σ characterises the form of the curve, given that it represents the spread of values around the mean value μ. If σ is increased, the curve flattens and widens. If σ is decreased, the curve becomes narrower and higher.

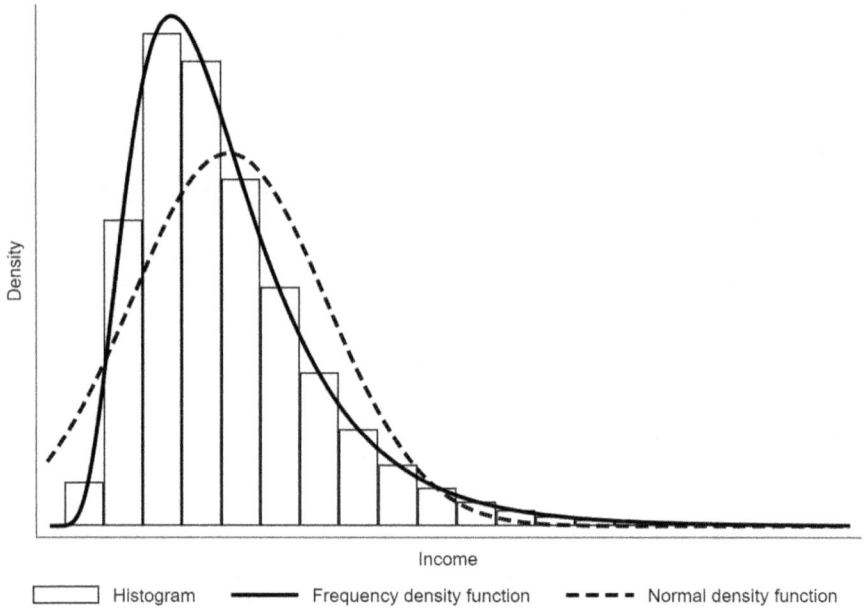

| □ Histogram | ▬ Frequency density function | ▬ ▬ ▬ Normal density function |

FIGURE 2   From histogram to frequency density function

In other words, it is calculated as a weighted 'local' mean – with weights decreasing as the distance between the generic income value and the point at which density is calculated increases – of the values that the $K(\bullet)$ function

assumes at the points $\dfrac{x - x_1}{h}$, ..., $\dfrac{x - x_n}{h}$.[7] The $K(\bullet)$ function is a density

function generally symmetric on either side of the origin known as the *kernel function*.[8] To increase its flexibility, the kernel function can be re-scaled with a scale factor of $h > 0$, known as the 'bandwidth,' which controls the weight of the observations that fall within the immediate surroundings of x. Choosing a value for h is one of the most delicate aspects of using a kernel method. A value too close to zero means the estimation will be erratic and will have an intolerably high variability. If the value is too high the estimation will be

---

7   In the formula, the divisor ensures that the value of the area below the density estimate is equal to 1 (or 100%).

8   There are different functions that can be used as the kernel function. One of the most common is the standardised Gaussian density, which possesses mathematical properties that make it convenient to use.

distorted and will not accurately reflect reality. A vast literature exists on the methods for automatically selecting the optimal bandwidth. In the following paragraphs we will use kernel density estimation with an automatic band-width selector for analysing the evolution over time of income distribution in Italy and globally.

1.3   *Global Income Distribution*

Figure 3 shows the evolution of 'global' income distribution over the last two centuries. The graph is based on estimations of mean income for each country (pro capita GDP). For comparability across countries and over time, incomes are measured in 2011 international dollars – a hypothetical currency that has the purchasing power of the US dollar in 2011. Global income distribution is indicated at three different points in time:

In 1800 only a few countries had reached a satisfactory level of economic growth. The graph shows that large parts of the world lived in poverty with an income similar to the poorest countries today. In 1975, 175 years later, the world had changed: it had become highly unequal. Global income distribution had become 'bimodal,' with the form of a double camel hump: one hump for income below the international poverty line[9] and a second far higher up the income scale. The world was now divided into the poor 'developing' world and the 'developed' world that was ten times richer. Over the course of the next four decades, global income distribution again changed radically. Now there was a convergence in incomes: in many poor countries, especially in Southeast Asia, incomes had grown at greater speed than in the richer countries. While enormous differences in income persisted, the world was no longer divided into the two neat categories of 'developed' and 'developing.' The two-hump line had become one-humped. At the same time, the distribution had shifted rightwards: the incomes of many of the poorest people across the globe had increased and poverty had decreased faster than at any other time in history (see below for further discussion).

The graph shown here takes as its unit of observation a whole country and uses the county's per capita income (GDP) without consideration of its pop-ulation size. In that sense, it compares countries as if they were each repre-sented by a single individual. The distribution displayed in Figure 3 is often referred to as 'global' income distribution, but it is in fact rather misleading to

---

9 On the meaning of the 'poverty line' and its different conceptualisations, see the section *Poverty: Definition and Measurement* below.

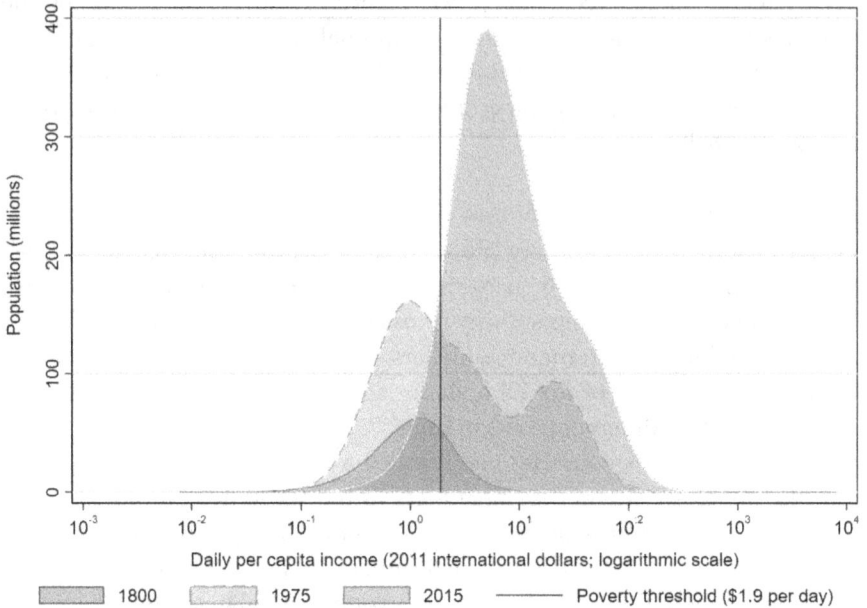

FIGURE 3   The global distribution of income in 1800, 1975 and 2015
            Note: The data can be accessed here (last accessed September 2021): https://www
            .gapminder.org/data/documentation/income-mountains-dataset/
            SOURCE: AUTHORS' ELABORATION USING DATA PRODUCED BY OLA ROSLING
            AND PUBLISHED ON THE GAPMINDER WEBSITE

refer to it as such as these calculations are not based on data pertaining to all
individuals on the planet (on this see Milanović, 2005). Lakner and Milanović
(2016) however take a different approach. They use data on mean income and
expenditure drawn from surveys of households across the globe to calculate
the actual global income distribution, with the individual as unit of analysis
and in disregard of national borders. This distribution, obtained through the
elaboration of data for the period 1988–2008 taken from surveys on income
and consumption carried out by Lakner and Milanović themselves, is illus-
trated in Figure 4. This graph essentially captures the end of a long epoch in
human history in which inequality was increasing, that began with the indus-
trialisation of Northwest Europe. In the wake of this technological revolution,
incomes in this part of the world began to increase, yet material prosperity in
the rest of the world remained at a very low level. While some countries were
able to follow Europe's lead in industrialising – first North America, Oceania,
and some parts of South America, then later Japan and East Asia – other countries in Asia and Africa remained poor. As a result, global inequality continued

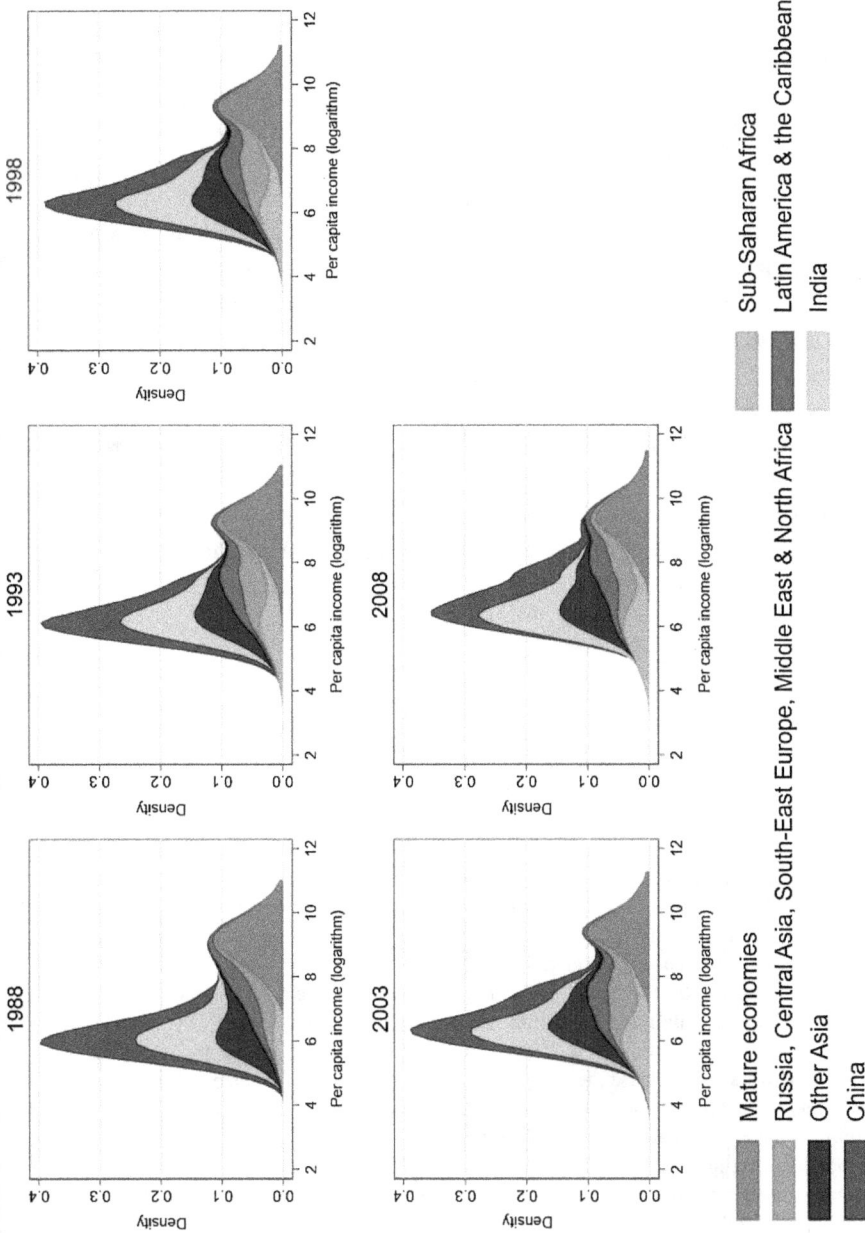

FIGURE 4 World income distribution, 1988–2008
Note: The data can be accessed here (last accessed September 2021): https://www.worldbank.org/en/research/brief/World-Panel-Income-Distribution
SOURCE: AUTHORS' ELABORATION ON DATA FROM LAKNER–MILANOVIĆ (2013)

to grow for a long period of time. And it was during the period analysed in Figure 4 that we began to see a change. With the rapid growth experienced by large parts of Asia in particular, global income distribution became more equal, and the incomes of the poorest half of the global population increased faster than the incomes of the richest half.

1.4   *Income Distribution in Italy*

Using data collected by the Banca d'Italia on Italian households, Figure 5 shows the non-parametric kernel estimate for equivalised income density in Italy between 1987 and 2016.[10] The diagram shows significant changes in personal income distribution over the last three decades: a reduction in the number of income receivers with incomes between €5,000 and €17,000 and an increase in the number of income receivers with incomes above the mean, which the 7,000-household-wide survey found to be around €18,600 in 2016 (and €17,400 in 1987). From a quantitative perspective, these shifts are evidenced in an increase in the inter-decile ratio P90/P10, which grew by about 15%, and by a rise in the Gini index from 0.32 in 1987 to 0.33 in 2016.[11] Inequality, after climbing sharply between 1991 and 1993, then remained substantially stable at levels above the 1989–1991 average. This upward trend in inequality since the mid-1980s is common to many OECD[12] countries, driven by a more than proportional increase in the incomes of the richest relative to the poorest.

---

10   As collection of data on household finances began only in 1987, Figure 5 shows the kernel density estimate for equivalised disposable income before tax or state benefits. Real values (at 2016 prices) have been obtained using the Italian state statistics agency's resident household consumption deflator. In order to present a clearer view of the lower-middle part of the income distribution, income values below zero and those above the €50 thousand threshold have been excluded.

11   The inter-decile ratio P90/P10 is calculated by comparing the 90th percentile (the first income value that falls above 90% of the total and below the remaining 10%) and the 10th percentile (the first income value above 10% of the total and below the remaining 90%). The Gini index is a standard measure of inequality that varies between 0 (when everyone has the same income) and 1 (when all income is held by one person). We look at this in more detail in our section *Economic Inequality*.

12   The Organisation for Economic Cooperation and Development (OECD) is an international economic research organisation for developed countries that currently has 36 active members.

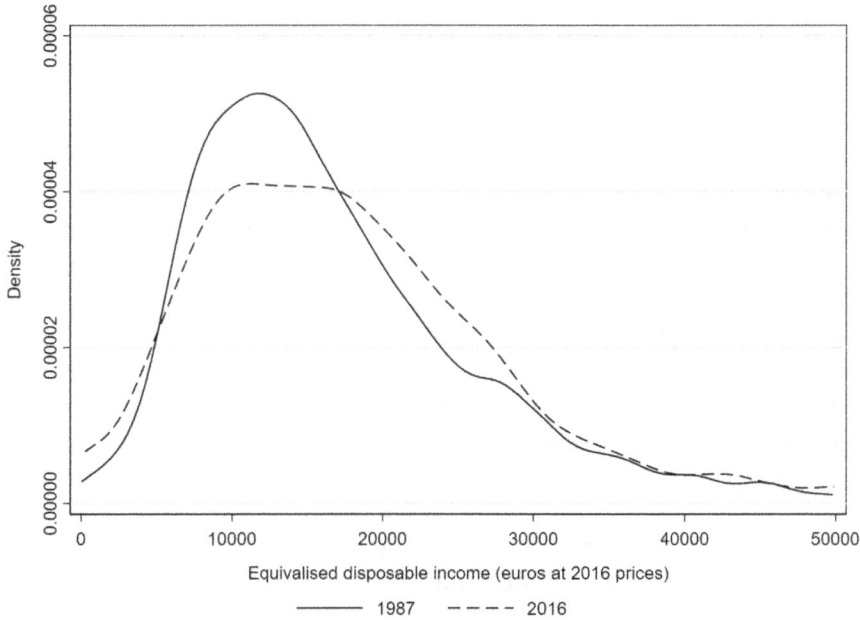

FIGURE 5   Income distribution in Italy, 1987 and 2016
            SOURCE: AUTHORS' ELABORATION USING THE BANCA D'ITALIA
            INCOME SURVEY

2   Economic Inequality

2.1   *Measuring Inequality*

Personal income distribution constitutes the basis for measuring the degree of income inequality in a given country, for analysing its development over time, and for comparing degrees of inequality in different countries.[13] In order to

---

13   Research on personal income inequality was first embarked upon by Pareto (1896, 1897a, 1897b) and then taken up by Lorenz (1905) and Gini (1912), later followed by various statisticians and economists in search of improved ways of measuring the concentration of income (see, e.g., Dagum, 1987). In our study of the principal elements of this line of analysis we will assume that an individual's standard of living is determined solely by the monetary variable, i.e. income. We will not discuss here other economic variables (income, consumption, or other factors) that can give us a better idea of the economic wellbeing of a household or individual, nor will we look at the 'multidimensional' approach to measuring inequality. Income is certainly a significant factor in determining living standards. Nevertheless, it cannot give us a complete picture of an individual or a household's wellbeing, which can consist in a variety of heterogenous components (see, e.g., Aaberge and Brandolini, 2015). Instead, we will touch on both of these questions

capture the essence of economic inequality in an objective manner, it is necessary therefore to use measurements that can provide a means of comparison
in an international context and a way of showing trends over time.[14] Despite
the great many ways of measuring inequality that have been suggested, the
most popular, generally standard in official statistical reports, is the index proposed by the Italian statistician Corrado Gini in 1912. Gini's index (or coefficient) is an indicator that offers a measure of the degree of concentration of
transferable quantitative variables, such as income, and is strictly connected to
the visual representation of income inequality by means of the Lorenz curve
(1905), which establishes a correspondence between proportions of individuals or households within a population and the proportions of the population's
total income that they receive. The graph in Figure 6, by way of demonstration,
has cumulative percentages of the population along the horizontal axis and
total income along the vertical axis. If the income distribution if perfectly egalitarian, meaning each percentage of the population receive the same percentage of income, the Lorenz curve will be a straight line. In Figure 6, the Lorenz
curve representing this scenario is the straight line cutting diagonally across
the graph, so at a 45° angle from both axes. The forms of the three Lorenz
curves representing three hypothetical income distributions (A, B and C) are
the more 'standard' forms that you see in analysis of real-world income distributions. Where income distribution is unequal, the Lorenz curve flattens as it

---

(concerning the choice of economic variable for evaluating living standards and on the
multidimensional approach to measuring wellbeing) in the subsequent section titled
Poverty: Definition and Measurement.

14   There are two approaches to this: a 'descriptive' approach and a 'normative' approach
(see, e.g., Sen, 1972). In the descriptive approach, the researcher has the objective of
simply describing the phenomenon of inequality rather than expressing any value judgement on whether it is good or bad. In this case, the measure of inequality is a mathematical formula that allows for impartial description of inequality as a deviation from a given
reference point, which could be a distribution where incomes are the same. The normative approach allows the researcher to make state whether a certain distribution is 'more
or less desirable,' according to an explicitly stated a priori value judgment. In other words,
the normative approach implies judgement as to whether inequality is good or bad, to
what extent it is good or bad, and to what extent society gains or loses out as a result of
inequality. As such, inequality measured in absolute terms is of less interest than a measurement on how far a real-world income distribution is from a supposed 'ideal' model or
situation that is not necessarily the extreme of all individuals receiving the same income.
In our analysis we will seek to avoid a strict dichotomy between the two approaches and
will take into account the wide variety of ways of measuring inequality that have been
proposed in the literature. For further reading on this topic the reader will find of use
Baldini and Toso (2009), Lanza (2015), and Alacevich and Soci (2019).

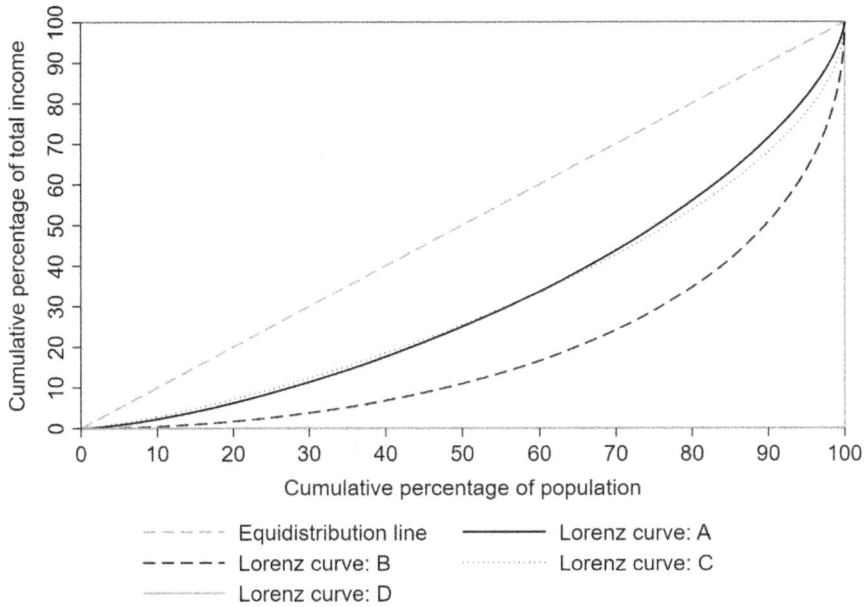

FIGURE 6   The Lorenz curve

moves rightwards, dipping below the straight line of equi-distribution. This shows that a percentage of the population received less than the same percentage of total income. The more the Lorenz curve departs from the straight diagonal line, i.e., the more it curves downward, the greater the degree of inequality. In other words, an ever-larger percentage of the population receives the same share of the total income, and an ever-smaller percentage gets all the rest. Figure 6 shows for example that the distribution represented by curve A is less unequal that the distribution represented by curve B.[15] The more inequality increases, the more the curve deviates from the equi-distribution line, until it reaches, in the hypothetical extreme, a situation where a single person (or unit) in a population (national or global) retains the entire total income. In

15   The ordering of income distributions by a Lorenz curve has the characteristic of being incomplete. If the Lorenz curve for two different income distributions intersect, nothing can be gleaned as to whether one is more or less unequal than the other. For example, in Figure 6 the Lorenz curve for income distribution C intersects with income distribution A. As such it is not possible to say which of the two income distributions is less equal, though we can say that total income in C is distributed more equally than in B. In the case of two Lorenz curves intersecting it is nevertheless possible to use well-known synthetic methods to ensure complete sorting in terms of more or less inequality.

this case the curve would become a sideways L-shape, running straight along
the horizontal axis right up to the final input (the person or unit that receives
everything) where it then rises in a straight vertical line, as represented in
Figure 6 by income distribution D.

With any Lorenz curve, the Gini index is geometrically represented by the
ratio between the area between the 45° equi-distribution line and the Lorenz
curve, and the area of the triangle subtended by the equi-distribution line. For
Figure 7, the following equation calculates the Gini index:

$$G = \frac{A}{A+B}$$

Since the area of the triangle $A+B$ is equal to $\frac{1}{2}$ – as it is half the area of a
rectangle – this means that:

$$G = 2A = 2\left(\frac{1}{2} - B\right) = 1 - 2B$$

In other words, the Gini index is equal to twice the area between the 45°
straight line and the Lorenz curve and also equal to 1 minus twice the area
subtended by the Lorenz curve. Given that $A = 0$ in the case of a Lorenz curve
that coincides with the equi-distribution line, in a situation of perfect equality
$G = 0$. It follows that in the opposite case of perfect inequality, represented
by the L-shape Lorenz curve, the area A is equal to $\frac{1}{2}$ and as such $G = 1$.

A Gini index therefore will have a value of between 0 (perfect equality) and
1 (perfect inequality). The higher the value the higher the levels of economic
inequality.[16] In this way, it is possible to give an immediate idea of the level
of inequality in a society using a single number, thus allowing also for spatial
and temporal comparisons. Additionally, the Gini index can also be calculated
algebraically, independently of the Lorenz curve, as the Gini index is equal to
half the mean of differences between all the income pairs divided by the mean
income. Or rather:

$$G = \frac{\sum_{i=1}^{n}\sum_{j=1}^{n}\left|y_i - y_j\right|}{2n^2\mu} = \frac{\Delta}{2\mu},$$

---

16   For the purposes of simplification, the Gini index is sometimes reported on a scale from
      0 to 100 rather than from 0 to 1.

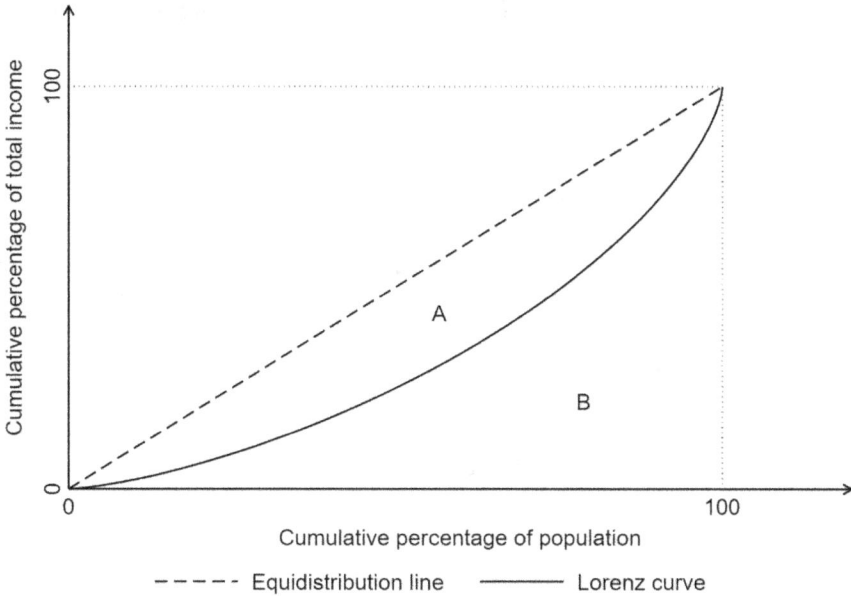

FIGURE 7   The Gini index represented by a Lorenz curve

Where n denotes the total number of observations, $\Delta = \dfrac{\sum_{i=1}^{n}\sum_{j=1}^{n}\left|y_i - y_j\right|}{n^2}$ is the mean absolute difference, and $\mu = \dfrac{1}{n}\sum_{i=1}^{n} y_i$ indicates mean income. The division by μ is necessary for G to be a number between 0 and 1.

2.2   Relative vs. Absolute Inequality

The Lorenz curve and the Gini index introduced above are 'relative' – rather than 'absolute' – measures of inequality. Put simply, according to the *relative* measure of inequality – widely considered the standard approach – if all incomes are raised in the same proportion, inequality does not vary (Kolm, 1976; Cowell, 2016). With the *absolute* view of inequality, incomes would have to be added to in equal amounts for inequality to remain unaffected. Absolute measures depend on absolute differences in living standards or levels of well-being, whereas relative measures are based on relative differences between incomes, i.e., ratios of incomes to the mean. By way of example, imagine a situation where one individual had $10, and another $100, and then both experienced an increase of 20%, so that the first individual now has $12, and the second $120. Relative measures of inequality would register this change as having no impact on distribution, since both incomes have increased by the same percentage, despite the fact that, in absolute terms, the difference in income has changed from $90 to $118.[17]

While from the point of view of measurement the choice between absolute and relative benchmarks is a normative choice, from an economic point of view the treatment of inequality as an absolute concept – the "leftist" view, that we ourselves will adopt in our subsequent chapters to show how the crisis and the pandemic have contributed to rising inequality – enables us to detect trends that otherwise would remain undetected. Indeed, an increasing number of scholars seem to be adopting this conception of inequality since it provides a convincing interpretation of diverse socio-economic issues, ranging from perceptions of inequality, to the trade-off between inequality and economic growth in the developing world, and, finally, to the relation between inequality and globalization.

In terms of the wider perceptions of inequality, relative inequality measures hinge upon a controversial axiom – the 'scale invariance' axiom, according to which multiplying the incomes of each member of a population by the same proportion leaves income inequality unchanged, a concept that is difficult to explain to a wider audience. Ravallion (2003: 741) illustrates this with a very simple example:

> Consider an economy with just two household incomes: $1,000 and $10,000. If both incomes double in size, then relative inequality will remain the same; the richer household is still 10 times richer. But the absolute difference in their incomes has doubled, from $9,000 to $18,000. Relative inequality is unchanged but absolute inequality has risen sharply.

---

17   Relative and absolute views of inequality are attributed, respectively, to "rightist" and "leftist" political opinions according to Kolm (1976). The "rightist" perspective holds that inequality does not change when incomes grow at the same rate as mean income over the course of economic development, whereas those in the "leftist" came maintain that the degree of inequality is constant when incomes increase by the same amount as mean income does. The "leftist" and "rightist" labels are connected to the French political context and the ideological differences between left and right-wing. Kolm (1976) introduced these expressions in reference to debates surrounding the Grenelle agreements that took place in 1968, which decreed the same proportional increase in wages for all employees. Kolm (1976: 419) reports that "the Radicals felt bitter and cheated; in their view, this widely increased incomes inequality". As shown by Bresson and Labar (2007), the "leftist" view implies a more egalitarian way of sharing additional incomes among individuals than the "rightist" view.

As the example shows very clearly, if we abstract for a second from the perspective of welfare measurement, it is complicated to convince a non-expert
audience that in this case inequality has not increased. This view that absolute inequality is closer to what people perceive as real inequality has gained
increasing attention in literature (Amiel and Cowell, 1999; Fehr and Schmidt,
1999; Leibbrandt and López-Pérez, 2012; Wade, 2013; Ravallion, 2018; Clementi
et al., 2019b), particularly in the behavioural economics strand.[18]

The different implications of absolute and relative approaches become even
more defined in discussions within development theory. One of the corner-
stones of development theory is the poverty/inequality trade-off faced by low/
lower-middle-income countries, i.e. concerning what happens in the ascend-
ing part of the Kuznets' curve (Kuznets, 1971). Less economically developed
countries seeking to reduce poverty (like most of sub-Saharan Africa) must
boost growth as options for redistribution are often limited. However, growth
will almost always be accompanied by an increase in inequality as the process
takes place in a highly unbalanced manner (Lewis, 1955). Interestingly, where
using absolute measures of inequality (Ravallion, 2005), this poverty/inequal-
ity trade-off hypothesized by Kuznets is empirically verified. If relative measures are used, however, the inverted U-shaped curve of growth and inequality
tends to barely register.

Another interesting example on how absolute measures give rise to a
very different interpretation of trends in inequality is the debate on whether
globalization has made the world more or less equal (Wade, 2004). Among
those using relative measures, a definitive answer has yet to emerge from
the scientific debate (Atkinson and Brandolini, 2010; Bosmans et al., 2014;
Bandyopadhyay et al., 2017). On the contrary, where absolute measures are
used, there is a broad consensus that both within- and between-country inequality has increased since the ascent of what we would call the 'age of globalization' (Niño-Zarazua et al., 2017).

2.3   *Inequality in the World*

Figure 8 presents a map of the world based on Gini indexes, showing economic
inequality country by country for the period from 1992 to 2019.[19] In Europe, the

---

18   For example, Celse's recent work (2017) shows that individuals derive utility largely from
      income comparisons but their utility is negatively correlated only to absolute inequalities.
19   For each country the Gini index value refers to the most recent year for which data was
      available within the period considered. The Gini index values are provided by the World
      Bank which collects data from each country for different years based on sample surveys
      on household wellbeing. For advanced economies and Latin America the data concerns

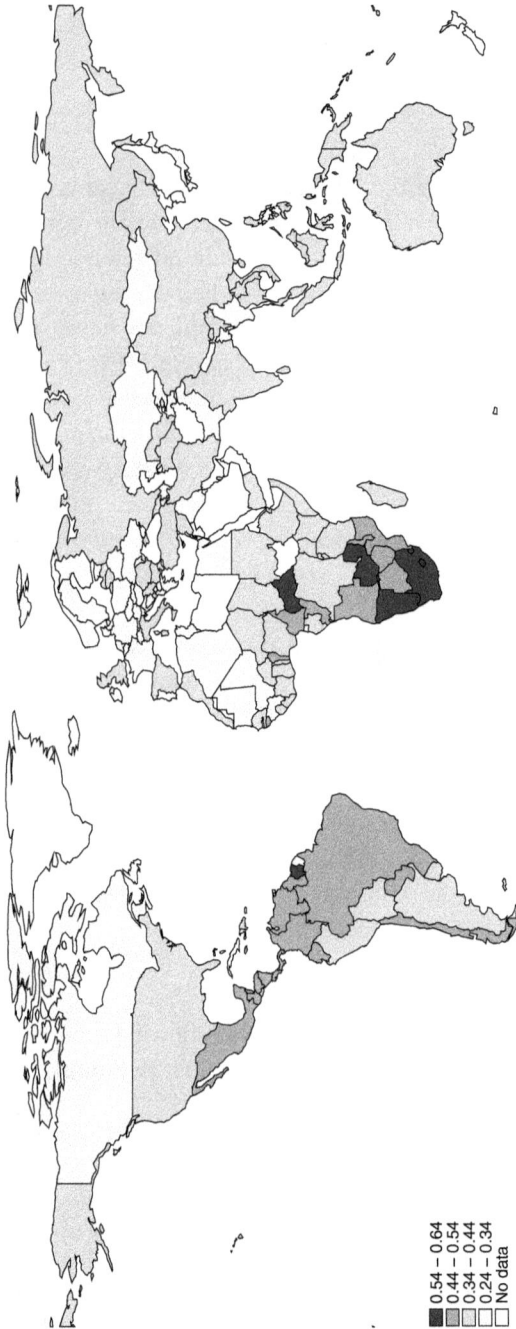

0.54 – 0.64
0.44 – 0.54
0.34 – 0.44
0.24 – 0.34
No data

FIGURE 8   Inequality in the world, 1992–2019

Note: Data can be accessed here (last accessed September 2021): https://data.worldbank.org/indicator/SI.POV.GINI

SOURCE: AUTHORS' ELABORATION USING WORLD BANK DATA

countries with the most equal income distributions – with a Gini index between 0.24 and 0.34 – are the Nordic countries (Denmark, Estonia, Finland, Island, Norway and Sweden), Western Europe (Austria, Belgium, France, Germany, Holland and Switzerland), and some Eastern European countries (Belorussia, Moldovia, Poland, the Czech Republic, Slovakia, Ukraine, Hungary). The countries with lower Gini indexes are found in Southern Europe, with a few others in the Balkans (Albania, Bosnia Herzegovina, Croatia and Slovenia) and one on the Iberian Peninsula (Portugal). In the rest of the world, the only G7 countries that have a low Gini index are Canada and Japan. In contrast, the countries with the highest levels of income inequality are Belize, Brazil and Suriname in South America; and Botswana, Mozambique, Namibia, the CAR, the Kingdom of Eswatini, São Tomé and Príncipe, South Africa and Zambia in Africa, all with Gini indexes of between 0.54 and 0.64. Russia and the Unites States share the same bracket – between 0.34 and 0.44 – and China and India are both close to the 0.4 mark (China at 0.39 in 2016 and India at 0.36 in 2011). In the Middle East, the data indicates that the UAE, Jordan, Iraq and Lebanon are the most equal countries in the region – with Gini indexes between 0.24 and 0.34 – while Iran, Israel, Syria and Yemen are the most unequal (between 0.34 and 0.44).

2.4 *Income Inequality in Italy*

Figure 9, again based on Banca d'Italia data, shows the historical trend in inequality in Italy for the period 1987–2016, measured using the Gini coefficient for equivalised disposable income.[20] As we see from the graph, inequality in Italy rose sharply during the late 80s and early 90s, with the Gini index shifting from 0.29 in 1989 to 0.33 in 1993. Following this, it remained relatively stable, finishing in 2016 at 0.34.

Compared to other OECD countries,[21] Italy has a higher-than-average Gini coefficient (Figure 10). While it is still far lower than the countries at the top of

---

household income. For the majority of developing countries the data concerns consumption. This obviously makes it harder to compare across countries, or rather across countries belonging to economically diverse regions of the world, and any such comparison should be used with great caution.

20 As the collection of data on income after tax or state benefits only began in 1987, Figure 9 shows inequality measured using equivalised disposable income gross of financial assets.

21 The Gini index values used in Figure 10 refer to the latest available estimates for the 35 countries for the period 2016–2019. The OECD average has been calculated from the available years. All OECD data can be freely downloaded from the OECD website (last accessed September 2021): https://stats.oecd.org/.

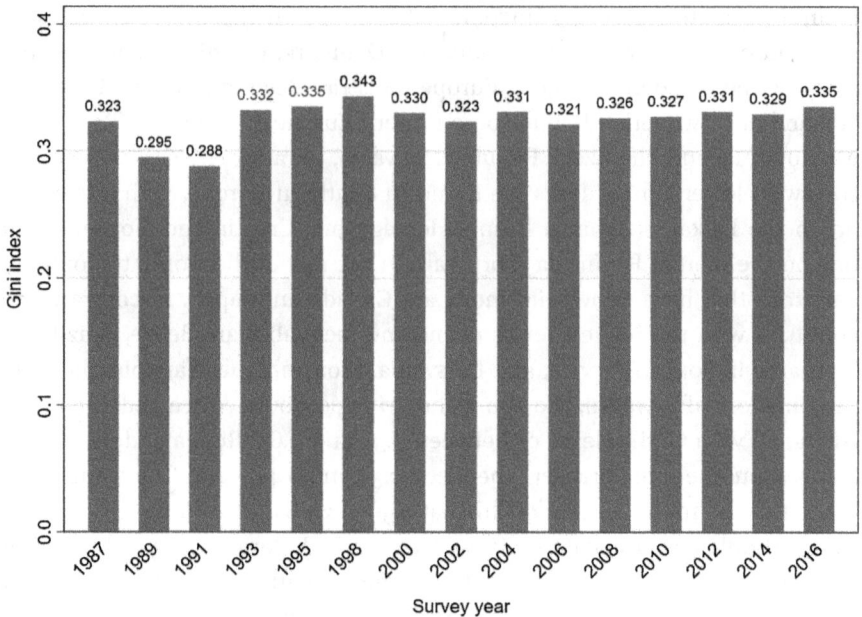

FIGURE 9   The Gini index of Italian income distribution, 1987–2016
            SOURCE: AUTHORS' ELABORATION USING THE BANCA D'ITALIA
            INCOME SURVEY

the range like Chile (0.46), Mexico (0.42), Turkey (0.40) and the US (0.39), inequality in Italy is significantly higher than countries like the Slovak Republic, the Czech Republic, Slovenia and Iceland (all around 0.25).

2.5   The Causes of Inequality

Economists have carried out a great deal of research into the causes of economic inequality, which include a whole variety of social, economic and institutional factors.[22] Income disparities can be the result of changes in the labour market, changes in other markets, changes to a series of social variables, and changes in the redistributive policies of the state. All these factors are so interconnected that any convincing explanation as to the how and whys

---

22   Such a complex topic will not be elaborated on here. For our purposes, we will discuss
      only the ways in which the different theories that have been put forward seek to explain
      both trends common to different countries and the evident differences. For any discussion beyond this we refer the reader to contributions such as Franzini (2007), Baldini and
      Toso (2009), Franzini and Pianta (2009, 2016), Dabla-Norris et al. (2015), and Nolan et al.
      (2019).

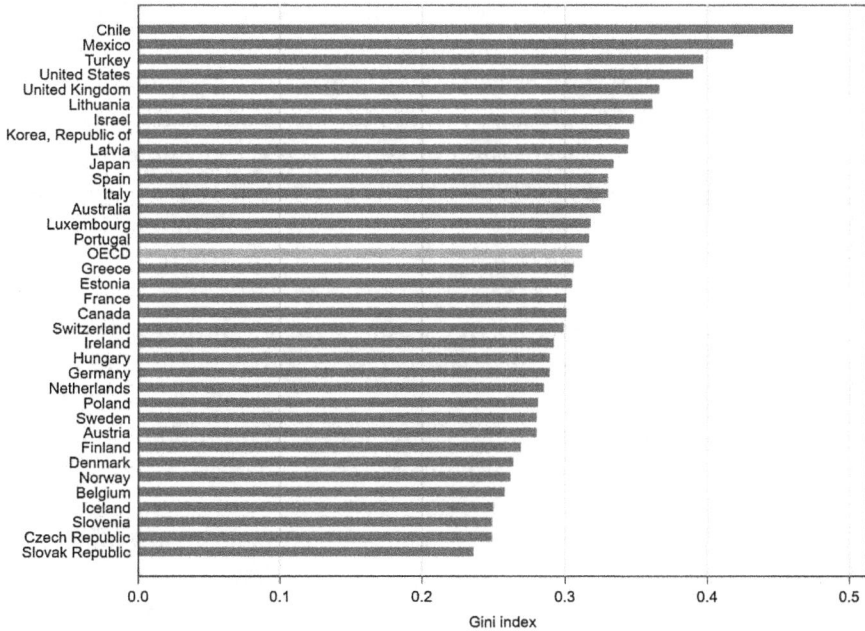

FIGURE 10   Italy's ranking according to the Gini index compared to other OECD countries,
2016–2019
Note: Data available here (last accessed September 2021): https://stats.oecd.org/
SOURCE: AUTHORS' ELABORATION USING OECD DATA

of inequality must necessarily take more than one factor into consideration.
Without embarking on an extensive theoretical discussion, we can nevertheless provide a summary overview of the principal causes of rising in-country
income inequality over the last 40 years:[23]

- *Technological progress.* New information technologies have no doubt
  brought about a significant increase in productivity and wellbeing. At the
  same time, however, they have played a central role in increasing wage inequality. This is because technological change can create demand for high-
  skilled or highly educated labour, widening the wage gap between these
  workers and lower-skilled workers (Acemoğlu, 1998; Card and Di Nardo,
  2002). The theory that increases in inequality are caused by technological
  change leaves some questions unanswered though. Most importantly, it
  is contradicted by the fact that in the wake of radical transformations in

---

23   We limit ourselves here to looking at in-country income inequality. While inequality
      between countries also warrants further analysis, this is beyond the scope of our cur-
      rent study.

productive technologies, advanced economies have not in fact experienced a significant increase in demand for qualified workers in relation to non-qualified workers. Instead, what we have seen is a sharp polarisation in the occupational structure of employment, with jobs concentrated at two ends of a scale, on the managerial or professional side and then the manual or unspecialised side. Job losses have been seen mostly in white-collar sectors and skilled crafts. This polarisation is evidenced in the distribution of wages in Europe. Here were see that a select group of top-level managers (classified as employees rather than capitalists) and professionals are earning unprecedentedly high salaries. At the same time, it is the lowest level wage categories that have been most affected by the proliferation of more precarious forms of labour – part-time, temporary, externalised, etc. – bringing more and more European workers into the class of the 'working poor.' The degree of wage polarisation also differs across different sectors, with the highest levels seen in sectors with the highest levels of employment, with high levels of university-educated employees, or where product innovation is most fundamental.

– *Globalisation.* Trade has been the motor for growth in many countries around the world, promoting competitivity and efficiency. However, the growth of international exchange in goods and services, in part triggered by technological progress, is frequently cited as the cause of rising inequality, especially in wealthier countries. In the advanced economies, businesses' capacity for innovating to reduce the labour necessary for production, as is also the case with the transfer of economic activity (or some of its stages) from high- to low-production cost areas (*offshoring*), has meant a fall in demand for lower-skilled workers, with a consequent increase in the wage difference between these workers and high-skilled workers. In this way, the globalisation theory would seem to converge with the technological progress theory (Feenstra and Hanson, 1996, 1999, 2003).[24] The globalisation

---

24   The process of globalisation regards not only trade in goods and services but also the liberalisation of capital markets. Financial globalisation can favour efficient global allocation of capital and promote a global distribution of risk. At the same time, the increase in financial flows – in particular of foreign direct investment (FDI) and portfolio investments – has led to a rise in income inequality in both advanced and emerging economies (Freeman, 2010). A potential explanation for this is the concentration of foreign assets and liabilities in technology-intensive sectors, which pushes up demand for high-skilled workers, and so pushes up their wages. Furthermore, FDI can encourage technological innovation relating to specific skills, which translates into a higher level of training required of the skilled workers employed in these jobs, widening the skills gap with lower-skilled workers (Willem te Velde, 2004). Finally, 'low-skilled' FDI, where originating from

theory also has its weaknesses, however. Specifically, it cannot account for the overwhelming empirical evidence that shows a slowing rate in income inequality in many countries from the 80s onwards, while neither technological progress nor the opening of new markets has slowed. Furthermore, where in the 90s inequality continued to rise, this was determined mostly by a sharp rise in the highest incomes relative to those in the middle ranges, and not by a relative decrease in the lowest incomes, which should have been the case as per the globalisation theory.

- *Changes in the institutional structure of the labour market.* Promoting greater flexibility in the institutional mechanisms that regulate the functioning of the labour market can incentivise economic dynamism by reallocating resources to more productive businesses and encouraging corporate restructuring. However, greater flexibility can also pose challenges for workers, especially lower-skilled workers, and as such can play a significant role in increasing income inequality (Alvaredo et al., 2013). A weakened labour movement, for example, reduces labour's contractual power, further exacerbating wage inequality (Wilkinson and Pickett, 2009; Frederikson and Poulsen, 2010). Equally, a reduction in the legal minimum wage relative to the average income results in greater income inequality (Jaumotte and Osorio-Buitron, 2015). In addition, studies have highlighted the role of higher percentages of part-time and temporary work in determining wage inequality in some advanced economies (OECD, 2012). When it comes to many labour market policies, such as reforms of employment protection legislation, the impact on inequality is less clear, inasmuch as they influence both wage dispersion and employment levels, in sometimes contradictory ways. In many emerging economies, the combination of rigid laws on hiring, firing and employment protection on the one hand, and weak wage protections on the other, often encourages the development of informal labour markets, which in turn feeds into wage inequality. On the whole, however, evidence from a broad range of countries suggests that labour market institutions (like legal minimum wages, unionisation, collective bargaining,

---

an advanced economy, can appear relatively higher-skilled FDI in a developing economy (Figini and Görg, 2011), stimulating demand for high-skilled workers within that beneficiary economy. Financial deregulation and globalisation are also cited as factors underlying the increase in financial wealth, the relative abondance of skilled labour, and the high salaries in the financial sector, one of the sectors that has experienced the fastest growth in advanced economies (Phillipon and Reshef, 2012; Furceri and Loungani, 2013).

social security contributions) tend on average to make for a fairer income distribution (Calderón and Chong, 2009: OECD, 2011).[25]

- *Changes in the functional distribution of income.* As the result of changes in labour relations and in the balance of forces between labour and capital, many EU countries have seen labour's share of GDP fall sharply, from the second half of the 70s to the second half of the 2000s. From 2003 onwards, a third of European workers experienced a decline in real wages. And not only have wages fallen in real terms, but since 2003 workers have seen their wages grow, on average, more slowly than the rate of increase in productivity. If workers are unable to access an adequate share of the benefits of increased productivity, often driven by technological change or by an internalisation of productive systems, problems arise. Market income inequality – based on pre-tax household earnings coming from the formal economy – has been negatively affected by these developments, due to rising inequality in the distribution of capital income (profits and rents).[26]

- *State redistributive measures.* The governments of the advanced economies have historically mitigated income inequality through taxation and spending. However, over the last few decades many developed nations have seen disposable income inequality increase, indicating a reduction in the state's redistributive activities. This decline in state redistribution can be traced back, at least in part, to a belief on behalf of policymakers that in a globalised world, progressive taxation is an obstacle to growth. Tax systems in some advanced economies have become less progressive in recent decades, with high-income households and firms now facing lower tax rates (Hungerford, 2013).

---

25   The presence of trade unions and of collective bargaining guarantees a certain homo-geneity of wages for a large number of workers employed in industry. However, over the course of the last thirty years in the advanced economies, we have seen the contributions of industry to the nation's wealth significantly scaled down, in terms of both added value and number of employees, while the service sector has vastly expanded. The service sector encompasses a highly heterogenous range of professional profiles, union density tends to be low, and collective bargaining practices less common (or even entirely absent). In some parts of the service sector informal employment can be widespread, meaning low salaries and no protections. In combination, such factors make for high levels of wage dispersion.

26   See Franzini and Pianta (2009, 2016). Other factors that have contributed to greater market income inequality have included the growing importance of income from self-employment – itself unequally distributed, especially in Italy – and some other social var-iables such as household composition, the number of workers per household and gender inequalities (see Baldini and Toso, 2009).

– *Human capital.* Education can play an important role in reducing income inequality as it decides a person's choice of profession and their access to higher-skilled jobs or promotions and so better wages. It is also a key marker of labour market productivity. The theory of human capital (Mincer, 1958; Becker and Chiswick, 1966) suggests that while there is an unequivocal positive link between education and income equality, the effect of higher levels of education on income equality can be either positive or negative depending on the evolution of the expected rate of return on education. In addition, there can be opposing forces at play that have to do with the composition of labour (or rather from an increase in the percentage of higher-paid workers) and with wage compression (or rather a fall in the return on higher levels of education in relation to lower levels). In general, the evidence suggests that the impact of education on inequality depends on a variety of factors, such as how much individuals or governments invest in education and what return they get for these investments.

– *The contribution of the rich to inequality.* A recent line of research has focused on changes over time to the right-hand tail of the distribution curve, which covers the richer end of the scale. Such studies have made significant contributions to our understanding of patterns in overall income distribution over the course of the 20th century, producing findings that are important for reading our present. It seems that in some countries, the US and UK in particular, the fact that the highest concentration of income was registered in the last few decades is connected to an extraordinary increase in the shares of total wealth that went to the rich. This phenomenon is also at the centre of studies by Atkinson and Piketty (2007, 2010) who looked at the incomes of the super-rich, or top incomes, in a number of countries over a long time period, allowing for evaluation of the effects of war, periods of economic depression, and the fiscal austerity regimes. The data appears to show that in the US, for example, there has been in recent times a sharp rise in the share of national income appropriated by a tiny proportion of the population (e.g. the 0.1%). Most importantly, what we see in recent decades is that the principal source of income for the super-rich is not capital but labour, though in the case of superstar performers or 'super-managers' this is not labour as conventionally conceived. These evolutions require us to rethink our ideas about how the labour market functions and which factors, aside from those identified by traditional economics, contribute to determining wages, especially higher wages.

– *Attitudes to inequality.* Lastly, a major role in deciding long-term trends in inequality is played by social norms or attitudes which regulate the degree to which inequality is tolerated within a given society at a given historical moment (Krugman, 2002). Measuring how these social norms change is a highly complicated and controversial affair. Nevertheless, there is no doubt that the current climate of relative permissibility has favoured the explosion in inequality.

3   Poverty: Definition and Measurement

There are many different policies that have an effect on people living in poverty and governments often design programmes specifically to combat poverty. It is of great importance therefore that policymakers are able to identify who is living in poverty, so they can test alternative policies through simulation and select those most effective. Before any of this can be done, however, it is first necessary to define poverty. When do we say someone is living in poverty? And how do we measure it?

3.1   *Defining Poverty*
When we think about poverty, we all have an intuitive idea of what this means but in actual fact its definition is difficult and can be controversial. Academics and experts have often found it necessary to adapt existing definitions or methods of measurement, over time or across space, or in accordance with specific economic, social or institutional contexts. Poverty can be defined for instance as the absence of some basic necessities (food, housing, etc.) considered necessary for mere survival (Watts, 1968). Alternatively, it can be defined as a situation whereby an individual or household lacks

> the resources to obtain the type of diet, participate in the activities and have the living conditions and the amenities which are customary, or at least widely encouraged or approved in the societies to which they belong.
> TOWNSEND, 1979: 31

Amartya Sen (1985) used the broad description of poverty as being a lack of the 'capabilities' needed to function in a given society. All these definitions refer to poverty as a state whereby a reasonable standard of living cannot be achieved. A synthesis of the various approaches was put together by the World Bank (2001) in the following manner:

> Poverty is the lack of, or the inability to achieve, a socially acceptable
> standard of living.

To fully grasp the scope of this definition, it is worth looking briefly at some of the keywords it contains:

Lack of – this is the basic definition of poverty: a situation in which an individual or family has no control over economic resources. Consequently, an individual would be considered poor if they do not have food or shelter, or, equivalently, if they do not have the income (or sufficient resources) to provide for these basic needs.

Inability – refers to a situation where an individual or family is unable to function in a society, a concept developed by Sen (1985). Sen's approach is based on the two main concepts of functionings and capabilities. *Functionings* are essentially 'states of being and doing' that are constitutive of a person's freedom to live as they choose. Put simply, freedom is the extent to which someone is able to do and be in their life. *Capabilities* represent the possibility and liberty to pursue and realise functionings. According to this perspective, poverty is a state characterised by the absence of the capabilities that allow someone to achieve their desired functionings, or by level of capabilities that in a certain society are unacceptably low. Disability, for instance, may not diminish an individual's ability to earn, but it would make it more difficult to convert earnings into functionings (though, in terms of income, this is potentially realisable).

Standard of living – With reference to standard of living, poverty depends on:
- What is understood within a given society at a given historical moment as "a socially acceptable standard of living." In a society where most people own cars, the use of public transport can be a sign of poverty. Not having a TV in a technologically advanced society could be a new indicator of poverty, while in other countries this is considered a luxury.
- How this standard is measured, i.e., what variable or set of variables are used to 'capture' standard of living.

3.2   *Uni- and Multidimensional Poverty*

Standard of living, and so poverty, can be represented by a 'unidimensional' indicator (e.g. income) or through a 'multidimensional' approach that positions the individual in relation to a set of dimensions of poverty (income, health, family status, etc.) In the first case, poverty is defined by income poverty and standard of living is defined within the sphere of economic wellbeing, a narrower concept than wellbeing in general. In the second case, where other indicators of wellbeing complement income in the definition of poverty, the concept of poverty is more closely associated with wellbeing in the broadest sense. Whatever approach is chosen, some methodological questions must be answered that are of particular relevance to the measurement of poverty.

- In the case the of the unidimensional approach, it is necessary to define which monetary indicator is most appropriate for representing standard of living. There are two natural candidates for this: consumption[27] and income. The choice of one rather than the other will have to do not only with theoretical considerations but also effective availability of reliable data.
  - Consumption is a common measure used to evaluate personal wellbeing. The reasons for this choice are both practical and theoretical. Among the practical considerations is the fact that in many developing nations it is easier to gain information on consumption than on income, due to the prominence of the informal economy and the scarcity of reliable data. In theoretical terms, using consumption as the benchmark for standard of living is based on two assumptions. Firstly, consumption is less influenced by fluctuations in income relating to changes in a person's employment (periods of unemployment, promotions, etc.) Secondly, consumption is less influenced by life events, or by the various changes in circumstance that characterise a person's existence (the young and the old are unable to earn but they must nevertheless consume the necessary to survive.) In short, consumption is impacted much less than income by the events that take place over an individual's lifetime and as such tends to remain more stable over time.
  - Income directly expresses the power to dispose of resources, and consequently is appropriate for describing the possibility for wellbeing independently of consumption. Though it fluctuates much more over a person's lifetime, it nevertheless has some benefits over consumption as a metric. Firstly, if people are unable over their lifetimes to maintain stable levels of consumption – due to a need to save or because they are using debt (or savings) to buffer cyclical variations in income – income can serve as a more reliable indicator of standard of living. Secondly, consumption reflects concrete opportunities for spending but it also reflects preferences, which could have the paradoxical result that a person of

---

27   Surveys on consumption in fact do not look at consumption but at expenditure, i.e. outgoings effected over a certain period to pay for goods and services.

higher income that lives a miserly life and spends little is mistakenly understood as living in poverty.

- In the case the of the multidimensional approach, it is necessary to set out the list of indicators most appropriate for describing and evaluating poverty, with the aim of obtaining a more comprehensive idea of what it means to be poor.[28] For example, if a person has a low income but is in good health, are they richer than a person who is sick but earns more? If someone is illiterate but in good health and with enough food to eat, are they poor? An alternative understanding of the multidimensional approach could be that it is a way of 'explaining' poverty via a range of indicators, leaving the task of defining how each factor links to poverty to statistical techniques. This however prompts the objection that simple correlation does not mean causality. Is someone poor *because* they are in bad health? Or are they in bad health because they are poor? How these questions are answered can produce very different policy approaches.

3.3   *Relative and Absolute Poverty*

In addition to the definitions discussed above, poverty can also be thought of as either 'relative' or 'absolute.' The concept of *absolute* poverty is based on the idea that it is possible to identify a selection of basic goods and services necessary for keeping someone out of a state of deprivation. This selection is often expressed in monetary terms, in order to determine an absolute level of spending serving as a threshold for deciding if someone lives in conditions of poverty. The concept of *relative* poverty refers to an individual's position within a distribution (income or consumption), so to a standard of living that is defined *in relation* to the norms of that particular society or social context (Streeten, 1984). From this perspective, poverty is fundamentally an indicator of inequality. For example, a threshold could be set according to which anyone whose income is less than half of the mean income is considered to be living in poverty. In this case, if the mean income increases because the richest are earning more, the number of people living in poverty could also grow. The concept of relative poverty thus automatically reflects a country's changing societal and economic conditions.

---

28   One of the most popular approaches for measuring wellbeing using a multidimensional approach is the UN's Human Development Index (last accessed September 2021): https://hdr.undp.org/data-center/human-development-index#/indicies/HDI.

3.4   *Poverty Lines*

What differentiates the analysis of poverty from the analysis of inequality is that the analysis of poverty presupposes the *identification* of actual individuals or households as being poor. The acknowledgment of this condition is traditionally based on the establishment of a poverty 'line,' i.e. a threshold that divides those who are poor from those who are not. Using one or the other of the concepts of relative and absolute poverty, it is possible to establish the following types of poverty line:

– *Absolute poverty line* – the absolute poverty line is a fixed limit that does not change if the distribution used to evaluate it (income or consumption) changes. This limit is often kept for long periods of time, until developments in standard of living require its adjustment. Some examples of this are: the World Bank's $1.90 a day earning threshold used to compare poverty across many low- to middle-income countries; the national poverty lines that exists in most developing countries, used to compare levels of poverty in the same country over time; the (almost) $15 a day standard that has been used in the US for almost 50 years. Absolute poverty lines are the most commonly used approach to comparing numbers of people living in poverty over time and across geographical space and are universally used in low- and middle-income countries. However, there are some practical issues associated with the establishment of an absolute poverty line. Firstly, several methods exist for deriving an absolute poverty line from a determinate set of observations, each of which may generate a different threshold. To some extent, therefore, the choice of absolute poverty line is arbitrary, something which could undermine its usefulness as an analytical tool. Secondly, when deciding how frequently to update the absolute poverty line, two conflicting options must be considered: whether to keep it fixed for a long enough period of time as to allow for observation of changes affecting poverty over time; or whether to update it frequently enough as for it to be reasonably consistent with prevailing circumstances.

– *Relative poverty line* – relative poverty lines represent a constant fraction of a particular measure of mean or median income.[29] They are often used in

---

29   In statistics, the median is the value that separates the top half from the bottom half of a data sample. For example, for the data set {1,3,3,6,7,8,9} the median is 6. The basic advantage of the median compared to the mean in describing the data is that its value is not affected by the presence of extremely large or small values in the sample and as such it gives a better idea of a 'typical' value. For example, in the case of household income statistics, a mean may be influenced ('distorted') by a small number of extremely high or

more advanced economies, where there is less concern over a basic minimum (absolute) being reached and more over social inclusion – for example, the national poverty lines used in the European Union are fixed at 60%
of the median disposable income for each country. However, this measure
too is not without its weaknesses. The definition of a relative poverty line
usually takes income as the sole indicator of poverty. As such, it generally
takes a unidimensional approach and does not give a more comprehensive
picture of poverty. In addition, if the poverty line is defined as a fixed percentage of a synthetic indicator of income distribution (mean or median),
eradicating poverty becomes impossible, unless a situation of perfectly
egalitarian income distribution is established.[30] Lastly, the nature of a relative poverty line means that the line itself (and the number of people or
households that fall below it) tracks the evolution of that society's mean
income over time. Relative poverty can therefore be pro-cyclical, meaning
it can increase in expansive phases of the economic cycle and decrease in
phases of contraction.

3.5   Measuring Poverty

After defining the alternative criteria for identifying numbers of people living in poverty, the economic analysis of poverty proceeds with an aggregative
phase where information on the incomes or expenditure of the people identified as poor are combined to obtain a 'poverty measure.' A poverty measure is a
number that represents levels of poverty within the (income or consumption)
distribution given the poverty line. In particular, one of the poverty measures
used most often in empirical studies, due to its simplicity, is the *headcount
index*,[31] defined by the relation:

$$H = \frac{q}{N} \times 100$$

Where q indicates the number of people whose income (or expenditure)
is below the poverty line and N refers to the total population. This index
thus represents the proportion of a population below the poverty line and is

---

low incomes. Median income, on the other hand, may be a better way of suggesting what
a 'typical' income is.

30   This concept was developed by Fiegehen et al. (1977: 14), who pointed out that with a
relative definition of poverty "poverty will always be with us."

31   There can theoretically be many poverty indexes, but only a few are commonly used. For
a more systematic rundown of poverty indexes see Baldini and Toso (2009).

generally referred to as the 'poverty rate.' For example, if H is 10% this means that one out of ten people in that society are below the poverty line. The index H can be anywhere between 0 and 100% (where everyone is poor).

3.6   *Poverty in the World*

By way of example, Figure 11 shows trends in the poverty rate by world macro-areas and for the world as a whole. The (absolute) poverty line used is the $1.9 World Bank standard. The time frame covered is 1990–2015.

What we glean from the graph is that in recent decades some progress has been made in reducing poverty. At the beginning of the 1990s, for example, 36% of the global population lived in poverty. In 2015 that percentage has fallen to 10%, corresponding to one billion people less than in 1990 (World Bank, 2018). Much of this progress is concentrated in East Asia and the Pacific, where the economic rise of China has helped bring millions of people out of poverty. East Asia as a region has gone from an average poverty rate per country of 61% in 1990 to just over 2% in 2015. More recently, South Asia has also made major advances, contributing further to reductions in the global rate. The number

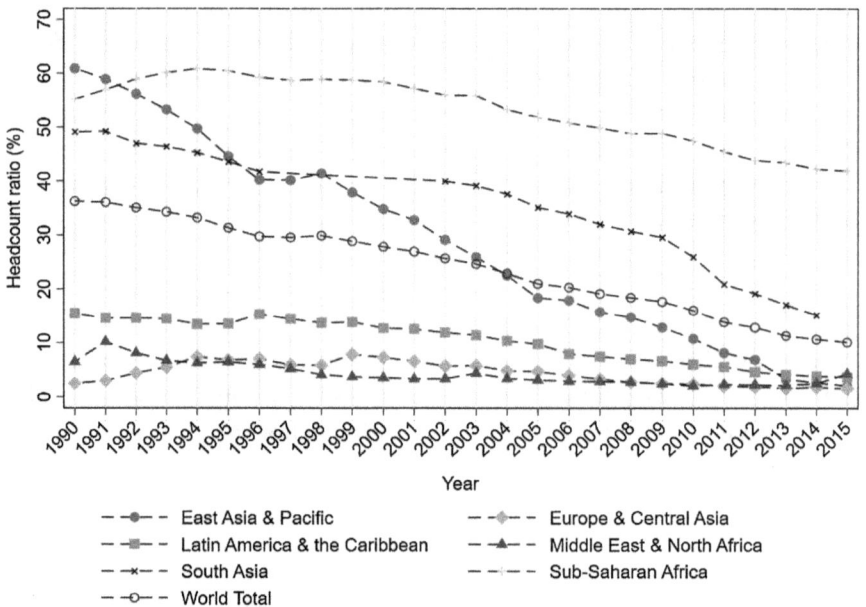

FIGURE 11   Poverty in the world, 1990–2015
            Note: Data available here (last accessed September 2021): http://iresearch.worldb
            ank.org/PovcalNet/home.aspx
            SOURCE: AUTHORS' ELABORATION USING WORLD BANK DATA

of people living in poverty in South Asia has fallen to 216 million in 2015 from more than half a billion in 1990 (World Bank, 2018). Not everywhere has such positive figures to report, however. The progress in Asia stands in sharp contrast to the slow rhythm of change in Sub-Saharan Africa, where poverty is becoming more of a problem due to slower rates of growth, instances of conflict, and weak state or other institutions. Today, most of the world's poor are in Sub-Saharan Africa. And unlike the rest of the world, the total number is growing. Where the average poverty rate for other global regions is less than 16%, in Sub-Saharan Africa it is around 42%. In addition, of the 28 poorest countries, 27 are in Sub-Saharan Africa, with poverty rates of over 30% (World Bank, 2018).

3.7   Poverty in Italy

The Banca d'Italia survey on household budgets can also give us information about poverty rates in Italy. Figure 12 looks at the evolution of the poverty rate among individuals. Poverty is defined in terms of equivalised disposable income and the (relative) poverty line is equal to 60% of the median equivalised income. The time period covered is 1987–2016.

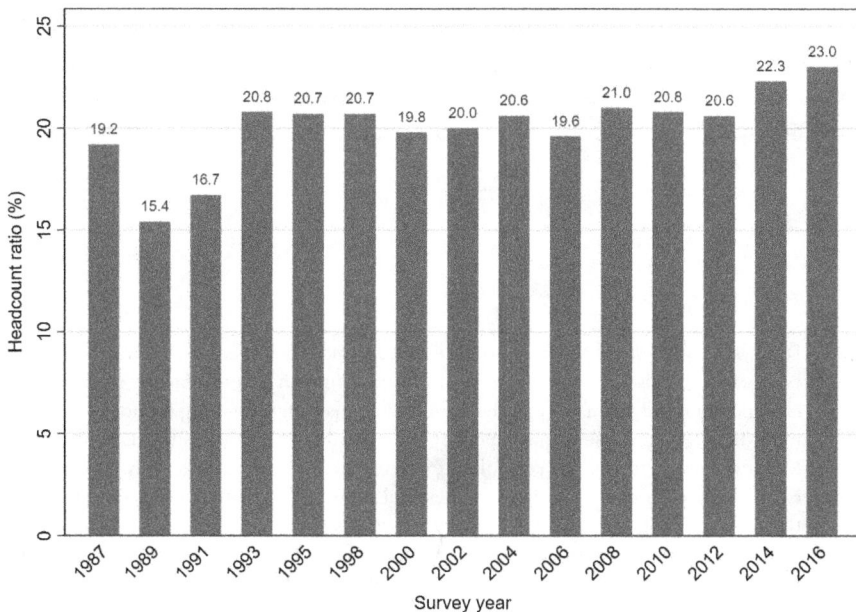

FIGURE 12   Percentage of poor Italians in relative terms, 1987–2016
SOURCE: AUTHORS' ELABORATION USING THE BANCA D'ITALIA
INCOME SURVEY

Over the course of this period, the pattern of relative poverty in the total population has developed in a similar manner to that of inequality. Following a slight drop during the late 80s and early 90s, the poverty rate subsequently began to rise again. From 1993 to 2012 it was essentially stable, but then towards the end of the period examined it reached levels that were far higher than at any other point. In 2016, 23% of the population was living in poverty, much higher than the 19% registered for 1987 and the 20% registered for 2006, before the global financial crash.

4   Income Polarisation

4.1   *Definition*

Income polarisation describes a process whereby income is concentrated at the two opposite ends of the spectrum: rich and poor. An increase in polarisation, often associated with the phenomenon of the 'disappearing middle class' (Levy and Murnane, 1992; Wolfson, 1994, 1997),[32] implies that there are less people or households in the middle-income brackets, and more at both the low- and high-income ends of the scale. Polarisation can happen when people or households in the middle-income brackets migrate up or down the scale, or if there is an increase in the population at one or other (or both) of the poles but not in the middle groups. It can also take place when high incomes become less variable – meaning that they move closer to the mean income within the high-income group – or if the same thing happens for low-incomes.

---

32   Discussion of what the 'middle class' means conceptually has been for the most part the concern of the discipline of sociology. In the economic literature, analysis of the middle class is important given the role the middle class plays in promoting economic development through investment in human capital, consumption and savings (Easterly, 2001). Moreover, where favourable conditions exist for the middle class, it is likely they will also exist for the poor as well, which favours social cohesion and mitigates tensions between the rich and the poor, making for greater political stability (Birdsall, 2010). Defining and measuring a middle class in precise terms is complicated however as the middle class is not a purely economic concept; the boundaries of what is or is not middle class are not determined only by income (or wealth). Deciding on unambiguous demarcations that allow for measurement and analysis of the middle class, even if only in the narrow domain of economics, is an arduous task with many obstacles in the way. For a better idea of the issues involved see Atkinson and Brandolini (2011).

4.2   *Inequality and Income Polarisation*

Inequality and polarisation are related but distinct concepts used to analyse income distribution.[33] While measures of inequality assess how income is distributed among individuals or households in the population, polarisation is a concept that concerns the presence of clusters within a distribution. Esteban and Ray (1994), for example, conceived of polarisation in the following terms:

> [...] a population of individuals may be grouped according to some vector of characteristics into "clusters," such that each cluster is very "similar" in terms of the attributes of its members, but different clusters have members with very "dissimilar" attributes. In that case we say that the society is polarized. [...] At the same time, measured inequality in such a society may be low'
>
> ESTEBAN AND RAY, 1994: 819–820

The following example gives us a good intuition of the meaning of polarisation and shows that changes in polarisation can differ from, and even move in opposition to, changes in inequality. We imagine first a population of 40 individuals distributed uniformly across ten different income values,[34] equally spaced as shown in panel (a) of Figure 13. Now we imagine that the distribution is concentrated around income levels 30 and 80, as shown in panel (b). The changes in the income distribution clearly imply a reduction in inequality, as the spread of incomes within the clusters has decreased in the transition from (a) to (b). However, in the second graph we see that the society now consists of two clear groups (or clusters), without a 'middle class' to bridge the divide between the two. In this way, this society is more polarised – the middle class has disappeared, and group identity has become much stronger.

---

33   While the study of inequality has a long tradition in economics, analysis of income polarisation has become formalised only in recent times. The first economists to analyse polarisation were Foster and Wolfson (1992, 2010), and Esteban and Ray (1994). Over the last few decades income polarisation has taken on greater importance in the analysis of income distribution. Some of the reasons for this are the role that it plays in the analysis of the evolution over time of income distribution (Duclos and Taptué, 2015), in analysis of conflict (Esteban and Ray, 1999, 2008, 2011; Chakravarty, 2015), and in analysis of economic growth (Brzeziński, 2013).

34   In probability theory and statistics, uniform distribution (or rectangular distribution) is a probability distribution that attributes the same frequency (number of observations) to each value of the set. In terms of Figure 13, the income distribution depicted in panel (a) is uniform because the same number of people (4) receive each level of income (10, 20, ..., 100).

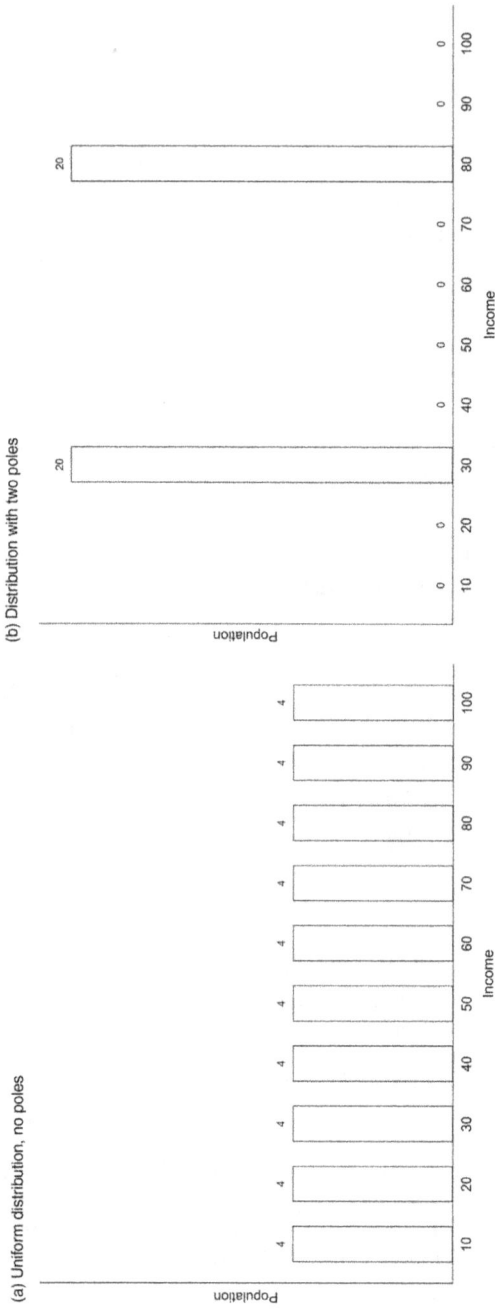

FIGURE 13   Inequality and polarisation

In measuring income polarisation, researchers consider two possible axioms. The first axiom, *increased* spread, implies that polarisation increases as the distance between the two groups either side of the median increases. Alternatively, the same thing happens if at least one individual with an income below the median becomes poorer, or one individual with income above the median becomes richer (i.e. if there is a regressive transfer of income across the median).[35] These changes thus also entail an increase in inequality. As the spread of the distribution increases, there is a rise in both inequality and polarisation. The second axiom is *increased bi-polarity*, referring to a situation in which incomes on the same side of the median move closer to one another. If the distance between incomes below and/or above the median reduces, these changes result in increased polarisation. An income distribution becomes more polarised, therefore, if incomes become more concentrated around values below or above the median, even where this means the poorest see a rise in their incomes. This latter case could therefore represent a situation of increased polarisation but decreased inequality. As such, income polarisation can imply greater inequality – captured by the principle of increased spread, where both polarisation and inequality increase – or it can imply greater equality – as in the case of increased bi-polarity, where polarisation increases but inequality decreases. Therefore, though there are complementarities between polarisation and inequality, there are also differences.

---

35   Traditionally, the phenomenon of income polarisation has been analysed with reference to a population divided into two sub-groups of individuals with income either above or below the median within the distribution. In this case, polarisation – also known as 'bi-polarisation' – is measured by the spread towards the two extremes either side of the median income value (Chakravarty, 2009; Deutsch et al., 2013). A broader concept of income polarisation sees it as a process in which a population 'clusters' around two or more poles within the distribution, regardless of where these poles may sit along the income scale (Esteban and Ray, 1994). Understanding income polarisation as a 'multi-cluster' (or multi-polar) context is an attempt to capture the potential conflicts inherent to such a situation (Esteban and Ray, 1999, 2008, 2011). The idea is that society should be considered as an amalgamation of clusters, where people within a cluster or group share similar attributes (i.e. there is some sort of reciprocal 'identification') and in terms of these same attributes they differ from members of other groups (i.e. there is a sense of 'alienation' from other groups). Social or political conflict is therefore more likely where these groups are more homogenous internally and distinct from one another, i.e., when income distribution within a group is more concentrated around its internal average, and when the distance between groups is larger.

4.3   *Measuring Income Polarisation*

One of the more commonly used indexes for measuring income polarisation was designed by Foster and Wolfson (1992, 2010) and Wolfson (1994, 1997).[36] The Foster-Wolfson index calculates how incomes are distributed around the median, meaning a highly polarised society is one in which fewer incomes are concentrated close to the median. The index is expressed as the following formula:

$$P_{FW} = 2\left[1 - L(0.5) - G\right]\frac{\mu}{m},$$

Where $L(0.5)$ represents the income share of the part of the population whose income is below the median (the poorest half of the population), G is the Gini coefficient, and μ and m are the distribution mean and median. The Foster-Wolfson index varies from 0 to 1, with 0 representing a case of perfectly equal distribution – where all incomes are equal – and 1 representing a perfectly bimodal distribution, where half of the population has no income and each member of the other half of the population has an income equal to double the mean income. Foster and Wolfson (1992, 2010) have shown that the index can also be expressed with the analogous formulation:

$$P_{FW} = 2\left(G_B - G_W\right)\frac{\mu}{m},$$

Where G_B is the component of the Gini coefficient that expresses inequality 'between groups' – calculated by replacing each observation within the two sub-groups on either side of the median with the group mean – and G_W is the component of the Gini coefficient that measures inequality 'within groups' – calculated as the weighted sum of the Gini coefficients for both sub-groups, with weights equal to the product of the subgroup's share of the total population and its share of total income. This formulation establishes a connection between Foster and Wolfson's concept of (bi-) polarisation (1992, 2010) and the 'identification-alienation' approach of Esteban and Ray (1994). Alienation – which positively correlates to inequality between groups, G_B – causes both inequality and polarisation to intensify, while identification – which negatively correlates to inequality within groups, G_W – reduces inequality but not polarisation.

---

36   Many different ways of measuring income polarisation have been proposed. Here we will limit ourselves to looking at the most common index. For an overview of other methods and of the concepts underlying income polarisation measurement see Duclos and Taptué (2015).

4.4   *Income Polarisation in Practice*

Figure 14 presents a map of economic polarisation in the world created using the Foster-Wolfson index for 52 countries over the period 1997–2019.[37] The data used to calculate the index comes from the Luxembourg Income Study, a research centre specialised in surveying household budgets in different countries, mostly in advanced economies.[38] The economic variable of reference is equivalised disposable household income, calculated by totalling the incomes of all the members of a household, after tax outgoings and social security incomings, and then dividing that sum by the square root of the number of household members.[39] To obtain unbiased estimates of income polarisation, the calculation of the Foster-Wolfson index takes into account a person-level weight assigned to each household included in the survey. This weight, obtained by multiplying the weight of the household by the number of household members, allows totals to be estimated for the entire population. As we see from Figure 14, the countries with the lowest income polarisation are Northern European countries (Denmark, Finland, Iceland, Norway, and Sweden), as well as Western European nations (Austria, Belgium, France, the Netherlands) and some ex-communist East European nations (Czech Republic, Romania, Slovakia, Slovenia, Hungary), all of which have an index of between 0.19 and 0.23. In contrast, the countries with the highest income polarisation are Estonia, Lithuania, the UK, Russia, Serbia, and Spain, with an index of between 0.27 and 0.35. Outside Europe, Guatemala, the USA, and Uruguay also fall into this bracket. Economic polarisation in the rest of Europe is less pronounced, with levels among the wealthier countries similar to Australia and Canada: between 0.23 and 0.27. The highest levels of income polarisation are outside Europe. In South America, Brazil, Chile, Colombia, Mexico, Panama, Paraguay, Peru and the Dominican Republic are all between 0.35 and 0.46,

---

37   For each country, the data used to calculate the Foster-Wolfson index refer to the most recent year for which data was available within the period considered.

38   Researchers at the LIS construct homogenous variables across countries, as much as is possible from the data available, in order to overcome the homogeneity of the single surveys and allow for comparative analysis. For security reasons, the micro-data is not free available to external researchers, however researchers can send processing programmes to the Institute which are then carried out remotely and sent back via email. See here for more information (last accessed September 2021): https:// www.lisdatacenter.org.

39   According to LIS's methodology (explained here: https://www. lisdatacenter.org/data-access/key-figures/methods/), all households with no disposable income, or where disposable income is exactly equal to zero, are excluded from the calculation of the Foster-Wolfson index. In addition, household incomes below 1% of median equivalised income, and those more than 10 times higher than the non-equivalised median disposable income, were replaced by values corresponding to the barrier thresholds shown above.

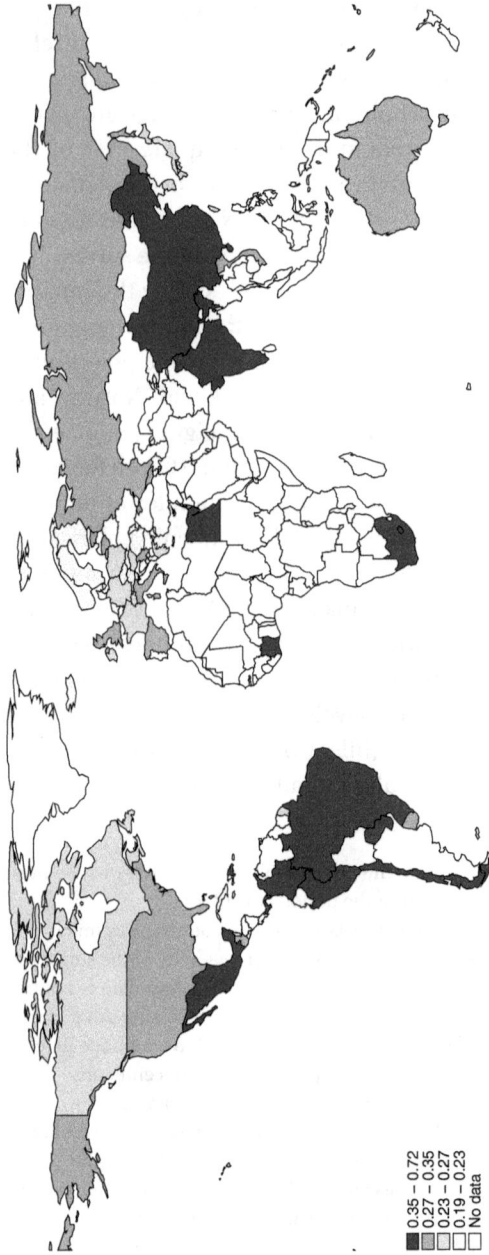

	0.35 – 0.72
	0.27 – 0.35
	0.23 – 0.27
	0.19 – 0.23
	No data

FIGURE 14   Income polarisation in the world, 1997–2019

SOURCE: AUTHORS' ELABORATION USING LIS DATA

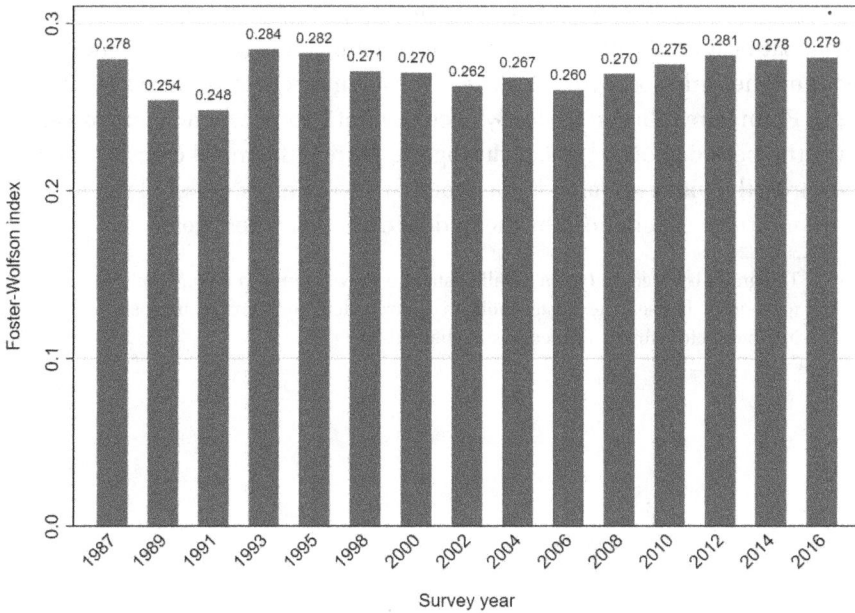

FIGURE 15   Income polarisation in Italy, 1987–2016
SOURCE: AUTHORS' ELABORATION USING THE BANCA D'ITALIA
INCOME SURVEY

while in Africa, the figures are even more extreme, ranging from Egypt with a low of 0.39 to South Africa with a high of 0.72, with other nations like Ivory Coast on 0.51 in between.[40] Asia, in comparison, appears to be more moderate in its income polarisation, with indexes of between 0.25 and 0.35 for South Korea, Japan, Georgia, Israel, Taiwan, and Vietnam. China and India stand out, however, with indexes of around 0.4 and 0.5 respectively.

---

40   Following the pioneering work on ten OECD countries carried out by Atkinson et al. (1995), the LIS study has become the benchmark for comparisons between countries based on micro-data. The LIS database, however, focuses mainly on rich countries, which for some is seen as an important limitation (Ravallion, 2015). Countries on the African continent (especially sub-Saharan Africa) are significantly under-represented, mainly because the national statistical offices of these countries focus their attention on collecting data on household consumption rather than income (Clementi et al., 2020a). This hampers possibilities for a more comprehensive (and comparative) analysis of recent trends in income polarisation in Africa, though studies using consumption data (Clementi et al., 2017, 2018, 2019a, 2020b) show sharp increases in polarisation over the last two decades, a period that has seen sustained economic growth.

Figure 15 shows income polarisation for Italy.[41] It demonstrates that income polarisation in Italy, like inequality, rose significantly during the end of the 80s and the early 90s, with the Foster-Wolfson index rising from 0.25 to 0.28 in 1993. From here it began to slowly decrease until 2006, where it shot up again over the period 2006–2012, i.e., during the years of financial crisis. From 2012 onwards, the index remains stable around the 0.28 mark, proof of the worsening conditions experienced by the middle class over recent years.

---

41   The graph is based on Banca d'Italia data and shows trends in income polarisation from 1987–2016. It uses the Foster-Wolfson index calculated from equivalised disposable income (before financial tax and state benefits).

CHAPTER 5

The Effects of the Crisis on Poverty and Inequality

1   More People in Poverty?

Our previous chapters have demonstrated that however you define poverty, relative and absolute measures being the best-known, determining clear-cut trends is not easy. Something we can be sure about is that while important progress is being made in some parts of the world – in particular in China, where the People's Republic has over the last few decades had major results in terms of bringing large parts of the population out of poverty – this is balanced out by very different dynamics elsewhere, especially in areas already plagued by serious and persistent poverty. However, the emergence of the crisis post-2007/2008 had the effect of putting poverty and inequality back at the centre of policymakers' concerns. This was because, in this period, countries that had thought themselves immune from serious poverty were now faced with scenes of misery unwitnessed since the aftermath of the Second World War. The causes of this rapid disintegration of the social fabric are multifarious and dialectically interconnected. Certainly, a significant factor was the more or less progressive dismantling of labour market regulation, prompted for the most part by the waves of social conflict that erupted in the 60s and 70s, a reflection of the more favourable balance of power (for labour) existing at the time. This gradual erosion of labour market regulation gave rise to a proliferation of the so-called 'working poor,' even in the most advanced economies. Or to put it more precisely, the breakdown of regulation allowed the global labour market to be flooded with wage workers who, despite working on a continuous basis, are *legally* forced to sell their labour-power for less than the subsistence minimum (and for casual or illegally employed workers the situation is generally even worse).

So, are more people living in poverty? As we have seen, determining the poverty line is crucial for defining poverty. The ILO divides those they determine to be poor into two categories: 'extremely poor workers,' i.e. those living in families with a per capita daily income of less than $1.90; and 'moderately poor workers,' families with a per capita daily income of between $1.90 and $3.10.[1] These measures, however, underestimate the phenomenon of poverty

---

1   These figures are expressed in PPP (purchasing power parity) terms.

in many respects, and are often contradicted by local research concerned with identifying threshold values per household that are unsurprisingly much higher. The Italian state statistical agency ISTAT, for example, has determined that a household of two people could be considered poor if the combined income was less than €1,000 monthly (around 1,170 US$ using the exchange rate as it was on 17/08/2021, so around $560 per head). According to the classifications used by the ILO and by international institutions generally, a worker is extremely poor if their monthly income is below $60, and moderately poor if it does not exceed $90. The difference in this case is stark, indicative of the fact that many measurements of poverty, starting with in-work poverty, underestimate the extent of the phenomenon, in some cases significantly. With this in mind, the most recent data from the ILO – from 2019, so before the pandemic – calculated that 8% of workers globally lived in extreme poverty, while 13% were moderately poor. And from the graph below (Figure 16) we see that the global distribution of poverty is still heavily weighted towards areas that had already had the highest levels of poverty before 2018.

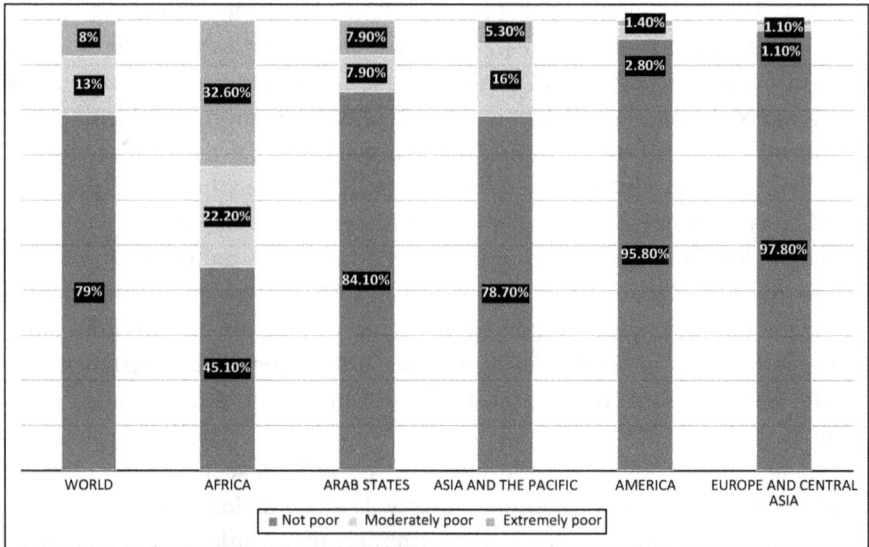

FIGURE 16   Global distribution of the working poor (2018)
             Note: ILO (2019) "The working poor or how a job is no guarantee of decent living conditions", ILOSTAT's *Spotlight on Work Statistics* No. 6, April. Available at (last accessed September 2021): https://www.ilo.org/global/statistics-and-databases/publications/WCMS_696387/lang–en/index.htm
             SOURCE: AUTHORS' OWN ELABORATION OF DATA TAKEN FROM ILO STATISTICS

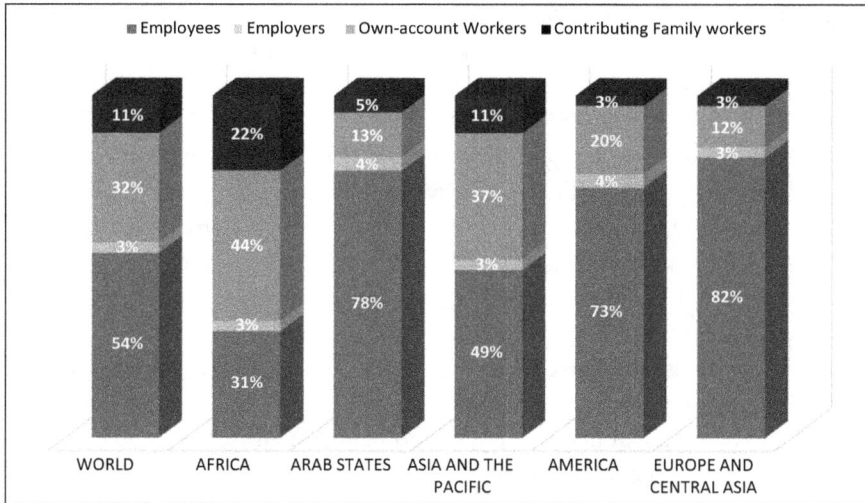

FIGURE 17   Distribution of employment by macro-areas (2017)
Note: https://ilostat.ilo.org/resources/concepts-and-definitions/ilo-modelled
-estimates/
SOURCE: AUTHORS' OWN ELABORATION OF DATA TAKEN FROM ILOSTAT – ILO
MODELLED ESTIMATES, NOVEMBER 2017

In addition to this data – particularly striking when looked at it from a macro-regional perspective, showing a truly dire situation in Africa – it is also useful to look at numbers concerning those considered 'at risk,' or 'vulnerable,' to poverty. According to the ILO definition, someone is vulnerably employed if they work for family or on their own account.[2] This definition clearly excludes many vulnerable types of wage-labour – that are also not included in the category of 'working poor' – and includes people who are in fact far from being vulnerable to poverty. Nevertheless, as the ILO has stressed, if some distortion is inevitable, it is usually compensated for, making for data that is in nonetheless valid and useful.

If we add, then, to the 21% of the global population in working poverty (about 11% of the total), even just a portion of the 43% in vulnerable employment, we begin to see a picture of a world that, even in the pre-crisis period of 2017–2018, was very distant from the descriptions we are generally presented with, and not just by the mainstream. Even without taking into account those categories of precarious wage labour, which, as the example above shows, are

---

2 In the case of contributing family work this usually means unpaid.

often included in national statistics but are not captured by the international data, around half of the global working class was living in conditions of vulnerability or in poverty of varying intensities. Focusing solely on Africa we see that on top of the fact that 66% of the population is vulnerably employed, over half of all workers are living in poverty. In other words, in the continent that has historically been most exploited by global imperialism, over 81% of those that work in any form were living in undignified conditions even before the pandemic. And when we then consider the significant numbers of people out of work (the industrial reserve army), we are confronted with a truly sombre picture (Figure 17).

These brief observations are useful first and foremost for demonstrating the extent of the phenomenon of poverty, a phenomenon that is functional to the capitalist system inasmuch as it is a phenomenon of class. They also help us to better understand how poverty must be interpreted as integral to the development of capitalism. As we have seen from the data reported in previous chapters (Figure 7), from the 90s up to 2015, if we pull together all the figures on extreme poverty, we see that it has fallen considerably. And this is even before we consider the World Bank's projections for 2030 that were highly optimistic right up to start of the pandemic (which bucked all these trends). From the early 90s figure of 1.9 billion people living in extreme poverty, over a period of 25 years the number fell to around 730 million (in 2015). However, there are two important points to note. Firstly, these figures use one of the more conservative measures of poverty, namely the World Bank $1.90 a day poverty line (expressed in PPP terms). Secondly, if we proceed with an analysis at the macroregional level, we see clearly that this reduction is thanks in large part to the spectacular growth of some Asian nations (China and India first and foremost), where previously a large proportion of the world's poor had resided. As we see in Figure 16, in the new millennium, China and India surpassed the USA and Germany respectively in terms of share of global GDP, consolidating their position as new superpowers on the global stage.

In Sub-Saharan Africa, however, the trend has been very different. Before the pandemic, the World Bank's projections (Figure 19) were that numbers of people living in poverty in Sub-Saharan Africa would continue to rise at a considerable rate. Post-pandemic, therefore, where the worst effects of the Covid-19 crisis were on the most vulnerable, the situation in Africa has become so disastrous that it could potentially be difficult to manage. What this shows us, then, is that the issue of poverty (in this case extreme poverty) needs to be approached from more than a single perspective. Far from being on the decline, it appears to be rooting itself ever more deeply in the same continent

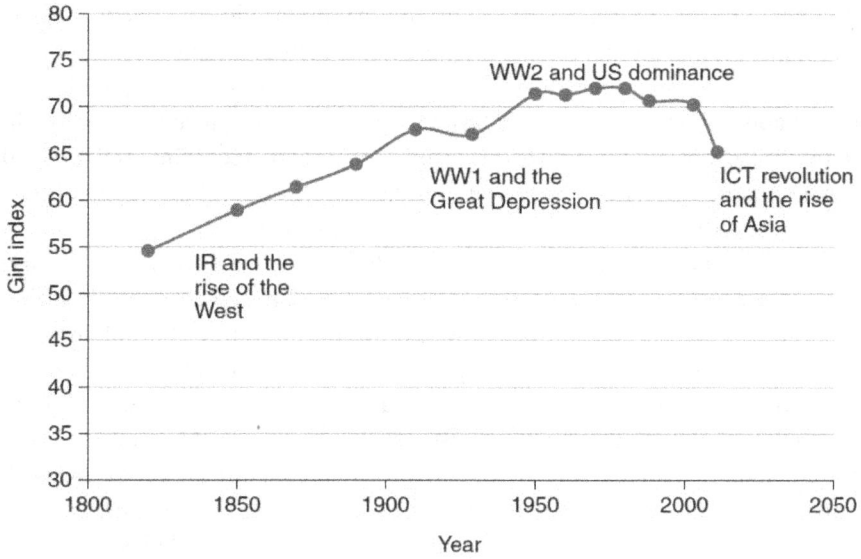

FIGURE 18   The performance of China and India over recent decades
SOURCE: MILANOVIĆ, B. (2019)

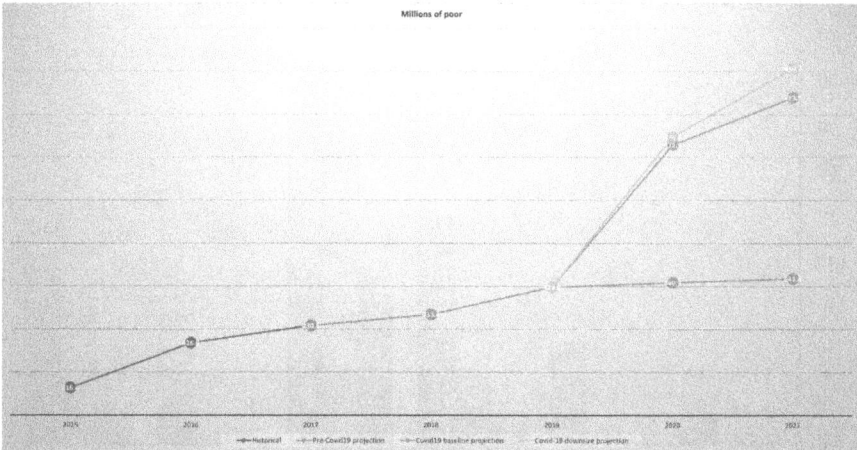

FIGURE 19   Extreme poverty in Sub-Saharan Africa (2015–2021)
SOURCE: AUTHORS' OWN ELABORATION OF DATA TAKEN FROM LAKNER
ET AL (2020) (UPDATED 19/08/2021), *POVCALNET, GLOBAL ECONOMIC
PROSPECTS*

that has suffered most historically and that paradoxically is the richest in the world in terms of the raw materials needed for industrial production.

In addition to this, if we move the poverty line upwards to an arguably more reasonable threshold of $3.10 or $5.50 daily income, the result is hugely different to the optimistic picture displayed in Figure 19. According to the World Development Index database (WDI), almost half the global population today lives on less than (PPP-adjusted) $150 a month, a quarter on less than $100, a 10th on less than $60. Yet again, when we focus only on Africa, the situation is dramatic to say the least, despite the supposed GDP growth of recent years.

Leaving aside the Global North – which was itself not free of problems even before 2020 – what emerges here is again a very different picture. With the $3.20 threshold, most African countries now see a figure of around 60% of the population living in poverty, rising to almost 90% in Madagascar, Mozambique, and the Democratic Republic of the Congo. If we move eastwards, we see that South Asia also has alarming figures, again in spite of recent growth figures. The percentage of people living in poverty in India is now 58%, in Bangladesh 57%, and in both Indonesia and Pakistan 37%. As such, though consistent GDP growth

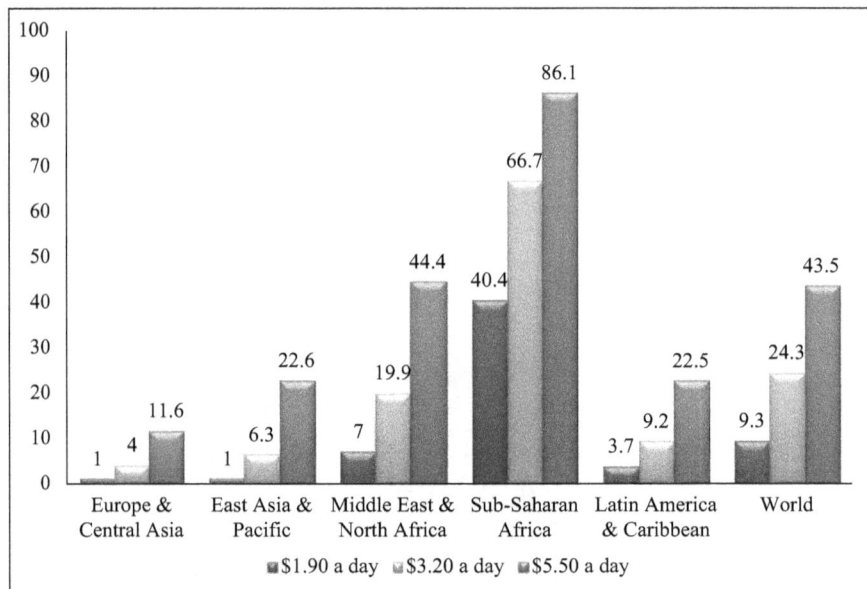

FIGURE 20   Poverty by macro-region according to different thresholds (2011 Int. PPP) (% of the population) – most recent data available
SOURCE: AUTHORS' OWN ELABORATION BASED ON THE WDI DATABASE (LAST UPDATED 30/07/2021)

has undoubtably improved standards of living for many Asians, at the beginning of 2020, poverty remained a serious and persistent problem (Figure 20).

These figures are therefore useful precisely because they are proof that if we limit ourselves to a single statistical perspective, our analysis will remain highly superficial, and our conclusions could potentially be very far from reality. In contrast to the claims of liberal commentators and the international institutions – and as much as some improvements may have been made, principally in China – the issue of poverty is absolutely central to our time.

One way of showing this is through the use of multidimensional indicators (Chatterjee, 2014), providing a much fuller conceptualisation of poverty by including of a range of factors that are not captured by economic variables. When the issue of poverty is approached from a multidimensional perspective, we see clearly that far from declining, it is potentially – especially following the 2007/2008 crisis – becoming more entrenched and more difficult to combat.

2   A Less Equal World?

The Covid-19 pandemic has undoubtably conferred on the question of economic and social inequality an unprecedented prominence, including in the media. Yet since at least a decade prior, there had been a growing realisation that inequality could pose a serious threat, including on an ideological level, to the progress of a system that has concentrated wealth in the hands of an ever-smaller group of people (the so-called global elite), while leaving behind a growing mass living in varying levels of poverty or vulnerability, struggling at times to provide even a single meal for their family. In many advanced capitalist countries, these masses of the poor have been increasing in number since the 1980s or even before, as a result of the progressive disappearance of the middle class. Here, large parts of the middle class have seen their standards of living drop to the extent that they now join the ranks of those living close to the poverty line (for a more in-depth analysis see Schettino and Khan, 2020; Nissanov and Pittau 2015; Schettino et al. 2021; Clementi and Schettino 2017; Schettino and Clementi, 2020). However, though a number of scientific and journalistic articles (from outside the mainstream paradigm) have contributed to a growing subjective perception that inequality is in fact rising, there are still pockets of resistance, mainly among free-trade advocates and the mainstream press, who are determined to convince us that both inequality and poverty are on the decline. In their view, the last century has been characterised by an unprecedent level of prosperity and a growing trend towards greater equality.

The roots of this discourse no doubt lie in an ideology that has been commonplace in the field of economics, and elsewhere, since the end of 70s. An ideology that, by instigating a series of highly questionable political choices, has propelled the entirety of capitalist development into a phase of serious crisis, appearing in full force a decade prior to the Covid-19 pandemic. Currently, while a free-market obsessed academic establishment continues to celebrate inequality as a stimulator of competition and efficiency, in the outside world economic disparity is more and more understood as a systemic problem that needs resolving. Representations of the phenomenon of inequality abound (see Banksy's Figure 21 as an example), some more effective than others, but though there is a general feeling that inequality is a bad thing, there is of course substantial divergence of opinion on the how and why it occurs.

The arrival of the pandemic arguably made more evident what these free-marketeer economists and experts have always tried to hide, hence further amplifying the distance between academia and broader social perceptions. It has revealed that the current distribution of income and wealth at the global

FIGURE 21   Depiction of global income distribution
SOURCE: COURTESY OF PEST CONTROL OFFICE, BANKSY, RICKSHAW, 2009

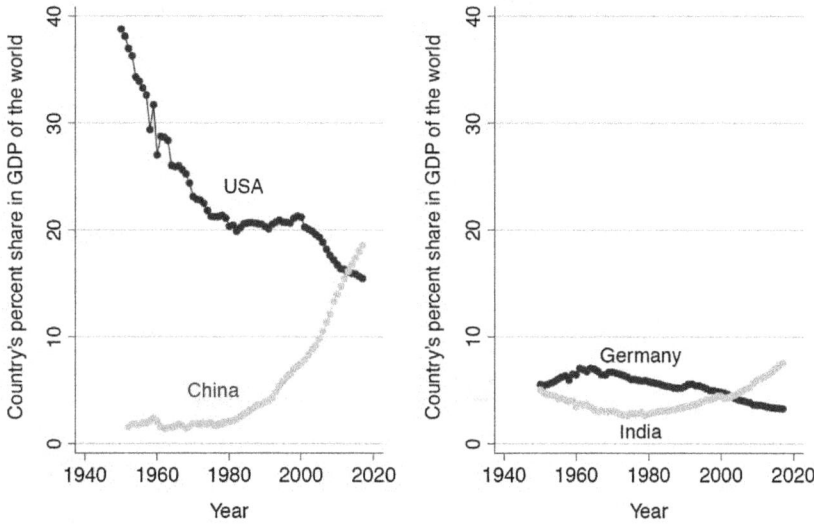

FIGURE 22   Trends in inequality 1820–2013
SOURCE: MILANOVIĆ, B. (2019)

level is profoundly unequal, and those differences have widened significantly over recent decades. The hypothesis generally accepted in scientific and academic circles, in contradiction to the daily reality of a large part of the global population, is that since the end of the Second World War, inequality has fallen, so that contemporary global society can be said to be no less unequal than at the beginning of the 20th century (see Figure 22). Yet if it is undeniable that the capitalist mode of production has developed the productive forces to an extent that at the end of WWII would have been impossible to even imagine, it is far more tenuous to assert that this unlimited growth has coincided with greater social harmony.

The inequality estimates shown in Figure 22 have been produced using the most widely known index, even among non-experts: the Gini coefficient (see the previous chapter for an explanation of what the Gini index is). As with any measure synthesising a complex phenomenon, by its nature, the index has both limits and advantages. While its advantages are widely accepted, to the extent that it has for many decades been the measurement of inequality *par excellence*, the limitations of relying exclusively on the Gini index are less commonly understood. Though it is able to capture in an exemplary manner the movements of the deciles around the central part of the distribution – i.e. the middle class – it is less good at adequately weighing against this the changes at the tail ends of the distribution, namely, among the very rich and very poor. As

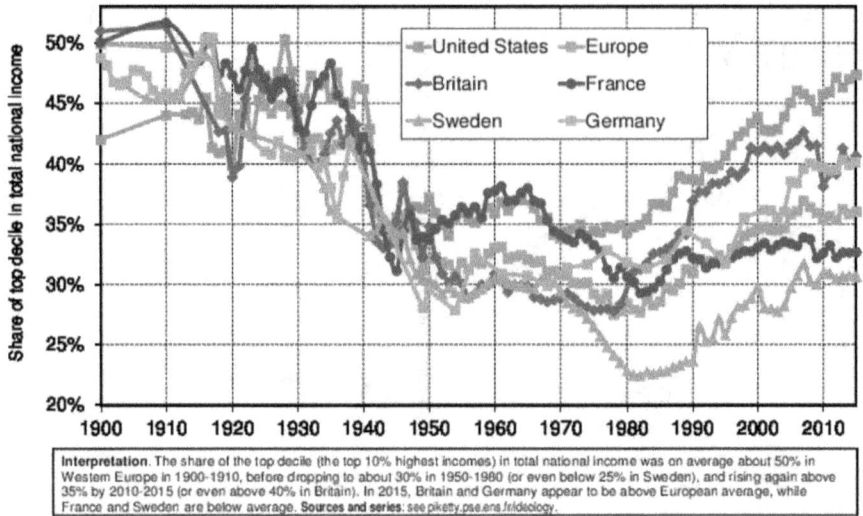

Interpretation. The share of the top decile (the top 10% highest incomes) in total national income was on average about 50% in Western Europe in 1900-1910, before dropping to about 30% in 1950-1980 (or even below 25% in Sweden), and rising again above 35% by 2010-2015 (or even above 40% in Britain). In 2015, Britain and Germany appear to be above European average, while France and Sweden are below average. Sources and series: see piketty.pse.ens.fr/ideology.

FIGURE 23   Income inequality measured differently
SOURCE: PIKETTY, 2020

we have said, there have been many solutions proposed to rectify this. Here, for reasons of brevity, we will address only a few of them.

Piketty's 2020 *Capital and Ideology* was likely the first time data from so many different parts of the globe had been collated and processed with such skill. Piketty provides much to reflect on, but what we will focus on here is how the simple choice of statistical measure can lead to very different results. Figure 23 shows trends in inequality measured using a different index to the Gini coefficient, which focuses principally on the percentage of income held by the top 10% of different societies over a period of more than a century. Looking at the graph we see quite clearly see a trend almost opposite to that shown in Figure 22, though the two graphs are mostly based on the same data. While Figure 22 shows inequality culminating in the 1950s then gradually reducing up to the present time, the graph developed by Piketty reveals a drop in inequality in the first part of the 20th century, followed by a rise in the accumulation of wealth by the richest portion of society from the 1980s onwards.

The premise that global inequality has fallen over the last half-century comes under even greater pressure when we extend our analysis further. Figure 24 for the most part would seem to support this mainstream interpretation, but it also allows us to isolate elements that would otherwise remain hidden by means of a simple statistical calculation.

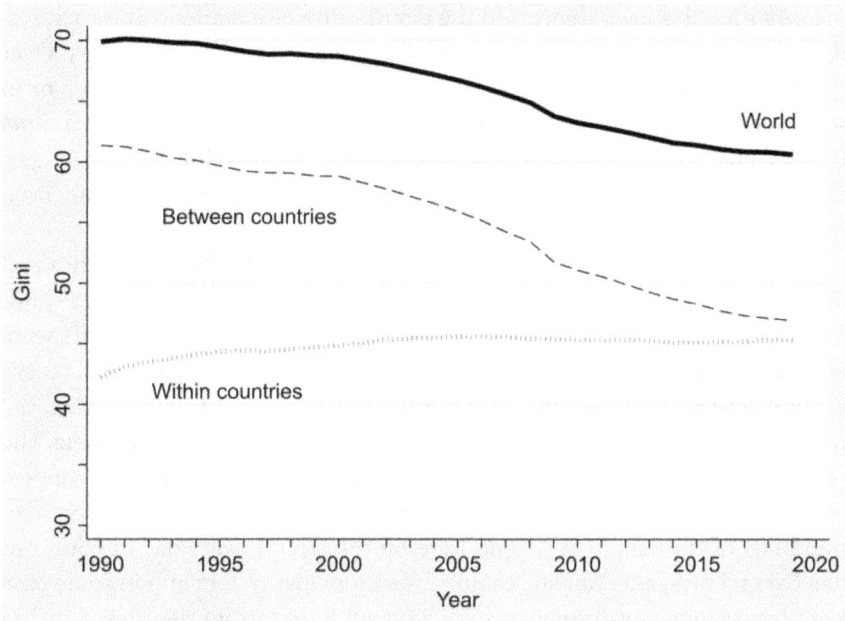

FIGURE 24   Global inequality
SOURCE: TARP (2017)

The solid line curve representing the Gini coefficient shows a significant reduction in inequality since at least the mid-1970s. As the previous chapter explains, the higher the value of this index, used ubiquitously in studies in income distribution, the greater the inequality. The lower it is, the more equal the society. However, while these initial values are unambiguous, we employ the Theil index – a statistical tool with similar features – in order to decompose this information into two parts: the so-called *between countries* effect and the other, the *within country* one. This calculation reveals something previously obscured: that where there has been a reduction in inequality this is applicable principally to inequality *between* countries. To put things simply, the reduction in inequality, which seems very likely to be due to the extraordinary growth of some Asian nations, captures the fact that, for instance, the average income of a Chinese, Indian, Nigerian, or Vietnamese citizen is today not as distant from that of the average Italian or German as it was in the past. As we are concerned here with averages, this information tells us nothing about inequality *within* each of these countries, but it does provide an account of the hypothetical phenomenon of 'catch up' (i.e. a supposed convergence between the Global South and advanced capitalist countries). The 'within country' component, on the other hand, shows changes in the distribution of income within each statistical unit, in this case countries. This data tells a very different story. Over the last 40 years economic disparity within each state has either grown or in some cases merely stayed unchanged for decades. What we see here, therefore, is that a change of perspective can make things look very different, leading us to make quite divergent conclusions to the optimistic projections we are used to hearing.

Indeed, this problem of the 'traditional' indexes' inability to capture real distributional changes also exists within less progressive circles, as there have been many cases where 'reassuring' statistics meant powerful interests were caught off guard by outbursts of social conflict. The most obvious and recent example of this – though certainly not the only one – is the Arab Spring, the protests that erupted in North Africa and the Middle East over 2010–2012. The protests were happening in places with inequality indexes that were supposedly positive, or at least that should not have been a cause for concern, yet hundreds of thousands of people were on the streets every day in countries like Egypt, Libya, and Tunisia, calling for a more just system and in some case even overturning governments that had been in power for decades. This has led some economists and statisticians to speak of the way the traditional indexes measure poverty as a structural problem. They are concerned that relative indicators, used in almost all cases (including in Figure 24), may not be as structurally advantageous over absolute indicators as is usually thought. As we have seen, most statistics relating to income distribution can be expressed in both absolute and relative terms. To give an idea of what the choice of one over the other implies, we can take the following two examples.

First, we imagine a society composed of only two individuals in which at the time t, the income of person A is $1 a year, while that of person B is $10,000 a year. This is clearly a very unequal society. If now imagine that the following year, $t+1$, person A's income grows to $2 a year, while person B's income grows to $20,000 a year. The situation remains undeniably very unequal, but at the same time it is important to be able to answer the question 'is the situation in $t+1$ more or less unequal in comparison to the previous year?' What we know is the following: 1) that both incomes have grown; 2) that both incomes have doubled and so have retained the same proportional relation to each other; 3) the absolute distance between person A's income and person B's income has grown from $9,999 in t ($10,000 – $1) to $19,998 in $t+1$ ($20,000 – $2). In simple terms, if we use a relative index (used in the overwhelming majority of statistics), the income distribution would not appear to have changed from t to $t+1$, as the proportional relation between the two incomes has remained the same – in formal terms the proportion in t is $\{10.000/1\}$, and in $t+1$ $\{20.000/2\}$.

Person	Leo	Julian
Assets		

FIGURE 25   Hypothetical distribution at point in time 1

Person	Leo	Julian
Assets		

FIGURE 26   Hypothetical distribution at point in time 2

The absolute indexes, however, would describe the society in *t+1* as much less equal than that in *t* because what counts here is point 3), i.e., the distance between the two incomes {*19.998>9.999*}.

We can also look not purely at monetary income but at property (Figure 25).

Again, this hypothetical society is composed of two people who own two very different assets in terms of economic value. Again, it is a very unequal society: Leo only has a bicycle and Julian has a luxury car.

As in the previous case, we see here a doubling of each person's wealth, meaning within the period from time 1 and time 2, Leo has acquired another bicycle and Julian another luxury car (Figure 26). It should be clear by now that measured with relative indexes, there would be no change at all from Figure 25 to Figure 26. In contrast, absolute indexes would more accurately capture the transformation, reflecting a trend towards greater inequality over time.

We should emphasise here that this does not necessarily mean that absolute indexes are inherently preferable to relative indexes, but rather that in conditions such as those described above, absolute indexes are more appropriate for

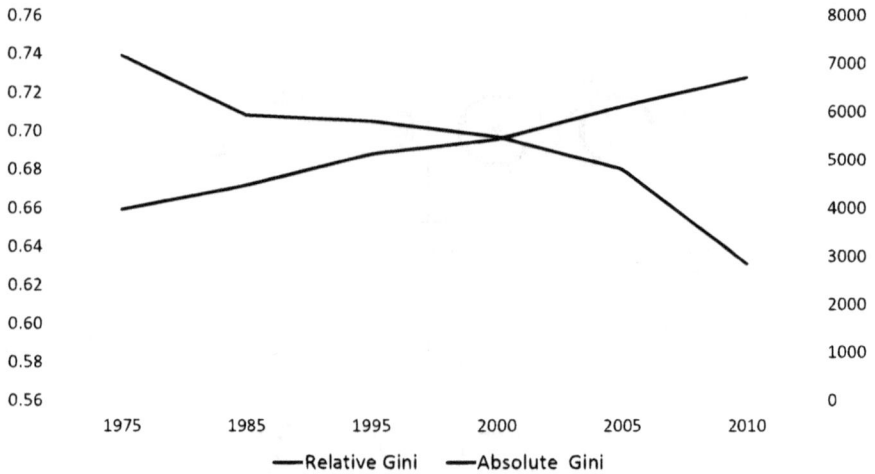

FIGURE 27   Global inequality: Relative vs. Absolute indexes
SOURCE: NIÑO ZARAZÚA ET AL. (2017)

capturing trends in distribution. Finally, returning to the Gini coefficient displayed in Figure 24, in Figure 27 the same *relative* Gini coefficient is displayed
next to a line showing the trend in the *absolute* Gini coefficient for global
wealth distribution.

As we may have expected, using the same Gini index, but this time the absolute rather than the relative version, the trend is entirely different. What we see
now is something much more reflective of the material reality lived by people
across the globe; it seems that inequality has risen steadily from at least the
1970s, accompanying the genesis of the more recent crisis and confirming once
again Marx's great intuition (Marx, 1867: 762–870) of two centuries ago that the
same capitalist law of accumulation generates the accumulation of both capital
and deprivation. Or in other words, it generates class (and income) polarisation.

And the same graph could be reproduced for a whole range of countries,
revealing a common trend that lay hidden in the data but is unveiled through
the application of the absolute Gini index. By way of example, we can look very
briefly at Latin America. Many analysts have struggled to explain the social
upheavals that regularly rock the subcontinent, as the studies suggest that
inequality has theoretically fallen over the last two decades (Figure 28) (see
also: Clementi and Schettino, 2015).

Here we see again that the downward trend in the relative Gini coefficient
(blue line) is entirely contradicted by a growth in inequality registered by the
absolute Gini Coefficient (red line).

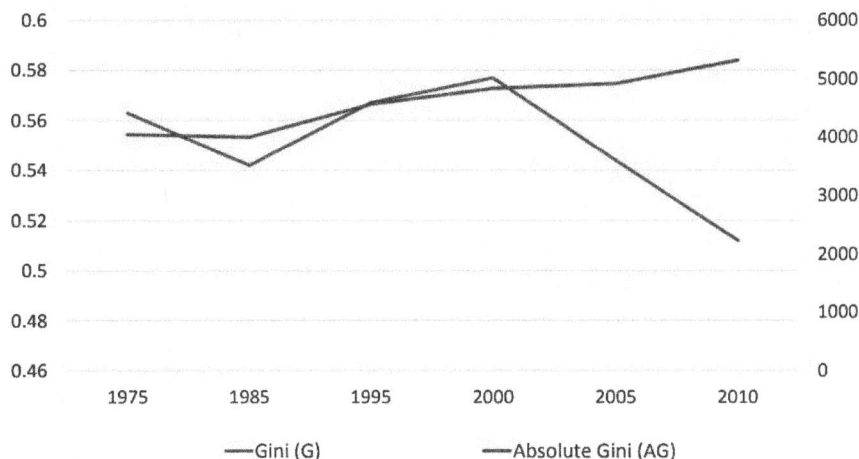

FIGURE 28   Inequality in Latin America
SOURCE: TARP (2017)

What we have attempted to outline here, therefore, is the dynamics of two key elements of capitalist development, poverty and inequality, in relation to the particular stage of development that has characterised the last few decades, namely the overproduction crisis that began to manifest itself from 2007/2008 onwards. Some studies, especially from more institutional or mainstream arenas, have for years been propagating visions of global levels of poverty and inequality that are entirely at odds with the material reality as perceived by populations in all corners of the globe. According to these analysts, both poverty and inequality are decreasing, following a trend that began more than a century ago, and the crisis of the last decade has had little impact in this regard.

Digging deeper into the data, however, the reality is very different. While it can be generally accepted that poverty and inequality are phenomena that have always accompanied the historical genesis of capitalism, from its earliest stages of life at both a local and global level, here we have shown that over the last half century – since the beginning of the previous protracted crisis in the 1970s – these phenomena have assumed a dynamic that is profoundly worrying. Though the rapid ascent of China, and to a lesser extent other Asian states, has objectively alleviated the profound poverty in which millions of people across the continent were living, in much of Africa by contrast, paradoxically in states rich in natural resources in particular, poverty is becoming ever more entrenched, and despite the attempts of the international institutions to play it down, the outlook here is tragic to say the least. And when it comes to inequality, when we switch to absolute measures we see an undisputable process of fragmentation of the (lower) middle classes dating back at least as far as the last decade. A process which for perhaps the first time in at least half a century also concerns the advanced capitalist economies.

At this point, therefore, what remains is to understand why poverty and inequality have always accompanied capitalist development, and why they become exacerbated in phases of crisis. As concerns poverty (both relative and absolute), it is important that we relate this to the concept of *relative surplus population* and therefore to the accumulation of capital. As Marx reminds us among the constant causes of crisis, the excess of wage labour

> is inseparable from the development of labour productivity [...] The more the capitalist mode of production is developed in a country, the more strikingly does the relative surplus population obtrude there. It is in turn a reason why the more or less incomplete subordination of labour to capital persists in several branches of production, and longer indeed than would seem to correspond at first sight to the general level of development; this is a result of the cheapness and quantity of available or dismissed wage-labourers [...]
>
> MARX, 1894: 343

In other words, when there is a clear problem with accumulation, competition among workers (employed or otherwise) undermines wages and generates increases the (absolute and relative) surplus-value produced (exploitation). Not only this, but the recent visible emergence of the working poor in mass numbers, including in the imperialist core, – a category which must also include those who earn a total wage that is some way above the national poverty line – corresponds to what Marx meant when he spoke of a "depression of wages below the value of labour-power," again as an antagonistic cause of the accumulation crisis.

When it comes to inequality it is necessary to take a more subtle and structural approach. Though by changing the way we measure inequality we can certainly present a more realistic and detailed picture, showing an undeniable widening of the gap in ownership, wealth and well-being among the inhabitants of the planet, when we look purely at monetary variables (income or consumption) we see only part of the problem. When we speak about distribution, we (almost) always mean in the *means of consumption* (monetary and/ or material). All the statistics we have spoken about here and in previous chapters have been concerned with monetary variables, yet in some respects these should in fact be considered as secondary, seeing as they are mediated by the market. In other words, the metaphor of the dividing of the pie, widely used to describe the phenomenon of distribution and its potential inequities, ignores the questions of how and by whom the pie is made. Therefore, in order to understand the roots of the problem of inequality, we should take a step back and try to analyse how the *means of production* are distributed. In other words, the very existence of a society composed of different classes, one owning the conditions of production and the other in possession only of their labour-power to be exchanged for a wage, cannot but generate an unequal society. It is therefore in the stage of production of goods and services, i.e., in the appropriation of unpaid labour (surplus-labour or surplus-value), that inequality is rooted, whose genesis and dynamics we then observe in monetary terms. Inequality is thus a *presupposition* of any class-based society, and not merely its result. As such, while the role of taxation in reducing inequalities remains important – though it concerns mainly redistribution within the working class – this can never structurally undermine what is the substance and very foundation of capitalist development: the appropriation of unpaid labour, i.e., the exploitation of labour within and through class domination.

CHAPTER 6

Pandemic, Crisis, Inequality and Conflict

1　　The Crisis Scenario Pre Covid 19

> Dear Reader, the global economy is at a delicate moment. The expansion of early 2018 has lost momentum, in large part in response to rising trade tensions. There are threats from rising financial vulnerabilities and geopolitical uncertainties. These challenges call for policymakers to avoid missteps and to take the right policy steps: at home, across borders, and globally.

At first glance, one could easily assume that this incipit was the introduction to a Marxist academic analysis of the current state of the global economic system. In fact, it was written by someone from a very different background, making it perhaps all the more interesting. The words are those of the acting manager of the IMF, David Lipton, published as the opener of its 2019 annual report. Paraphrasing Lenin, what this tells us is that while the radical left is forever distracted by the search for the next theoretical big thing, it is the ruling class itself that provides the most accurate material analysis of capital's current condition.

The IMF report, published at the end of 2019 (IMF, 2019), echoed alarm bells that had been growing louder for some time, as many analysts came to recognise that 2020 might well be the year in which the financial bubble that had been ballooning since 2008 exploded with unknown force. A key warning in this respect was an event that took place on the 17th of September 2019. Deliberately passed over in silence by most of the world's media, it nevertheless put fear into all financiers with sound knowledge of the dynamics of the markets. And while it may not tell us much for now, it could easily turn out to be a historic event.

What happened on 17th September 2019 was that in spite of all the liquidity that had been pumped into banking systems across the globe from 2008 onwards through the various QE programmes, estimated to amount to around twenty thousand billion dollars in total, the US interbank market suddenly ground to a halt for lack of cash flow, though interest rates were zero or even negative in some cases. More specifically, some repo[1] rates jumped to 10% at

---

1　Also known as Repurchase Agreements: https://datahelp.imf.org/knowledgebase/articles/484377-what-is-a-repurchase-agreement.

the same time that official interest rates remained around 2–2.25%. This spread between repo rates and official rates is in theory a typical sign of blockage in the system due principally to loss of confidence among operators involved in lending and returning capital, mainly in overnight trading. In other words, it seemed to be a repeat of the months leading up to the 2008 explosion, symbolically represented by the Lehman Bros. collapse.

To avoid a collapse in the system, the Federal Reserve was therefore forced to intervene with yet more cash, amounting to around $260 billion (at that point a historical record) over the two months that followed ($75 billion of this was just the immediate response on the same day). It also cut interest rates by a quarter of a point. In this way, the Fed dramatically reversed the course it had embarked over the previous six months which consisted in an attempt to 'normalise' the money market, or rather to slowly drain it of supply.

In spite of the evident similarities with pre-2008 conditions, there were some elements of the 17th of September crunch that were characteristic of a new phase of development, whose beginnings we can trace to around five years prior to 2019. Confirming the generalised crisis of accumulation, financial instruments had been evolving, moving towards models that allowed investors of (both large- and small-scale) fictitious capital to save on brokerage fees. As such, in the period immediately preceding September 2019, there had been an explosion in so-called 'passive investing,' involving instruments such as index funds, investment funds set to track a chosen financial index. Put simply, if the value of this particular index rises, the value of the fund rises, if the index drops, so does the fund.

In a period in which markets globally were reaching record highs (something which in fact continued well into the pandemic), index funds could generate significant results in terms of profits, and could themselves contribute to this spectacular growth. At the same time, however, this kind of investment, by tying investment performance to that of a market index, becomes entirely disconnected from what is termed the 'underlying' market, more simply: the real economy, or material reality. In synthesis, exactly as happened just before the 2008 crash (see previous chapters), many speculators were buying up securities they knew very little about, aside from the basic fact that their value is tied to a stock index. From a quantitative perspective, this fuelled the expansion of financial bubbles across the globe and promoted widespread ignorance regarding the financial products being bought and sold, as their performance was not connected to the fortunes of any particular company but rather to something entirely exogenous to the production and circulation of goods and services. As a result, such instruments may be appealing to investors looking to save on brokerage fees, but they in fact work undermine the already very delicate structure of the financial markets.

On top of this, considering the growing numbers of actors in the credit market (especially short-term credit) that do not belong to a financial institution – meaning they are able to evade a lot of banking regulation but are also that they are unable to access Fed liquidity directly (the lender of last resort) – a monetary squeeze in the US at the end of 2019 was beginning to seem highly impractical. To put it bluntly, from almost as soon as the 2008 crash ended, a fresh house of cards made was being constructed, based on junk securities apparently anchored in the real estate market, with the difference from pre-2008 being that the decisive moves were being made by 'unconventional' actors, capable of evading all existing regulation. A system that was already structurally dependent on injections of liquidity, was now hostage to actors capable of manipulating thousands of billions worth of securities without any oversight. Faced with this scenario, the strategy of drying up the money markets became highly risky. However, how this could be dealt with remains to be seen, as with the arrival of the pandemic the issue simply became dwarfed by the ensuing chaos.

Leaving aside the more technical details, what concerns us most here are two contradictions that emerge from these details with force. The first regards the fact that despite the twenty thousand billion dollars of new liquidity that had been pumped into the economy between 2008 and 2019 (more or less the equivalent of the USA's annual GDP), the market remained constantly at risk of stalling for lack of accessible cash (a 'credit crunch'). The second, a broader and more systemic consideration, relates to the role that QE has assumed over the years, and the dependence that the system has come to have on this type of expansive monetary policy.

So how do we make sense of these contradictions? Starting with the first, in both the US and the EU, QE, or rather an expansive monetary policy, was presented by bourgeois economists as the panacea that would vanquish the so-called credit crunch: the hypothetical lack of access to credit that financial operators encountered over the period 2007/2008, which in the economist's view was the cause of the disaster that followed the Lehman collapse. In simple terms, a flood of liquidity was supposed to bring the cost of borrowing down to zero (or even below zero in real terms), stimulating consumption and investment on the part of financial actors. The theory, invoking the 'eternal' Keynes, was that monetary policy as a tool of intervention would indirectly stimulate demand. Consumers would be able to access loans and mortgages at lower rates, or access credit lines more easily to pay for basic necessities or luxuries, and businesses would be able to borrow in a more sustainable manner, giving a boost to the global economy. The idea, never openly set out but which nevertheless underpinned the whole programme, was to create an effect similar to that of 'helicopter money,' i.e., money simply rained down on the economy, as depicted literally in the recent series *Money Heist*. However, if this was the theory, the reality was very different. This staggering amount of dollars, euros and yen, far from ending up in the wallets of workers and small business owners, instead became concentrated in the hands of a tiny group of individuals, in line with the general laws of capitalist accumulation, exacerbating an existing trend towards a monopoly in the production and circulation of credit.

To illustrate the extent of this, suffice to note two simple figures: in the US, the Federal Deposit Insurance Corporation reported that almost 90% of the excess liquidity created has ended up in the hands of 1% of American banks. And just four banks possess almost half of this. In Europe, before the QE programme, loans to families and businesses amounted to just over €10.4 trillion. After almost ten years of expansive monetary policies this had risen to no more than €11.1 trillion. In other words, for every 100 euros 'injected' by the ECB into the economy, only 27 were used for lending to families and businesses.[2] At this point, it is easy to guess where the rest ended up.

If many remained ignorant to this reality, the authors of this book had been warning of the potential dangers since as early as 2011, stressing that as this was a crisis produced by the overproduction of value, the credit crunch was not the real problem, or rather was only superficially the problem, affecting some people but not others (see also Schettino, 2011, 2013, 2015, 2018; Schettino and Clementi, 2020). What was really going on can be best expressed in Marx's words:

> But if this new accumulation comes up against difficulties of application, against a lack of spheres of investment, i.e. if branches of production are saturated and loan capital is over-supplied, this plethora of loanable money capital proves nothing more than the barriers of *capitalist* production. The resulting credit swindling demonstrates that there is no positive obstacle to the use of this excess capital.
>
> MARX, 1894: 639, emphasis in the original

Once we understand this, we understand that an expansive monetary policy would have had only marginal effects in terms of real accumulation, expanding the financial markets and further detaching them from the production of value.

---

2   Data taken in January 2020 from the websites of the FDIC and the ECB.

However, looking at the causes of the systemic need for QE, the injections of liquidity were *necessary* inasmuch as they allowed for a dizzying growth in the profits of fictitious capital, which remains, in a world mired in crisis, the only sphere in which decent profits can still be made, reflected in the inevitable regrowth of the speculative bubbles. To fully understand the question, therefore, we must turn the mainstream discourse on its head. The crisis is not the result of an increase in the use of speculative instruments (or 'financial instruments,' as they are commonly known). On the contrary, since it is impossible to accumulate money in the sphere of production and circulation of goods (M-C-M'), the speculators simply circumvent this, seeking to valorise their capital through the mechanism of M-M', i.e., through gambling on the stock exchange. Speculation therefore becomes the *consequence* of a real crisis and not its *cause* (as much as this then serves dialectically to aggravate the crisis).

To give an idea of the magnitude of the problem, in case this is not yet clear enough already, we can look at the MSCI World Index, which summarises the performance of global markets. Over the course of 2019, this grew by 26%, surpassing 1,800 points for the first time in history. In the same period, global GDP growth was just over 3%, one of the worst figures since the end of WWII. According to IMF data (World Economic Outlook, October 2019), the advanced capitalist states were seeing their GDPs grow by an average of only 1.7%. In the USA, with the NASDAQ and S&P 500 on +30%, the real economy grew by a modest 2.1%. The same was true for Italy, where, while the Milan Stock Exchange was surging (+28.28%), Italian workers were facing another year of hardship due to stagnant GDP growth (+0.5%). Even Greece, finally experiencing a modest recovery from the devastation wrought on it by transnational capital, was seeing stock market performances (+43%) way beyond real production (+2.2%). And the arrival of the pandemic did not upset the trend. In 2020, while the economy was shaken to its core by the inevitable volatility, stock markets continued to thrive (NASDAQ Composite +43.63%, Nikkei 225 + 16%, S&P 500 +15.61%, Dow Jones +7%, and so on). Whichever way we look at it therefore, it is clear that the speculative market (the fictitious market) has over the last decade been the only place in which it was possible to realise consistent profits, even in the midst of the Covid-19 epidemic. At the same time, however, the system of fictitious capital does not create new goods or *new*-value (so value and surplus-value). As such, the game cannot continue forever. Indeed, the widening gap between stock market values and GDP growth is a very effective way to measure the precise extent of the speculative bubble, or bubbles, that up to 2019 had so far managed to avoid any snags, though which were looking as perilous as ever. So much so that at the start of 2020, many imagined that the trend was on a course to disaster.

2   Epidemic, Misery, Inequality and Conflict

When we look at the striking estimates for the global economy produced by the international institutions during the first wave of the pandemic, it is therefore important to bear in mind that at the end of 2019 the global economy was already in a highly precarious state. This is significant because when the Covid-19 pandemic arrived, it became easy cover, a scapegoat to which could be attributed sole responsibility for the catastrophe in act. Figure 29 shows OECD data produced half-way through June 2020 – i.e., at the moment the first wave was subsiding – and relates to estimates for real GDP by country. The estimates were uniquely dramatic for every single country measured, though there was of course some heterogeneity among the results. The double bars were used to show estimates with and without a potential second peak in infections, something which was already seeming very likely (indeed, not only did this become reality in many parts of the world towards the end of 2020/ beginning of 2021, but at least one other wave followed after that). Focusing on the performance of the countries with the highest GDP and then on the global average (Figure 30), however, another detail of interest emerges. The estimates for Italy, France and the UK were the worst, while those for China – official Chinese government data in fact predicted weakly positive growth, figures way off the OECD estimates – were much less severe, despite the fact that China was the first country to face the full force of the Covid-19 pandemic. The US was also predicted to do worse than the world average. Other macroeconomic variables all reflected the same trend, presenting a starker situation than even the post-2008 period, more akin to the immediate aftermath of the War.

As is often the case, though it is rarely spoken about, the pessimism of these predictions was in fact not borne out by reality, or at least where it was this was only in a minority of countries. For the most part, the estimates were largely disproved by the unfolding of events. Indeed, by the second half of 2021, considering the figures for 2020, all the world's major research centres have significantly revised their previous estimates.

Figure 31 shows clearly that the sudden dive in the second quarter of 2020, the result of the explosion of the pandemic, had by the third quarter already effectively been absorbed in those countries most affected. The anomalous case of China aside, on the whole, the global economy, and countries like Japan, the US etc., were able to overcome the problems created by the pandemic, at least momentarily. The UK seems to have lagged behind in this regard, but even so, it seems set to surpass pre-Covid levels of real GDP by the first quarter of 2022.

Nevertheless, this vast discrepancy between forecasts and reality, however positive it may have turned out to be for the global economy, should not be put

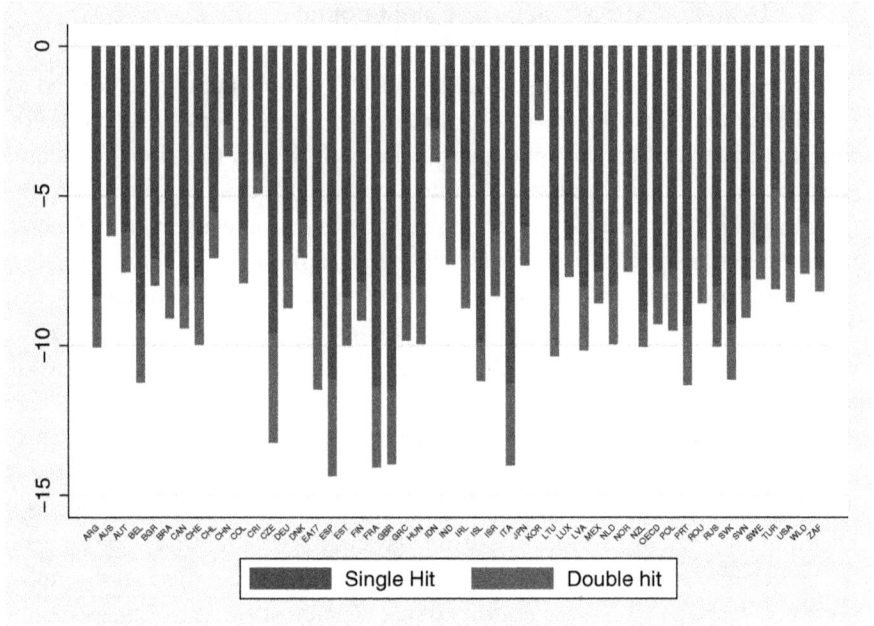

FIGURE 29   Predicted GDP growth as a percentage for 2020 (50 countries)
SOURCE: AUTHORS' ELABORATION USING OECD DATA

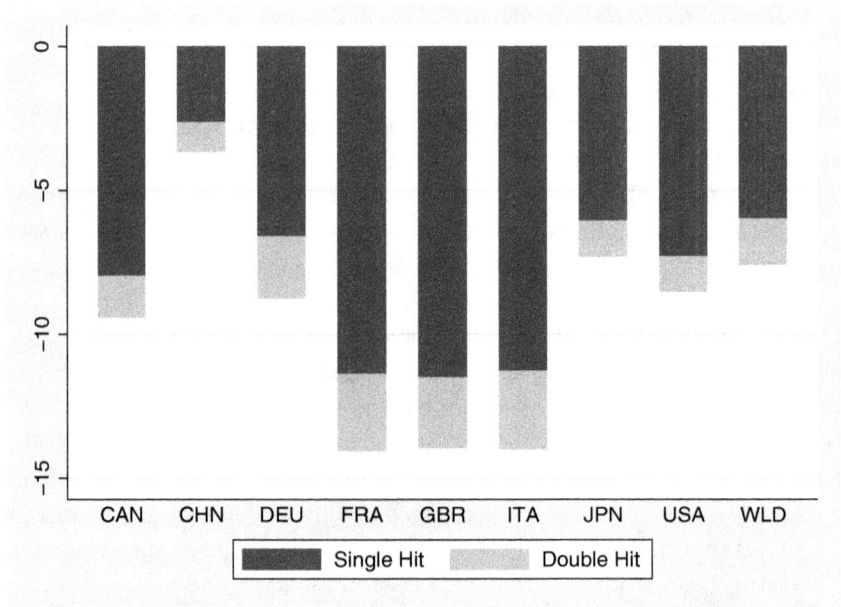

FIGURE 30   Predicted GDP growth as a percentage for 2020
SOURCE: AUTHORS' ELABORATION USING OECD DATA

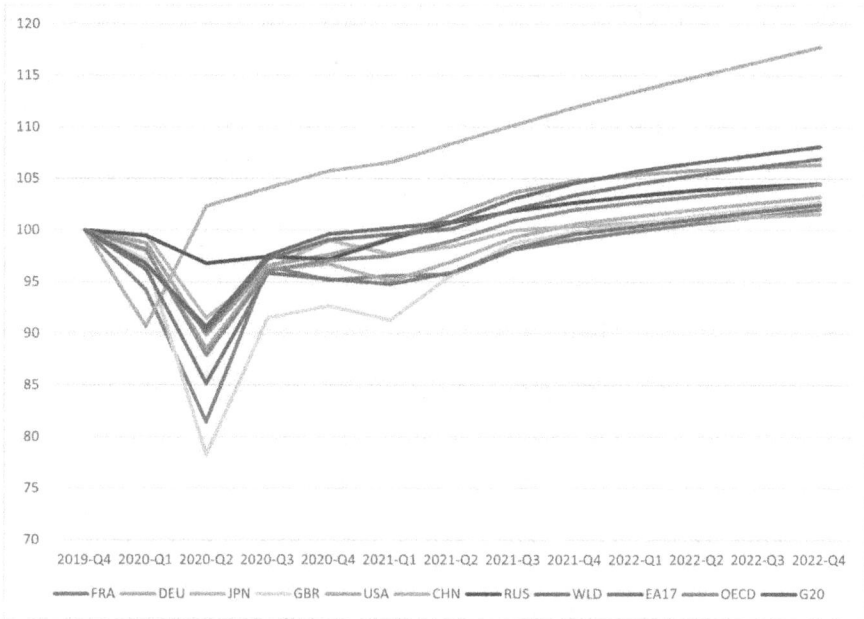

FIGURE 31   Real GDP Forecast
Note: "Real gdp forecast" (indicator), available at (accessed on 13 November 2021): https://doi.org/10.1787/1f84150b-en
SOURCE: OECD

down to a simple error on the part of the analysts: attributing the mistake to a mere formal miscalculation ignores the seriousness of the matter. There is no doubt that drawing up estimates at a national or global level is a tricky business, especially in a historical moment as chaotic and confusing as has been 2020 and some of 2021. It is only reasonable therefore, that in a continually changing context we should expect a higher margin of error. Yet the contrast between Figures 29 and 30 and then Figure 31 is so great that there must be something more at play. To understand what was going on, it is worth changing our angle and looking instead at the consequences such alarming forecasts had on the turn of events – forecasts, we should remember, that were unanimously agreed upon by all the international research organisations.

   First and foremost, there was the race to develop a vaccine capable of mitigating the spread of the pandemic. In the view of some experts, it was the precisely the vaccine roll-out that prompted the rapid turnaround in economic fortunes. While there is undoubtably some truth in this, at the end of 2021 the percentage of people who have received a vaccine in large parts of Africa and Asia is still minimal, testament to the logic of capitalist property relations which means that protection against the virus will only be guaranteed to those who can afford it. As such, while for some countries the vaccine may have played a part in the economic recovery (France and Italy are emblematic in this respect – they have instituted a legal vaccine or testing requirement for entry into all workplaces), it should not be understood as the decisive element (indeed, as we will see, the vaccine could have the effect of widening the gap between social classes).

The other key consequence of the dire predictions was state intervention. Acting in continuity with the agenda set by the 2007/2008 crisis, the institutions of the state took it upon themselves to intervene in order essentially to stop the ship going under, again working to conceal the real and structural roots of the problem. However, if we can say, for reasons previously stated, that during the financial crash it was the central banks that took on the burden of action (despite legal restraints, mainly in the case of the ECB), in the case of the pandemic it was governments, from national down to local, that assumed a predominant role by embarking on the most monumental fiscal programme in the history of capitalism. Places that had always been religiously committed to the doctrine of the free market – a chimera of ever thinning substance, essentially existing only in academic textbooks and the discussions of the servants of the ruling class – now made Keynesianism their own, throwing vast amounts of public money into the real economy by various means. In 2021 alone, the so-called Biden Stimulus has put about $1.9 billion into the pockets of US citizens, roughly the equivalent of Italy's yearly GDP. Around the same time, the EU, its infamous red tape notwithstanding, was able to inaugurate Next Generation EU, which should see around €750 million going to European citizens.

In other words, the role of the bourgeois state has been revived in order to save the capitalist market from asphyxiating itself under the weight of its own structural conditions, a dichotomy that reveals itself in all its falsity. Alongside these large-scale and better-known programmes, local governments across the globe have also been enacting measures to favour capital (essentially big capital, but also small and middling), which have likely provided the basis for the rapid recovery seen in Figure 31, where in some countries figures for 2021 are already looking better than 2019. It is useful to reiterate, therefore, that the state, whatever its role in the economy or within the dominion of the capitalist mode of production, remains (in a period of crisis more than ever) the expression of the ruling class and a "'special force' for the suppression of the oppressed class" (Lenin, 1917b: 57). Understanding this is vital if we are to stamp out the misunderstandings widespread in the common consciousness, creating a kind of "superstitious reverence for the state," as Engels put it (1891: 190), leading to such dead-end thinking as the idea of the state/market binary which is a distortion of reality: under capitalism no such thing can exist.

As we have said many times before, in order to best observe a phenomenon, we must look at it from a variety of perspectives. GDP has the merit of proving a precise measure of the annual income of a country, understood as a unified whole. However, this *corporatist* perspective has the effect of eliminating what in fact is the key to understanding the question: class. Therefore, we can get a much better picture if we complement general GDP statistics with data from other spheres, such as the labour market. Right at the beginning of the pandemic, the ILO was already indicating that around 40% of the global workforce could see job losses or significant cut-backs in their hours and wages (ILO, 2020a). Most of those affected would be from the poorest sections of the working class. The same study showed that around 60% of those employed in the informal sector globally (around 1.6 billion people) had already seen large reductions in terms of earnings. And most of these workers, as we know, live in low-income countries. For this reason, according to the ILO, the parts of the world that would pay the highest price for the pandemic would be African and Latin American workers (81% of the total), with serious repercussions for global poverty. Businesses as well, especially smaller and more vulnerable businesses, and also the self-employed, were predicted to suffer, a sign on the one hand of the fierce conflict that exists among the capitalist classes, and on the other of the necessity of understanding some of these categories (mainly forms of self-employment) as in reality much closer to the condition of the salaried worker.

If the forecasts for GDP and other macroeconomic indicators were excessively pessimistic, perhaps for instrumental reasons, as we have seen, the prospects for labour were much more on the mark. Without wanting to focus too much on the quantitative side, it is useful again to mention some numbers. The ILO's 2021 report (*Trends 2021*) tells us in no uncertain terms that in the face of the tragedy of 2020, the labour market did not rebound in 2021 in the same way as the sphere of accumulation. In the month in which the pandemic exploded, hours worked globally fell by just under 9%, the equivalent of around 225 million FTE jobs.[3] Of this, around half were taken from workers that retained some form of employment, while the rest represents people who lost their jobs and were unable to find other work. In comparison to the previous year, around 144 million more workers were laid off from their jobs. And the heterogenous restarts of 2021/2022, the report continues, will counter this catastrophe only

---

3   Full time equivalent.

in part. The ILO predicts that by the end of 2021, the equivalent in hours of 100 million full time jobs will not have been recovered. Moreover, most of the jobs being lost are characterised by low productivity, poor quality and – we add ourselves – very poor pay and conditions. Only in the advanced capitalist countries will pre-Covid levels of productivity be restored, while the least developed countries will see a reduction in labour productivity, something that the ILO believes could seriously jeopardise the 2030 poverty eradication targets. Therefore, as we have said before, it would be a serious mistake to ignore the ways in which the impact of the pre-Covid19 crisis, as well as the pandemic itself, has been profoundly heterogeneous, working to increase social inequality and poverty in countries already historically affected by these problems. As the ILO report lays out, small and medium-sized businesses, workers in the informal economy (found for the most part in the poorest parts of the globe), the young, women, and migrants are paying and will continue to pay the highest price.

The conclusion we draw from this is that, with the help of the state and using the excuse of the pandemic, the crisis – a crisis of capital which dates back to long before the pandemic – has been entirely offloaded onto the shoulders of the most vulnerable classes, and to a lesser extent onto a part of the capitalist class that was less protected. Yet again, a crisis of capital has been transformed into a crisis of labour through the mobilisation of all means available to the state, including that of intervention in the real economy through fiscal measures (beloved of the Keynesians), thus increasing the public debt and making it necessary to cut back on the public services that make up the indirect wage of the working class. When we look at which social classes are paying the most (in terms of job losses, deteriorating working and living conditions for themselves and their families), it becomes reasonable to imagine that the post-Covid world will be more unequal than ever, the numbers of the poor and marginalised greater than at any time before. The existence of the public debt as leverage, which for many years has meant that private capital is the biggest shareholder in the bourgeois state, and which is already being used to finance a (much needed, from the ruling class's perspective) restructuring of capital, can nevertheless only be of use in the short-term. As we have seen, many of the measures adopted to mitigate the crisis have had a weighty impact on the public debt. Without going into detail concerning individual countries (the figures are constantly being updated and always getting worse), it is clear that in Europe, without a profound change of direction (which for now seems impossible), these accumulating amounts of public debt will need to be paid off if the parameters laid down by the treaties are to be reinstated. Those parameters are currently (in 2021) suspended, but at some point, they will have to be revived. In other words, the EU's founding values and norms notwithstanding, once the health emergency has abated, it will be the costliest public services to come under the attack, as contradictory as that may seem. Though the pandemic laid bare the extent to which privatisations and under-funding had eaten away at our health services, meaning it hit all the harder, we can be sure that further cuts and sell offs will become a requirement if the EU rules on sovereign debt are to be upheld.

If the fate of our public services, the indirect wage of the working class, seems sadly set in stone, what is less certain is what the consequences will be of the restructuring taking place within international capital. In a context of deep and pervasive crisis, inter-capitalist conflict intensifies in all its forms – regional, sectoral, or between capitals of differing scales. While the attacks on China and the WHO by the two most recent US administrations for their handling of the pandemic is a clear sign that US capital is set on proceeding with the currency conflict, perhaps less evident is the sharpening of tensions between Europe's North and its Mediterranean South. The clash between the Italy/Spain/France axis on the one hand, and Germany and Holland on the other, which emerged during the negotiations over the EU's financial response to the pandemic, were viewed by many as a mere conflict between national identities. In fact, nothing could be further from the truth. Such confrontations purely concern factions internal to the capitalist class; the working classes of those countries gain, if any, only indirect and unsystematic benefit, and through no will of their own. They are disputes that concern different groupings operat-ing at different stages of the international production chain according to geo-graphical location, with different interests and desires to profit from money made available through tax revenues and public debt. Put simply, therefore, the conflict that has emerged among member states of the European Union was not a conflict between German and Italian workers, but rather between national bourgeoisies, such as northern Italian producers of white goods and their competitors headquartered in Germany or Holland.

Within this mass of figures and observations, put together in an attempt to explain phenomenon that would otherwise seem highly contradictory, the only indicators that would seem to run counter to the trends, aside from pub-lic and private debt, are the US market indexes (followed by market indexes globally) which already in May 2020, only three months from the outbreak of the pandemic, had returned to their (excessively high) pre-Covid levels. Once again, we see sound confirmation of an expanding gulf between fictitious cap-ital and the production of value (what is also referred to as the *real economy*), and of the fact that the liquidity injected into the economy through the new pandemic-busting QE programmes has mostly gravitated towards, as is its habit, the stock markets, i.e. towards speculative activity. And these new sums dwarf the programmes of the post-Lehman response. Fitch Ratings (2020) has estimated that it amounts to around $6,000 billion in the US just up to the first half of April 2020, a sum that was already being added to in the weeks immediately following. On a slightly more modest scale, the ECB, in line with the pattern set by post-2008, injected €120 billion into the European economy, provoking the ire of the German authorities among others, who wanted strict adherence to the rules of the treaties that would in theory exclude such action.[4] And the aim is to reach €6,000 billion before the end of the year (compared with the Fed's target of $10 trillion). The UK and Japan of course had to follow suit, though with lower figures (£200 billion and the equivalent of $118 billion respectively).

As more evidence becomes available, it is becoming increasingly clear that the negative effects of COVID-19 are disproportionately borne by those who were already disadvantaged and vulnerable before the pandemic hit (Hill and Narayan, 2020; Berkhout et al., 2021). In the United States, for example, average life expectancy has declined as a result of COVID-19, but the decline disproportionately affects minorities who were already disadvantaged – Black Americans and Hispanics lost two to three years, while the White population lost 0.7 years on average (Andrasfay and Goldman, 2021). These differential reductions in life expectancy are attributed to both higher COVID-19 mortality rates and greater susceptibility to COVID-19 on the part of minorities.

There are several reasons why existing inequalities could be exacerbated by the pandemic.

Firstly, in terms of the direct effect of the virus on people's health, poor and vulnerable citizens have a greater risk of contracting the virus as they tend to be more exposed. Poor people are more likely to live in cramped conditions, without the means to maintain safe levels of hygiene, e.g., regular handwashing, and have less money to spend on things like masks or gloves. Poorer people are also more likely to live in multi-generational households, increasing the transmission risks to vulnerable older people who cannot be isolated from interactions with others at home. The working poor are more likely to be engaged in client facing activities, and are less likely to receive adequate protective equipment, thereby increasing their risk of exposure. Furthermore, poor populations are more susceptible to becoming severely ill with COVID-19 as they are more likely to have underlying health conditions – in the United

---

4 The recent decision of the court of Karlshrue (*Bundesverfassungsgericht*) is illuminating in this respect and likely foreshadows the future direction of the EU (see De Sena and D'Acunto, 2020).

States for instance, the richest American men live 12 years longer than the poorest men, while the richest American women live 10 years longer than the poorest women (Isaacs et al., 2021). Finally, poorer sections of societies may have limited access to medical treatment, not least because the cost of consultations with doctors and expenses for treatment are beyond their financial means. And even in countries where medical care is freely provided, COVID-19 has become a disease of the poor. In the United Kingdom, for instance, the Office for National Statistics has shown that those living in the most deprived neighbourhoods have been more than twice as likely to die from COVID-19 as those in the least deprived.[5]

Similarly, the economic impact of COVID-19 has also seen the poor and vulnerable disproportionately affected by income losses due to lockdowns, unexpected health expenses, or because these sections of society have reduced access to social safety nets. Poorer populations are more likely to be employed in jobs that cannot be done from home (Garrote Sanchez et al., 2020). Indeed, the ability to work from home correlates with income, as white-collar jobs are more suited to home-working and wealthier households are more likely to have access to a good internet connection. Poor and less-educated workers, by contrast, tend to be employed in sectors where it is difficult to observe social distancing and thus carry a higher risk of contracting the virus and consequently losing their job. As a result, younger or poorly educated workers and those on temporary contracts are least likely to be able to work from home and as such are more vulnerable to the labour market shocks caused by COVID-19. Joyce and Xu (2020), for example, have found that low-income earners in the UK are seven times as likely as high-income earners to have been working in a sector shut down entirely by the lockdown (see also Bradley et al., 2020).[6]

---

5   See   https://www.ons.gov.uk/peoplepopulationandcommunity/birthsdeathsandmarriages/
    deaths/bulletins/deathsinvolvingcovid19bylocalareasanddeprivation/deathsoccurringbetw
    eenimarchand17april (accessed on 5 November 2021). Amongst the poor, women are especially vulnerable, and COVID-19 is affecting women more than men mainly because women are disproportionately represented in sectors negatively affected by the crisis (Azcona et al., 2020; Madgavkar et al., 2020). Whilst indications suggest that more men than women are dying of COVID-19, women have a higher risk of infection because they are more likely to be work in health professions (Boniol et al., 2019).

6   For the European Union, early findings suggest that the risk of job loss is highest in southern Europe and France (Doerr and Gambacorta, 2020; Pouliakas and Branka, 2020). At the country level, young, low-educated, low-income workers appear to face the highest income and employment risk (see Galasso, 2020, for Italy; Adams-Prassl et al., 2020, for Germany; Beland et al., 2020, Cajner et al., 2020, Cho and Winters, 2020, Mongey et al., 2020, and Shibata, 2021, for the United States; and Aum et al., 2020, for South Korea).

Finally, poor individuals are also more likely to have jobs that come with fewer social protections, tending more frequently to be employed in the informal sector, and much less frequently in the public sector which, unlike the private sector, has largely been able to resist lay-offs while managing to continue to pay salaries.

The consequences of the COVID-19 crisis on income distribution raise serious concerns. The increases in poverty and inequality caused by the pandemic have narrowed the scope for a rapid recovery, as they are detrimental to economic growth (Madsen et al., 2018). Moreover, a perception that the better off have been able to navigate the pandemic relatively unscathed while the most vulnerable are left coping with the brunt of the impact, has exacerbated tensions in society. Economic projections confirm that the number of people living in extreme poverty globally will increase by between 119 and 124 million as a result of the pandemic, representing an unprecedented setback on the global effort to end extreme poverty (Mahler et al., 2021). Furthermore, the existing evidence suggests that the COVID-19 crisis will lead to a generalized increase in income inequality in a number of countries, both developed and developing. Palomino et al. (2020) estimate that the Gini coefficient will grow by 2.2% in Europe. And income inequality is expected to rise in low-income and emerging economies as well (Cugat and Narita, 2020; International Monetary Fund, 2020; Malpass, 2020). Moreover, historical data suggests that past events of this kind, even though much smaller in scale, have led to significant, persistent increases in the Gini coefficient (by 1.25% five years after a pandemic) and have raised the income shares of higher income deciles (Barro et al., 2020; Furceri et al., 2020; Ma et al., 2020). There will also be intergenerational consequences, that will play out mostly in terms of loss of schooling. Children of poor and vulnerable households will pay the highest price in terms of loss of schooling, and the disruption to learning associated with school closures will lead to a loss of human capital and to stronger educational and income inequality in the future (see, e.g., Lustig and Tommasi, 2020).

The unequal impact of the pandemic and its exacerbation of existing inequalities will have consequences for planning in the post-COVID period. Sustainable recoveries will require growth that benefits all people, and not just those in positions of power. In an interconnected world, where people are more informed than ever before, this pandemic of inequality – with rising poverty and declining incomes – will increasingly be a threat to the maintenance of social order and political stability, and even to the functioning of democracy.

Therefore, the post-Covid world will likely be very different to what we have known before, if there will even be a clear end to the pandemic phase. Not only in terms of the ways of living and freedoms that billions of people across the globe had for many years been accustomed to, which have already changed and will continue to transform further over time, but because a process of restructuring has begun that is potentially the most extensive reorganisation of the capitalist mode of production as a whole ever seen in history, guided by the ruling class and the state. Capital, starved of its oxygen and in a much worse state than even 2008, will once again take aim at labour, the source of social wealth. So-called labour market reforms will aim at lowering wages where possible, at intensifying work, prolonging the working day, and generating a relative surplus population. In other words, the last card capital still has left to play in its attempt to kick start a new cycle of accumulation before the next crisis comes along is a profound precaritisation of working conditions at the global level, particularly for less skilled workers who are already at breaking point. Sadly, the first bits of data to emerge since the easing of pandemic restrictions would seem to confirm this.

Nevertheless, due to the contradictions inherent to the process, existing conflicts will inevitably be exacerbated. The ongoing fragmentation of the middle class in all parts of the globe (see also Clementi and Schettino, 2015; Clementi et al., 2017, 2018, 2020a; Schettino and Khan, 2020) will likely be accelerated with a push towards the mass proletarianization of significant sections of society even in the advanced capitalist countries. Those who up to some decades ago were able to make a decent living from the crumbs of imperialism will find themselves a dying breed. At the same time, the vast swathes of people living in poverty or situations of vulnerability will become less visible while also increasing in number. They will be progressively more alienated from the opportunities available not only to the possessors of capital but also to specialised salaried workers, creating a gulf that will become difficult to bridge. And the ruling class's remaining weapon against the kind of structural change that is becoming increasingly necessary, will be the despotic management of the impoverished masses and of the growing levels of inequality.

However, history has taught us that it is precisely in those places where social conflict seems to have been repressed once and for all that the contradictions of the capitalist system continue to multiply, sparking the regeneration of mass movements aspiring to real systemic change. This aspiration can be made real, but only if these movements evolve to assume progressive and class-specific forms, expanding worldwide and prefiguring objectives far more ambitious than the demands that initially gave rise to them. Only in so doing will these movements acquire the strength necessary to close the final doors on human prehistory and set us on a new historical trajectory free of the exploitation of man by man, free of classes, of crises, and of inequalities and poverty.

CHAPTER 7

Afterword

Socialism or Barbarism: Where Do We Go from Crisis, Inequalities and Poverty?

Haider A. Khan

1 Introduction

It is now mid-August 2021. We are in the midst of a new variant of COVID 19 virus. This so-called delta variant is so far proving to be the most dangerous one. Given the analysis of the deep underlying dynamics of global capitalism that this book has laid bare, what can we expect? To answer this question, we can take – like the authors of this book – uneven and combined development (UCD) and stress points of the contradictory global capitalist system (GCS) as a point of departure. The move towards authoritarianism by some fractions of the capitalist class in many advanced capitalist countries should be viewed in light of this dialectical and historical materialist approach. But politics and economics both – most importantly, politics – requires concrete analysis of concrete conditions. The authors of CRISIS, INEQUALITIES AND POVERTY have done this admirably; I will clarify some aspects of the connections among WCS (World Capitalist System), UCD, inequality and poverty, and draw some tentative conclusions about the possible future trajectories of GCS. More importantly, I will try to assess the prospects for moving away from the class divided racialized and patriarchal capitalist class societies towards a higher form of socio-economic system after the current crisis.

Many of us, including the authors of the present book, have explored how the crisis-ridden dynamics of uneven development, particularly for developing economies, emerges as part of the normal GCS dynamics. This can be done within a conceptual context of complex systems dynamics in the GCS that includes a metropolitan centre and its opposite, the periphery. In between the two there can be a small group of emerging economies–exemplified earlier by the East Asian tigers and now by the special case of the PRC which is discussed later in contrast with COVID-crisis affected capitalist countries.

1.1   *On Crisis, Inequalities and Poverty within a Global Ecological*
        Imperialist Political Economy with Real Competition

In my other works in the reference section, I have covered systematically and
sequentially the following areas that are dialectically interrelated:

– Uneven Development in the semi-periphery and periphery
– Real Competition and Uneven development in the semi-periphery and
  periphery
– The East Asian Strategy of Capitalist Development in the periphery and
  semi-periphery
– Limits of the East Asian Strategy of Capitalist Development in the periphery
  and semi-periphery. What could at least a partial democratic socialist development be?
– The ambiguous case of industrialization and innovation in PRC

Much of this work has clear points of contact with the arguments developed
so admirably by the authors of CRISIS, INEQUALITIES AND POVERTY. Why the
PRC case is ambiguous in systemic terms even when it has succeeded on so any
fronts including recovering from COVID crisis will be explained after I cover
China's success in contrast with the capitalist countries' failures in some detail
necessary for looking at possible futures.

In GCS, there can be much disorder at the micro level and yet there can
also be the emergence of order at the macro level out of this disorder. This
pattern of the capitalist order/disorder dynamics in the developmental economies can be explored theoretically by a series of real abstractions from the
experience of developing economies within the uneven GCS development
itself. This theoretical approach can explain some of the key stylized features
of the components of the system. Some limits of policies and of the so-called
developmental state capacities can also be identified through this analysis.
The transnational dimension which was always important from the beginning
of WCS has assumed an increased cross-border trade and finance in the age of
monopoly finance capitalism.

As the book points out:

> The transnational concatenation that changed the configuration of inter-
> imperialist struggle so that it was no longer cleanly divided along nation-
> state lines, has resulted in capital seeking greater penetration into the
> global market. As such, the predetermination of an investment's asso-
> ciation with a currency area has come to override its mere geography,
> something that would also explain why some financial centres develop
> at the expense of others. [...] On the one hand are grouped the charac-
> teristics of a desperate pursuit of the 'real economy' within the current

international division of labour: production chains; dislocations; out-sourcing, subcontracting on a global scale; Euro-Asian corridors and other transport infrastructure; talk of 'competitive advantage'; central-isation and transformation in international ownership structures; the upending of the relationship between supra-state organisms and nation states; privatisations (where they are seen to be more efficient); the list could go on. On the other are the features of a 'monetary economy' where the struggle is for a hegemonic redefinition of the currency areas towards a 'unified' global market.

As Arrighi (1994) among others has pointed out in his superb history of global capitalism in his 1994 book, *The Long Twentieth Century*, the financialization of capitalism in ever increasing scale has been a constant element in the evolu-tion and expansion of global capital.[1] It is important to understand the trans-national nature and specificities of the current crisis, however. The authors are right when they write:

> The media depiction of currency conflict as a simple question of the prices of different currencies – resulting from mere exploitation of the exchange rate – is useful for the ruling classes because it obscures the fierce conflict between 'hostile brothers' (factions of capital), which in the current phase has developed into a struggle to subsume the largest number of dominated countries within a currency area, in the hope of countering the natural compression of the rate of profit. This is done by working to lower the cost structures of financial holding companies in the dominant countries in relation to the final sales prices. However, as this can only incidentally alter the mass of new value produced, espe-cially in a phase of acute crisis such as that which we are currently liv-ing through, its effect is to damage in inverse proportion other capitals' capacity to accumulate in an already sluggish environment.

The book, CRISIS, INEQUALITIES AND POVERTY has presented a lucid case of failures of the GCS in handling the COVID crisis and the implications of this colossal failure. The book has also explored by using modern concepts and

---

1   For further analysis and as background for the discussion of the Chinese case, see also Arrighi (2007); Arrighi, Giovanni, Po-keung Hui, Ho-Fung Hung and Mark Selden (2003); Arrighi, Giovanni and Beverly J. Silver. (1999); Braudel F., (1958); Gunder, Frank A., (1998); De Vries, Jan (2008). Hayami, Akira (2015). Sugihara Kaoru. (1996). Sugihara, Kaoru. (2003). Smith, Adam. (1776).

measurement techniques for inequality and poverty, the dire impact of COVID crisis which stemmed from a mixture of both exogenous and endogenous factors and, other, endogenous crises of the GCS, particularly in its neoliberal ideological form. In this afterword, it may be helpful to look at the performance of a complex political economy which is at least quasi-socialist but also has developed some capitalist features. This is China and a concrete theory-based multisectoral empirical examination of the Chinese case can contrast meaningfully with the analysis of current capitalist order offered in CRISIS, INEQUALITIES AND POVERTY. In this analytical and factually-grounded analysis – and counterfactual analysis via an appropriate model – we can pose the question of alternative futures scientifically. Some may be surprised to see that such contrastive analysis, consistent with the dialectical dissection of the WCS in CRISIS, INEQUALITIES AND POVERTY, analytically supports the prescient prediction of Rosa Luxemburg on the eve of the first world war. The choice in the 21st century just like it was in the 20th century is between the WCS and breaking away from the WCS towards a saner society and mode of production. Only, given the ongoing ecological crisis, the crises are more multidimensional and the choices are even more stark in our century.

It is interesting to note that approaches like the above are actually rooted in classical analysis of Marx and Lenin. I have tried to trace the lineage of this line of work including my own work on ecological imperialism in this manner. Let me give the reader a summary picture of this lineage including Anwar Shaikh's work (2016) on real competition and crisis which I have developed elsewhere. This will make the nuances of the case study of China that follows clearer.

Marx never made a systematic theoretical and empirical analysis of the development of capitalism in the non-capitalist parts of the world in his time. One widely quoted remark found in the preface to the first edition of *Capital* has been seized on by many scholars as Marx's definitive position:

> ... the country that is more developed industrially only shows, to the less developed, the image of its own future.

Yet Marx was aware of the complexities of the actual development of capitalism in specific countries, for he avers in the same preface that the backward country "suffers not only from the development of capitalist production but also from the incompleteness of that development." A uniform law of the development of capitalism in each country would be particularly attractive to a positivistic social science. But was Marx a positivist? On the basis of a particularly clear statement by Marx (reproduced below) and other internal theoretical evidence in Marx's writing, Miller (1984) pronounces Marx to be a non-positivist. According to Miller, in the following passage Marx "emphasizes two features of his theory of history that would rule it out as unscientific if the positivist account is right."

In several parts of Capital, I allude to the fate which overtook the plebians of ancient Rome. They were originally free peasants, each cultivating his own piece of land on his own account. In the course of Roman history, they were expropriated. The same movement which divorced them from their means of production and subsistence involved the formation not only of big, landed property but also a big money capital. And so one fine morning there were to be found on the one hand free men, stripped of everything except their labour power, and on the other, in order to exploit this labour, those who held all the acquired wealth in their possession. What happened? The Roman proletarians became not wage labourers but a mob of do-nothings; more abject than the former "poor whites" in the South of the United States, and alongside of them there developed a mode of production which was not capitalist but based on slavery. Thus, events strikingly analogous but taking place in different histori- cal surroundings led to totally different results. By studying each of these forms of evolution separately and then comparing them can easily find the clue to this phenomenon, but one will never there by using as one's master key a gen- eral historical-philosophical theory, the supreme virtue of which consists in being super-historical.[2]

Furthermore, in *Capital* Marx also argues that the development of capital- ism or any economic structure for that matter may show "infinite variations and gradations in appearance which can be ascertained only by an analysis of empirically given circumstances."

If Miller's interpretation of Marx's historical method and Marx's own state- ments are taken *prima facie*, then Marx's view of the development of capital- ism in previously non-capitalist parts of the world after the first flowering of industrial capital as a social relation in England, must be seen as fairly com- plex, in principle. What Marx discovered were some crucial (and approxi- mately true) general tendencies of the development of capitalism. However, he had no explicit theory of development in the periphery and semi-periphery in the GCO. However, elsewhere I have tried to articulate this with the help of Marx's concept of the circuits of capital and their uneven development. Without rehearsing these again here we can move to what is perhaps the first

2   (Letter from Marx to the editor of the *Otecestvenniye Zapisky*, Nov. 1877, *Marx and Engels Correspondence*; International Publishers (1968)).

significant Marxist analysis of capitalist development and underdevelopment in, what we will call today, the semi-periphery of GCO in the late 19th century.

In Lenin's *Development of Capitalism in Russia* (1899) one already finds a superb analysis of capitalism in a backward country. Some dependency theorists have actually sought the authority of this book to give a 'Leninist' flavour to their views.

In arguing against the Nardoniks' position of instant socialism in Russia, Lenin presented a two-sided argument in 'the Development.' On the one hand, contrary to the Nardoniks' claim he argued that capitalism was developing in Russia. At the same time and because of this (uneven) development, the possibilities for development of proletarian politics and a complex transition path to socialism under concrete conditions were also there. This view, quite plausible within the then existent Marxist tradition, is not without a certain internal tension, however. For the moment, let us note the special features of capitalism in late 19th century Russia which Lenin discovered. The data showed the capitalist development of Russia to be real. Nevertheless, the rate of this development was extremely slow and the extent was quite uneven.

The latter feature was not surprising in itself, since the development of capitalism in Western Europe was also marked by unevenness. But the tardiness of the development and the persistence of traditional, seemingly pre-capitalist forms (another discovery of Lenin), needed explanation. Here Lenin relied on both an analysis of the internal development of class structure in Russia and the external factor of competition from Western European capitalism and at the same time a capital inflow from the centre. The striking feature of this early analysis is the way Lenin combines the external with the internal. The capital from Western Europe accelerated the industrialization and helped the emergence of a bourgeoisie in Russia. At the same time, the weak and dependent nature of the Russian bourgeoisie, partly a result of its domination by foreign capitalists, prevented the development from being rapid and widespread. As Palma correctly points out, Lenin actually gave a great deal of weight to the survival of traditional structures in Russia in his explanatory scheme. Quoting Marx's earlier remark regarding the incompleteness of capitalist development in a backward country, Lenin refers to the "abundant survival of ancient institutions that are incompatible with capitalism". At the same time, Lenin notes the linkages, at least in production, between the factory and the handicraft industry or more generally the traditional, pre-capitalist and the modern, capitalist organizations of production. Thus, we can detect an uneven and turbulent dynamics of the circuits of capital in Russia.

In summary, Lenin in 1899 saw the development of capitalism in Russia as a slow-motion replay of the development of capitalism in Western Europe. At the same time there is recognition of a complex interaction between the external and internal factors. The political conclusions drawn by Lenin from *The Development of Capitalism in Russia*, as well as his subsequent studies including *Imperialism: The Highest Stage of Capitalism* form the subject of a separate paper and will not be pursued here. What is important to emphasize is that capitalism from its very inception has been a system with expansionary drive rooted in real competition. Therefore, the global scope of capitalism is a logical development of inherent tendencies of capital. However, it takes place within a historically and politically determined spatial configuration. In modern capitalism, this has been the system of nation states. Furthermore, capitalism both in this global system and within nation states develops unevenly over time through a turbulent process. A crucial aspect of this uneven development is the increase in inequalities *ceteris paribus*.[3]

1.2   Real Competition, Uneven Development, Crisis and North-South Divide in the Age of Pandemics

However, there is one lacuna in Lenin's classical work that is relevant to mention here. Like most Marxists of his time, he did not see the role of what Shaikh calls real competition in the classical political economy tradition, as crucial albeit in a highly uneven context in the development of capitalism in Russia and other underdeveloped parts of the world. Here indeed, the idea of GCO comes into its own. In many ways, as Marx's chapters on primitive accumulation in *Capital Vol. 1* discuss, capitalism has been tendentially a global order right from its beginning. Yet, the historic development of a GCO did not reach its maturity till the end of the 19th century. More than any other historic event, the conference in Belgium for the partition and plunder of Africa can be seen as the crucial historical marker for the maturity of GCO. Given the views of the 2nd international and Lenin's mentors such as Plekhanov, it is not surprizing that Lenin did not see the real competition as the dynamic factor in mature capitalism and its earlier evolutionary stages as well. Perhaps what should come as a pleasant surprize is that even without a sufficient theoretical anchor – or to put it more strongly, with a partially wrong and largely economic determinist anchor – Lenin empirically identified both external competition and complex internal factors working dialectically to produce a puzzling array of development and underdevelopment in Russia. Later, Gerschenkron would develop some of these ideas – without analysing the implications for revolution – in his famous works on "the advantages of backwardness".

---

3   This was observed in classical Marxian literature.

In chapter 6 of his *magnum opus, Capitalism: Competition, Conflict, Crisis* (2016), Shaikh takes up the idea of profitability and its relations to capitalism before moving to the second part of his book on "real competition" in classical political economy. Chapter 6 delivers an analytical definition of capital, discusses the determination of aggregate profit, and the details of their measurement. With this analytical apparatus at hand, in chapter 7 Shaikh points out correctly:

> Capital is a particular social form of wealth driven by the profit motive. With this incentive comes a corresponding drive for expansion, for the conversion of capital into more capital, of profit into more profit. Each individual capital operates under this imperative, colliding with others trying to do the same, sometimes succeeding, sometimes just surviving, and sometimes failing altogether. This is *real competition*, antagonistic by nature and turbulent in operation. It is as different from so-called perfect competition as war is from ballet.
>
> The mobility of capital is inherent in its existence. Capital tied up in labor, plant, equipment, and inventories is fixated and must be used up or sold off before it can adopt a new incarnation. But fresh money capital, borrowed or garnered as profit, always looks over the available list of avatars before making its choice. The profit motive rules in all cases.
>
> Real competition is the central regulating mechanism of capitalism. Competition within an industry forces individual producer to set prices with an eye on the market, just as it forces them continually try to cut costs so that they can cut prices and expand market share. Cost-cutting can take place through wage reduction, increases in the length or intensity of the working day, and through technical change. The latter becomes the central means over the long run.
>
> SHAIKH, 2016: 260

More than any modern Marxist theory of imperialism – Leninist or otherwise – the theoretical concept of real competition explains why under some conditions which are quite plausibly present particularly during the expansionary phases of capitalism in advanced centres, there is a tendency to expand abroad. But strikingly, the tendency is present – indeed it might be a compulsion – for capitalists of the centre to invest abroad even during downturns as profitability sinks lower and lower in former centres of accumulation. But there is also a tendency to hoard capital, or with state fiscal-monetary intervention without tightened financial regulations, pursue speculative financial activities.

Shaikh further draws out the implications of real competition that will have important roles to play in the interpretation of our formal models in the appendix – the most important of these formally being the idea of turbulent equilibration:

> Real competition generates its own characteristic patterns. Prices set by different sellers are roughly equalized as each tries to gain an advantage over the other. Profit rates on new investments are also roughly equalized over somewhat longer periods. Both of these processes result in perpetual fluctuations around various moving centers of gravity. This is the classical notion of *turbulent equilibration*, very different from the conventional notion of equilibrium as a state-of- rest ... Supply and demand are part of the story, but their roles are not decisive since both can change in response to profit opportunities (Sraffa, 1926: 538–539).
>
> The notion of competition as a form of warfare has important implications. Tactics, strategy, and resulting prospects for growth are central concerns of the competitive firm. In turn, the relevant profit must be that which is defensible in the medium term, which is quite different from the notion of short-term maximum profit emphasized in neoclassical theory. *In the battle of real competition, the mobility of capital is the movement from one terrain to another, the development and adoption of technology is the arms race, and the struggle for profit growth and market share is the battle itself ...*
>
> It is important to understand that price equalization due to competition between sellers, as well as profit rate equalization due to competition between investors, always give rise to unintended outcomes. Prices tend to equalize because buyers gravitate toward the lowest price, which forces other sellers to adjust their own prices. Similarly, profit rates tend to equalize because investors flock to higher rates of return. This accelerates supply relative to demand in the favored industries and drives down their prices and profits. The rush toward riches closes the gaps that initially motivated the agents while opening up new gaps which feed new arbitrage movements. The turbulent equalizations of prices and profit rates are quintessential emergent properties.
>
> SHAIKH, 2016: 260; emphasis added

This mobility of capital globally with turbulent equilibration tendencies and emergent properties is the disordered 'order' of capitalism globally. What mainstream economists after WWII chose to call the then new field of development economics can be more realistically and scientifically viewed as one part of the turbulent evolution of GCO. Let me elaborate by looking critically at the most important early 'classical' model of dualism by W. A. Lewis and refer to a new formal version of a 'dual-dual' model that pushes it more in the direction of the real external and internal competition approach discussed above.

Lewis himself was aware of the quasi-Ricardian roots of his model. Without rehearsing the details, we can recall that the modern sector is the capitalist sector and generates growth. In this process of 'development' surplus labour is released by the traditional agricultural sector. One can add a Harris-Todaro type migration model and arrive at a fully specified general equilibrium with straightforward linearized dynamics.

There are several problems with Lewis's and all subsequent formulations of dualism, however. Just to mention two that I think are most critical, the absence of capitalist development in agriculture is analytically misleading and historically inaccurate. Without such a dynamic capitalist – at least tenden-tially – agriculture, the source of surplus labour seems to be overpopulation. This is unhelpful analytically. With dynamic capitalist agriculture, reverse migration from urban to rural areas particularly during downturns may be quite significant. At any rate, this lack of dynamic thinking about an explicitly dynamic problem points to a second, even deeper theoretical problem. This has to do with equilibration. Although Lewis starts out by invoking classical ideas, his equilibria are entirely neoclassical. This is made clear in the subse-quent versions of Ranis, Ranis and Fei and Fields models. In Svejnar-Thorbecke (1986), there is an ambiguous formulation that could be interpreted as a devi-ation from the neoclassical formulation, but no explicit analytical statement is made by these authors. Khan (1983) was the first theoretical generalization of dualism multisectorally. More importantly, chapter 2 of this work drew out his-torically the roots of dualism and formulated an early turbulent equilibrium-seeking version, later refined in Khan and Thorbecke (1989) and Khan (1997a, 1997b). Jung and Thorbecke's empirically implementable dual-dual structural CGE model (2001) is refined and extended further technically and conceptu-ally by Khan (2004, 2006, 2007) in the direction of turbulent equilibria in a dual-dual model.[4] What is important in this debate is to realize that a classi-cal model of capitalist development in the formerly non-capitalist parts of the world can be formulated within the GCO via the concepts of real competition and turbulent equilibria. Judzik, Khan and Spagnolo (2016) extended this anal-ysis to capabilities transformation in a learning economy. Keeping this overall

---

4 The formalizations of all these models can be found in the references listed in the bibliography.

dynamic framework in mind, let us now turn to the interesting case of PRC since the COVID crisis began.

1.3   *From Crisis, Inequalities and Poverty within a Global Ecological Imperialist Political Economy with Real Competition to the Contrastive Case of China and Global Futures: Socialism or Barbarism*

The case of China in responding to the economic and public health crisis of COVID-19 stands out for a number of reasons. While the initial outbreak of COVID-19 was first identified in December 2019, the national health crisis had peaked and gradually stabilized after about mid-March of 2020. From January to February of 2020, the Chinese government imposed a series of strict containment measures including large-scale lockdowns and social distancing protocols across China. The timeliness and uniformity of these containment measures are identified to have successfully 'flattened the curve' of infections across China's mainland (Peirlinck et al. 2020). However, acute economic shocks resulted from these containment measures.

Although the impacts of COVID-19 have weakened their economy, China had emerged in a stronger economic position relative to the rest of the world. The effectiveness of the government in containing the pandemic enabled the relatively quick recovery of the economy at a time when other major economies in Europe, and the Americas, and even Japan lagged far behind China in terms of pandemic containment and re-opening. A partial reopening of the economy coupled with the provision of industrial subsidies enabled the rapid recovery of fixed-asset investments, leading to a V-shaped recovery in economic activity. In a global sense, the restoration of industrial production in China connects their own economic recovery with that of the Asian region as a whole and many foreign countries in Latin American and Africa with which trade links are strong.

In contrast to investment spending, domestic retail sales had recovered at a more stagnant pace throughout 2020, reflecting the weakened state of domestic and foreign demand (Sutter and Sutherland 2021). Retail expenditures have seen a substantial jump in early 2021 thanks to seasonable consumption patterns though this rebound has not been sustained through the year as growth rates for both retail sales and investment spending peaked in January and declined steadily after. These trends may point to a corrective process as China's speed of recovery stabilizes at a slower pace. However, the growth of retail sales expenditures by April 2021 have failed to meet expectations, leading to growing concerns among experts of the unbalanced nature of the present recovery and doubts as to its stability over the medium-run (Cheng, 2021).

Although investments remain the most important component of aggregate demand in China, the domestic market has increased in importance in recent decades. This is particularly true after 2010 with the appreciation of the Renminbi, rising wage rates, and the saturation of export markets with Chinese goods (Lau, 2020). Accordingly, policy measures aimed at stimulating recovery from the impacts of COVID-19 have shifted attention from employment stabilization toward demand-side management. This shift in policy measures are core components of the newly-emphasized Dual Circulation policy, announced in the Central Committee's May 2020 Report on the Work of the Government (Keqiang, 2020).

The term 'Dual Circulation' traces back to fundamental reforms in the late 1970s and 1980s which led to the liberalization of the economy and China's turn toward export markets. In leveraging a relatively low-cost labour force to develop export-intensive industries, China's internal economic development ('domestic circulation') would be driven by export-led growth and the expansion of 'international circulation.' The original usage of the term stressed the relative importance of 'international circulation' in supporting the development of 'domestic circulation.' In practice, this involved large flows of foreign direct investment (FDI) in China, concentrated mainly along urban centres on the coast starting with the export-oriented special economic zones (SEZ). Comparatively, investment in Western interior provinces and rural areas had been geared for the development of primary industries to secure flows of raw materials for urbanization and the development of coastal industry (Fan, 1997).

At the same time that exports as a share of GDP have increased since the 1980s, China has seen some of the fastest recorded growth rates in recent history. This rapid growth of output is behind the secular increases in standards of living and substantial declines in the level of absolute poverty observed in the process of China's development. However, this period has also seen substantial increases in income and wealth inequality. Among the main identified drivers of inequality in China are the rural-urban income gap, which is based on differences in access to education and the growth of skill premia in urban agglomerations.

China's guiding export-led vision of development was challenged with the onset of the 2008 global financial crisis. Collapsed export markets and their weak recovery called into question the long-run sustainability of export-led growth. Turning inward, the government initiated a program of subsidizing the expansion of domestic markets and promoting the development of interconnections between domestic markets and industry. This was done using tax breaks for the production of manufactured goods for domestic consumption, as well as direct subsidies to rural households for the purchase of domestically-produced goods (Wilde, 2021). Thus, in a dialectical fashion the contemporary usage of 'Dual Circulation' came to refer to the state-subsidized growth of domestic markets as a buffer of support for export-led sectors in times of global crisis.

Since 2015, Dual Circulation has increasingly taken the form of supply side reforms including import-substitution-industrialization (ISI) in high-tech manufacturing. The overall goal of these reforms is to pursue independence from foreign markets in critical 'bottleneck' areas like energy, chemical products, and semi-conductors. The overall threat of supply chain shortages for import-intensive sectors has been realized with the onset of COVID-19 as a global pandemic. With a combination of demand and supply-side shocks the pandemic has interrupted global recovery and generated lasting economic impacts across global markets and key trading partners. Aside from the immediate concerns of hunger prevention and targeted poverty reduction, responding to the pandemic with a view toward sustainable recovery will necessitate the expansion of domestic markets and indigenous innovation in high-tech manufacturing, biopharmaceuticals, and energy. Of critical importance for the treatment and containment of disease in China is the role played by indigenous knowledge systems (IKS) in healthcare including the development of vaccines and innovation in the use of traditional Chinese medicine (TCM) for the treatment of COVID-19. As we demonstrate in a related paper (Khan and Szymanski-Burgos, forthcoming) further investment in IKS will be an important component for improving economic and social resilience to future pandemics.

Beyond the acute impacts of COVID-19, there are a number of additional factors behind the weakness in consumption expenditures such as uneven growth of output and employment across regions, an increase in household and corporate debt, and the onset of trade frictions that threaten to undermine China's export-led growth strategy. One persistent barrier to the recovery of consumption expenditures are structural inequalities between urban and rural populations and across regions. The impacts of the pandemic are known to make economic and social inequalities worse (Pires et al. 2020). On one hand, low-income communities find themselves more exposed to infection due to public-facing employment and housing circumstances that make social distancing prohibitively difficult. On the other hand, the loss of incomes during the pandemic-driven recession disproportionately affects workers in the informal sector, low-skilled workers, service-sector and construction workers, and the self-employed.

Although the spread of infection to rural communities in China was relatively minimal, these communities have experienced disproportionate economic

impacts including high unemployment, loss of household income, price inflation, and disrupted student learning (Wang et al. 2021). Unemployment in the
early months of the pandemic are estimated to have risen to virtually 100% for
many rural villages in Central China where residents were entirely dependent
on working in cities (Wang et al. 2020). Even after quarantine protocols were
lifted, rural unemployment remained very high (upwards of 60%) through
March and April, implying substantial and lasting effects on income loss for
rural households. China's large proportion of rural residents are an important
driver of economic activity and constitute an enormous source of drag under
extraneous conditions. These estimates suggest that economic recovery in
rural areas has been significantly slower than in urban areas in spite of the
stabilization of urban employment opportunities for migrants.

    The goal of this article is to provide a strategic framework for sustainable
demand-led recovery. Our framework is framed at the outset by a socially-
embedded intersectional capabilities approach (SEICA) (Khan 1998; Khan
2021). This approach views development as a democratic process where
important feedback loops link macro-level outcomes with the material well-
being of disadvantaged and minority groups. We aim to assess and help direct
the strategic allocation of resources for counter-COVID-19 fiscal expenditures
in light of China's Dual Circulation policy. This is done on the basis of socio-
economic modelling using input-output (IO) multipliers. As a complement to
Khan and Szymanski-Burgos (forthcoming), we focus on both immediate and
medium-run impacts of direct economic stimulus by exploring a range of economic multipliers and modelling the employment effects of direct fiscal injections as part counter-COVID-19 expenditures. The following section focuses
on a break-down of the Chinese response to the public health and economic
challenges of COVID-19. Next, we provide a detailed description of multiplier
analysis using a national 153x153 input-output (IO) table for 2018 and discuss
the possible integration of indigenous knowledge into our schema. Then, we
turn to an outline of findings regarding the structure of the Chinese economy
and on this basis, identify *counterfactually* key strategic areas where targeted
spending could generate the widest benefit, particularly for the disadvantaged
and vulnerable groups.

2   Time Horizon for Optimal Planning

To inform optimal decision-making we highlight three distinct time frames
specific to the case of China's exposure to the public health crisis and the economic impacts represented by the COVID-19 shock:

1. Addressing the immediate crisis from the initial outbreak through to the first quarter of 2020 (December 2019 – February 2020),
2. The restorative phase during the gradual reopening and restoration of economic activity throughout the year (March 2020 – March 2021),
3. Planning for going beyond 2021 consistent with China's long-run economic goals specified in the Chinese Communist Party's (CPC) 14th Five-Year Plan (2021–2025).

Of the three time periods, the first two were the most critical in terms of overcoming the challenges of containing the spread of infection, preventing shortages, and implementing incentives to ensure an optimal restorative path.

3   The Immediate Crisis: December 2019 to February 2020

On January 25th, 2020, the Central Committee issued a series of nationwide pandemic control protocols requiring all public spaces, businesses, and schools to close down and implementing strict stay-at-home orders and travel restrictions. These measures coincided with the ongoing Lunar New Year festivities, a time when millions of migrant workers had travelled home to rural areas or were caught in the process of returning when lockdowns were introduced. Travel restrictions and pandemic controls lasted through late February and early March, with regional quarantines easing at variable rates depending on local severity.

The strict January and February nation-wide lockdowns and containment measures were successful in preventing the spread of infection to critical levels in both urban and rural areas. The public health response in China is distinguished for its effectiveness in preventing the spread of infection and the Chinese case is increasingly used in the epidemiological literature as a benchmark for rapid containment.[5] Yang et al. (2020) highlight the critical importance of the timing and uniformity of lockdown implementation. They estimate a five-day delay in implementation would have tripled the number of infected, while lifting the province-wide Hubei quarantine prematurely would have resulted in a dramatic second peak and extended the pandemic into late April. Another point of distinction in the public health response relates to the fact that the Chinese government has traditionally not ignored the role of traditional knowledge systems in employing locally-viable solutions for indigenous communities. TCM is widely encouraged and sanctioned by the government

---

5   See Yang et al. (2020), Peirlinck et al. (2020), and Wangping et al. (2020).

for use in preventative healthcare and for use in public health crises as during the 2003 SARS epidemic and COVID-19.

3.1   *Economic Impacts and Countervailing Policies from March 2020 to March 2021*

By the end of March, the majority of Chinese provinces (with the exception of Hubei and Beijing) had significantly eased restrictions and begun the process of overall recovery. However, the COVID-19 shock led to acute economic impacts with the potential to present lasting effects on recovery. In total, national output declined by 6.8% on a year-to-year basis with disproportionate impacts across sectors in the first quarter of 2020 (Huang and Lardy, 2020). The most affected industries were in the accommodations sector, followed by the wholesale and retail, construction, and transportation sectors (Liu, 2021). National lockdowns and travel restrictions led to sharp drops in travel flows and national tourism revenues, which severely impacted the most affected industries. Because of the interdependence of various sectors through backward and forward linkages, most sectors in the economy experienced declines in economic activity to various degrees. In addition, the overall public health crisis significantly depressed consumption across much of China. Though many migrant workers were able to return to urban areas to find work, unemployment rates in rural areas are estimated to have remained quite high for several months even after travel restrictions were lifted on account of lingering fears of infection and decreased propensity to travel (Wang et al. 2020).

Thanks to early success in pandemic containment, China exhibited a remarkable turn in economic trends, reporting positive economic growth by the end of June 2020. Declines in fixed-asset investments hit their lowest point in February of 2020 before bouncing-back fairly rapidly by the end of the second quarter and into the rest of the year. This recovery was orchestrated in part by fiscal and monetary policy measures targeting the corporate sector much more so than households.

Measures including tax and interest rate cuts, state subsidies, and waived social security contributions were aimed at supporting production through medium, small, and micro enterprises (MSMES) and state-owned enterprises (SOEs), which altogether provide the majority of China's employment base (Zhang, 2019; Liu, 2019). The growth of fixed-asset investment experienced a further jump in early 2021 above pre-pandemic levels thanks to lagged positive effects from 2020 investments and the partial recovery of global markets. Retail expenditures have also seen a substantial jump in early 2021 during the shopping season. However, this rebound in both investment and retail sales has not been sustained in more recent months as growth rates for both indicators peaked in January and declined steadily after.

While proportionately small, expenditures targeted toward households include unemployment and emergency relief (including food and shelter aid) oriented toward the most vulnerable households. Largely at their own initiative, local governments in China engaged in modest efforts to support regional spending through the distribution of prepaid consumption vouchers; however, the magnitude of household transfers remained small and locally-specific. Notably absent from the present stimulus were direct unconditional federal transfers to households that we have seen in the stimulus programs of advanced economies around the world. For some observers of China, the lack of demand-side stimulus during 2020 is a key factor behind the unbalanced recovery (Tang, 2021).

We argue that a key component of any successful demand-led recovery requires addressing structural factors that constitute a source of drag in aggregate demand. One such structural source of drag is the large level of income and consumption inequality between rural and urban residents and within urban areas in China (Gradín and Wu, 2020). Recently, the Chinese government has made significant efforts to make labour market supports more inclusive for rural and migrant workers, in particular with the extension of emergency aid for rural residents and unemployment insurance for migrant workers. These efforts have been important for protecting incomes in particularly vulnerable communities. Additional priority is being given to the poorest workers to secure employment through state-provided "welfare jobs," presently responsible for employing a large percentage of impoverished rural and migrant workers.

There is still much work to be done on this front. Greater efforts are necessary to generate high-value development and income growth in rural and interior areas. Such an effort would best involve significant public investments in developing an economic base in the tertiary sectors in rural areas, including tourism and accommodation as well as upgrading in the primary sector to higher value-added products in the agricultural and food processing sectors. Notably, high-level development plans are being implemented which include a focus on developing the manufacturing base of key interior regions, like machinery manufacturing in Guangxi Zhuang Autonomous Region. As we will see, assuming necessary imports are drawn largely from within China, such a boost in rural manufacturing promises to generate growth in employment within rural provinces and across China.

3.2   *Going Beyond: The 14th Five-Year Plan*

The growing size of China's urban middle class is poised to provide a steady future consumption base (Barton et al., 2013), though the COVID-19 shock has imparted considerable drag on the consumption component of GDP. Despite the recent surge in urbanization and rising living standards, China's poorer rural households continue to make up a huge portion of China's population and are likely to require additional government support during the longer-run recovery phase to support the much slower recovery of rural households' consumption.

Rising labour costs in China are beginning to drive patterns of structural change observed in advanced economies. Although the share of service sector employment has not reached the level of Japan or the US, the manufacturing share of employment in China is estimated to have peaked in 2012 (Hou et al., 2017). As the service sector share of employment continues to grow in coming years, government economic policy must prioritize household consumption and industrial upgrading. In line with the longer-run goals of Dual Circulation, recovery policy over the end of the second period and into the third period appears to have shifted from employment stabilization toward demand-side management while simultaneously engaging in supply wide reforms through major public investment projects over the next five years. Key areas of focus for public investment are in technology-intensive infrastructure projects such as 5G telecommunications infrastructure, comprehensive national high-speed rail networks, electric car charging stations and other 'green energy' infrastructure (Liu, 2021).

3.3   *Methodology for Modelling and Counterfactual Experiments and Scenarios*

The data used for this analysis come from the 2018 national IO table for China, which offers a set of interindustry flows for 153 production activities. This level of disaggregation provides a unique level of details regarding the identification of important sectors and linkages in the economy. Final demand is divided into rural and urban household consumption, government consumption, gross fixed capital formation (investment in fixed assets), changes in inventory, and exports. Total value-added is then distributed among factors of production in the form of workers' compensation, gross operating surplus, production taxes, and capital depreciation.

Although the data does not presently allow, augmenting our IO for indigenous knowledge sectors would be useful for modelling indigenous innovation sectors and identifying the inflow and outflow of resources for this sector. We propose a method for integrating indigenous knowledge-based innovations

within a social accounting matrix (SAM) for South Africa. By delineating total
knowledge production into two sectors, non-indigenous (NIK) and indigenous
knowledge (IK), it would be possible to derive their respective production
functions and identify the consequences and complementarities between NIK
and IK production.

3.4   Matrix Algebra of Multiplier Analysis

The basis for input-output multiplier analysis is the matrix of interindustry
transactions. This matrix offers a model of interindustry flows of products
and resources within an economy as well as resources flows to institutional
accounts including households, taxes, capital incomes, and exports. The interindustry transactions matrix describes the total output of each production
sector in the economy as it is distributed among purchasing sectors as intermediate goods and among households and other agents as final goods. Data for
interindustry flows are necessary for multiplier analysis because it enables the
derivation of the matrix of direct requirements for the economy, describing
the direct sector requirements in terms of inputs of sector i for a unit of total
output in sector j. Algebraically, this produces a system of equations with the
general form (1) and matrix notation (2):

$$x_i = a_{ij}x_j + y_i \tag{1}$$

$$x = Ax + y \tag{2}$$

where a_{ij} is the technical coefficient representing the per-unit monetary value
of input from sector i required to produce a monetary unit value of output in
sector j. In the matrix notation, x is a column vector of total output produced
by each production sector, y is a column vector of output generated by final
demand, and A is a square matrix of technical coefficients a_{ij}. A fundamental
assumption with the use of input-output tables is that, for a definite length
of time, interindustry resource flows from sector i to sector j depend entirely
on the total output of sector j for the same period of time. Conventionally in
IO analysis, we assume this ratio is constant according to a fixed-proportions
production function with constant returns to scale.

If the vector of final demand y is known, the total output of each sector
needed to supply both intermediate and final demand requirements may be
found as the solution to the following equation:

$$x = (I - A)^{-1} y \tag{3}$$

where I denotes the identity matrix, and the inverse matrix $(I - A)^{-1}$ gives the matrix of total requirements coefficients. The product of the total requirements matrix and the vector of final demand y give the necessary output required from each of the sectors to satisfy total demand in the economy. The elements of the total requirements matrix describe the direct and indirect sector output effects for change in final demand. By specifying some change in the elements of the final demand vector for instance, along the lines of an increase in government consumption in a given sector, we can use the total requirements matrix to perform an impact analysis of the induced increases in output across sectors.

Summing the elements of the total requirements matrix in column j gives the output multiplier for sector j. Formally, the output multiplier is defined in the following equation where l are the elements of the total requirement matrix for a given column (Miller and Blair, 2009).

$$m(o)_j = \sum_{i=1}^{n} l_{ij} \qquad (4)$$

The output multiplier refers to the amplified effect of an economic stimulus considering all the indirect effects as money is spent and re-spent over several rounds. For a given sector, the output multiplier measures the combined effect of a unit change in sector output on the output of all industries in which that sector purchases inputs. To produce an additional $100 worth of machine parts requires the additional purchasing of local inputs (e.g., steel, electrical components, and transport services) as well as the purchasing of local labour services. These kinds of relationships are referred to as *backward linkages* (Hughes, 2018). Information regarding these backward linkages is captured in our model and used to derive Type 1 output multipliers which together describe the total effects of both direct and indirect increases in sectoral output. An output multiplier of 1.5 indicates that an additional $100 in demand for machine parts will generate $150 in total output spread throughout sector linkages.

An increase in the purchases of local labour inputs following an increase in demand leads to higher household incomes and additional consumption expenditures. Consumption linkages present an additional multiplier effect on the basis of induced increases in output from increased household expenditures. By 'closing' our model with respect to households we can derive Type 2 multipliers, which describe the total multiplier effect of direct, indirect, and induced increases in sector output. Closing our model with respect to households refers to the inclusion of consumption linkages as an endogenous sector by including an additional row for labour compensation and an additional column for household consumption in our intermediate matrix that we use to calculate our technical coefficients table.

In order to assess the Chinese government's counter-COVID-19 expenditures we focus also on identifying counterfactually the employment *and income* effects of the current stimulus. In addition to our output multipliers, we derive also employment and income multipliers for each sector. For a change in final demand $y' > y$, we can calculate the necessary increase in labor demand *and household incomes* across all sectors corresponding to these multipliers.

To derive our employment multipliers, we construct a vector of employment coefficients ε denoting the base-year value of employment in each sector divided by the level of sectoral gross output, shown here for a two-sector example where x_i^0 denotes

$$
\varepsilon = \begin{bmatrix} e_1 / x_1^0 & 0 \\ 0 & e_2 / x_2^0 \end{bmatrix} \tag{5}
$$

The employment multiplier describes the sector-to-household linkages through the labour market, where its value denotes the direct and indirect increases in the monetary value of labour inputs expenditures. In order to estimate domestic employment effects for an increase in government spending, we multiply our employment requirements matrix ε by y' and then integrate average wage data by sector to produce estimates of employment effects in terms of physical units of employment.

Income multipliers represent the economic impacts of a change in final demand on household earnings and describe how the benefits to growth are distributed to households. By considering household expenditures as endogenous, these multipliers capture information regarding the magnitude of induced output effects which appear in our Type 2 output multipliers. Income multipliers are derived using the technical coefficients for direct labour requirements when the IO model is closed with respect to households. The calculation involves weighting each element in the direct labour requirements (households) row by the output multipliers of the corresponding sector and taking the sum. This relation is described formally in Miller and Blair (2009)

where $a_{n+1,i}$ are the row elements of household income receipts from labour compensation by sector as:

$$m\left(h\right)_j = \sum_{i=1}^{n} (a_{n+1,i})\left(l_{ij}\right) \tag{6}$$

Viewing the results of income multipliers from a socioeconomic lens enables the identification of critical sectors which can be leveraged to pursue strategic commitments for sustained inclusive growth for those in poverty and for disadvantaged groups. The major limitation of IO data in this respect is the lack of delineation between various income or skill groups, accounts which prominently feature in SAMs.

3.5   *Some Illustrative Results and Interpretation*

The identified panel of input-output multipliers describe the production structure of the economy and its relation to household income and consumption expenditures. The average output multipliers in our model are 2.83 (Type 1) and 3.6 (Type 2). These relatively high values for average economy-wide multipliers are indicative of the level of development of backward and forward linkages in the Chinese economy. These average multipliers suggest that a 1 trillion yuan injection in the economy will return between 2.8 trillion and 3.6 trillion in total additional sectoral output. These estimates are meant to reflect the lower- and upper-bounds of our modelled stimulus where the actual outcome depends on which sectors receive an increase in government spending as well as households' propensity to consume.[6]

Secondly, we find an average employment multiplier of 10.1[7] and an average income multiplier of 1.24. The high value of the average employment multiplier suggests that aggregate employment growth in China is relatively responsive to changes in final demand, where the increase of 1 job for the average sector may directly and indirectly support up to 9 *additional jobs throughout the economy*. This high average is not representative of the typical sector however. Due to particularly robust backward and forward linkages, high employment multipliers are typically concentrated in tradable sectors like manufacturing, information technology, and professional services, which bring revenue flows and capital from outside a local community.

In income terms, every additional dollar of final demand in the average sector may be expected to stimulate additional household expenditures by $1.24 dollars. An average income multiplier greater than 1 in our case indicates that household expenditures indeed provide a significant channel for augmenting

---

6   Households' propensity to consume is taken as constant and uniform across income or social
      groups in the standard analysis of input-output multipliers.
7   Outliers excluded.

the effects of economic multipliers. However, the magnitude of income multipliers by sector varies substantially, indicating significant differences between the consumption linkages of different sectors.

Table 1 presents a full table of output, employment, and income multipliers for the top 10 value-added sectors of the economy. Observing our table, we see that the real estate sector contributes the largest share of value-added (VA), followed by the wholesale trade sector, financial services, the public administration sector, and the broad agricultural products sector. The output multipliers for the top 10 VA sectors are generally strong, indicating that they are well-integrated in the economy through backward and consumption linkages. The highest output multipliers are found in the residential construction (3.84), business services (3.79), and agricultural products (3.29) sectors. Notably at this level of disaggregation, all top 10 VA sectors are non-manufacturing.

The real estate sector appears to have modest output multipliers relative to rest of the top 10 VA sectors while exhibiting a relatively strong income multiplier (1.18) and the highest employment multiplier (8.79) of the group. These results indicate that the economy-wide impact from a change in final demand for the real estate sector occurs mainly through the employment channel as employment gains in this sector tends to support employment gains in other sectors, mainly through local household expenditures. The relative size of the real estate, financial services, and business services sectors indicate the increasingly central importance of the finance, insurance, and real estate (FIRE) sector in the modern Chinese economy. This fact reflects one of the drivers in income inequality in China: the rise of skill premia. Jobs in the FIRE sector typically require high levels of formal education and are concentrated mainly in financial centres like Beijing, Shanghai, and other highly urbanized areas. These urban skill premia are largely inaccessible for China's large population of rural and migrant workers with comparatively less access to higher education.

Other note-worthy sectors in terms of employment multipliers are residential housing construction (7.56), road cargo transportation services (7.92), and wholesale trade (5.45). Residential construction and road cargo transportation services are sectors employing relatively large numbers of workers and exhibit particularly large employment multipliers. Gains in output and employment in these sectors may be expected to be distributed somewhat more evenly across regions and support employment for both less-skilled urban and migrant workers since construction and transportation activities are not as concentrated as the FIRE sectors. The present stimulus explicitly targets spending in infrastructure construction across various provinces. As we will see, the multipliers for residential housing construction are similar to construction activities

TABLE 1   Multipliers for top 10 by VA (in ten thousand yuan)

	Real estate	Wholesale	Financial services	Public administration and social organization	Agricultural products
Sector VA	¥ 681,344,741.76	¥ 497,784,169.53	¥ 488,219,705.16	¥ 429,894,799.64	¥ 401,199,459.53
Rank	1	2	3	4	5
%GTVA	7.39%	5.40%	5.29%	4.66%	4.35%
Type 1 Output Multiplier	1.595	1.848	1.976	2.036	1.853
Type 2 Output Multiplier	1.994	2.503	2.688	3.160	3.291
Employment Multiplier	8.796	5.445	5.378	4.001	4.746
Income Multiplier	1.178	1.460	2.005	0.529	2.166

	Retail trade	Residential housing construction	Education	Business services	Road cargo transportation services
Sector VA	¥ 379,287,792.70	¥ 326,818,539.27	¥ 315,788,793.37	¥ 245,740,789.85	¥ 208,613,515.71
Rank	6	7	8	9	10
%GTVA	4.11%	3.54%	3.42%	2.67%	2.26%
Type 1 Output Multiplier	1.815	3.079	1.724	2.829	2.313
Type 2 Output Multiplier	2.679	3.835	2.795	3.792	2.892
Employment Multiplier	4.261	7.563	4.008	5.047	7.923
Income Multiplier	1.289	0.153	0.573	2.058	0.975

SOURCE: AUTHORS' CALCULATION FOR 2018 IO TABLE

in infrastructure and other civil engineering projects. Therefore, we should expect significant direct and indirect gains from increased output in construction and related sectors.

The highest income multipliers for the top 10 VA sectors are in agricultural products (2.17), business services (2.06), and financial services (2.01). These values indicate that the induced effects on output of increased labour demand in these sectors are quite high, however this effect occurs for different reasons. In the business and financial services sectors, this effect arises due to the high average wages earned by the relatively skilled workforce, leading to high induced output effects from the spending of these workers. While the FIRE sectors altogether make up 14% of value-added, they account for less than 7% of total employment. The business services sector however has the 5th largest share of total employment (5.5%). Since actual employment gains in these sectors and their respective income effects may be limited by education requirements and geographic location, the realized economy-wide effects depend largely on the higher propensity to consume of higher-wage earners in these sectors.

In agricultural products, where wages are much lower, this effect occurs because production in this sector remains quite labour-intensive and absolute employment numbers remain high. From the 153 production activities in our dataset, the agricultural products sector[8] commands the largest share of total employment at 13.2% despite a share of total value-added at 4.4%. As would be expected, the broad agricultural sector forms the bedrock for rural economies in China providing large numbers of rural households a source of primary or supplementary income.[9] Though wages are low relative to skilled workers in urban areas, any gains in the incomes for agricultural workers can have significant output impacts on rural communities given the outsized importance of consumption expenditures in rural economies. Moreover, since most employment in the primary sector typically require little formal education actual employment gains may very quickly be realized through increases in final or intermediate demand, meaning that investments in this sector can lead to positive economic effects in the short-run and contribute to addressing acute hunger and poverty. Finally, since rural areas provide markets for domestic goods in other regions, may lead to significant economic impacts that are spread

---

8   This sector specifically references agricultural crops and excludes livestock, fisheries, forestry, and miscellaneous animal husbandry products. Altogether the agricultural sectors make up roughly 25% of total employment in China.

9   As in the case of migrant workers who work seasonally in urban factories or construction sites and return for work in rural agricultural production for the rest of the year.

TABLE 2   Multipliers for pandemic-sensitive services (in 10 thousand yuan)

	Meals and food services	Accommodation and hotels	Resident services
Sector VA	¥ 117,503,013.34	¥ 43,119,338.74	¥ 88,016,448.74
%GTVA	1.27%	0.47%	0.95%
Type 1 Output Multiplier	2.639	2.452	2.016
Type 2 Output Multiplier	3.592	3.321	2.993
Employment Multiplier	6.908	5.019	4.107
Income Multiplier	0.654	0.556	0.511

SOURCE: AUTHORS' CALCULATION FOR 2018 IO TABLE

more evenly throughout the economy. However, these income effects do not generally lead to significant impacts in terms of sustained employment gains in other sectors because agricultural products have few backward linkages.

Using production accounts Liu (2021) shows that the some of the largest sectors by share of value-added: wholesale trade, retail trade, and road cargo transportation services were among the most impacted by the COVID-19 shock. The collapse of wholesale and retail trade coincided with the sudden disruption of intercity and interregional commerce and transport flows on account of strict lockdowns. This particular impact of the pandemic has tended to concentrate in regions most affected by the pandemic (Chen et al., 2020). Accordingly, a significant portion of employment losses have been concentrated in broadly pandemic-sensitive service sectors like wholesale and retail trade, business services, and the transportation sector in addition to accommodation and meals, and other related service sectors. Altogether, job losses in these sectors represent the loss of mainly middle and low-skill jobs (citation needed).

Table 2 reports multipliers for a set of three service industries that have experienced significant employment losses during the pandemic. Here we find output and employment multipliers that are generally higher than would be expected for service sectors. Notably, we find higher than average employment multipliers in the meals and food services, and accommodation and hotels sectors. These results highlight the relative importance of these sectors in supporting overall economic activity across regions and as a major source of employment in both urban and rural areas. Declines in service sector output and employment left lasting impacts on the revenues and employment of various other sectors throughout the economy. Given this context, one of the principal challenges of the COVID-19 shock then is to restore domestic demand to pre-pandemic levels in order to boost employment in these and interconnected sectors.

Major employment losses also resulted from manufacturing plant shutdowns in early 2020 (see also below). The wider impacts of these shutdowns can be traced in Table 3, which shows the estimated multipliers for the largest manufacturing sectors in China by VA. The largest manufacturing sectors are electricity and heat production, steel rolled products, coal mining products, metal products, and petroleum and natural gas mining. These sectors feature among the largest estimated output and income multipliers among the manufacturing sectors.[10] Judging by their large employment multipliers manufacturing sectors contribute substantial spill-over in terms of direct and indirect employment effects. Given that manufacturing requires a wide-ranging list of inputs, stable manufacturing employment tends to support a large volume of additional output and employment in related sectors and local communities. The sharp decline in manufacturing activity constituted a major drop in demand for intermediate goods throughout the wider economy.

When considering global value chains and uneven development, where manufacturing is largely concentrated in China's Eastern provinces and in cities, the total magnitude of large national employment multipliers may not always refer to employment created domestically within-country or evenly across regions. Taking national employment multipliers for manufacturing at face value assumes that all value-added activities in manufacturing and ancillary sectors take place within-country and that value-added are distributed evenly across regions. Distinguishing regional employment effects would require the use of a multi-regional input-output model. Here we can distinguish national employment effects of manufacturing by observing the final row entry for the sectors on Table 3 reporting the level of imports as a percentage of sector VA. We find that the largest manufacturing sectors with the greatest dependence on imports are the petroleum and natural gas, electronic components, and automobiles. The magnitude of import exposure in these and other sectors dependent on imports should raises doubt as to the full effect of the reported employment multipliers since an increase in demand for these sectors raises demand for imports and employment abroad.

An important set of non-tradable sectors for the Chinese economy are in construction and allied industries. Table 4 reports multipliers for three

---

10   The notable outlier is the refined petroleum and nuclear fuel products sector with an exceptionally large employment multiplier of 61.05.

TABLE 3   Multipliers for top 10 manufacturing sectors by VA (in 10 thousand yuan)

	Electricity and heat production and supply	Steel rolled products	Coal mining and processing products	Metal products	Petroleum and natural gas mining products
Sector VA	¥ 203,934,895.87	¥ 142,840,345.00	¥ 121,462,438.75	¥ 118,112,728.75	¥ 90,126,121.46
Sector Imports	¥ 167,346.58	¥ 10,748,552.80	¥ 17,067,535.54	¥ 8,933,652.91	¥ 181,295,520.27
Rank	1	2	3	4	5
%GTVA	2.21%	1.55%	1.32%	1.28%	0.98%
Type 1 Output Multiplier	2.813	2.808	2.236	3.127	1.838
Type 2 Output Multiplier	3.403	3.352	2.932	3.788	2.257
Employment Multiplier	11.863	16.267	5.925	9.586	10.316
Income Multiplier	1.875	0.744	1.003	0.367	1.085
Imports as % of VA	0.08%	7.5%	14.1%	7.6%	201.2%

	Whole cars	Refined petroleum and nuclear fuel processed products	Electronic Components	Waste resources and recycling products	Auto parts and accessories
Sector VA	¥ 88,125,836.21	¥ 85,757,375.11	¥ 72,060,214.58	¥ 72,006,612.70	¥ 70,833,823.84
Sector Imports	¥ 11,054,482.11	¥ 90,126,121.46	¥ 23,247,565.52	¥ 24,256,644.04	¥ 24,209,119.43
Rank	6	7	8	9	10
%GTVA	0.96%	0.93%	0.78%	0.78%	0.77%
Type 1 Output Multiplier	3.428	2.560	3.789	1.276	3.492
Type 2 Output Multiplier	4.015	2.935	4.450	1.669	4.142
Employment Multiplier	7.157	61.050	15.845	6.414	15.181
Income Multiplier	0.351	1.194	1.569	0.466	0.704
Imports as % of VA	40.2%	29.0%	341.3%	17.3%	27.3%

SOURCE: AUTHORS' CALCULATION FOR 2018 IO TABLE

TABLE 4   Multipliers for construction and allied-industries (in 10 thousand yuan)

	Professional technical services	Railway, road, tunnel and bridge construction	Building decoration, decoration and other construction services	Other civil engineering construction
Sector VA	¥ 133,478,272.08	¥ 114,579,968.71	¥ 67,731,788.85	¥ 60,496,539.27
%GTVA	1.45%	1.24%	0.73%	0.66%
Type 1 Output Multiplier	2.724	3.100	2.990	3.102
Type 2 Output Multiplier	3.567	3.898	3.795	3.896
Employment Multiplier	5.467	7.139	6.496	7.207
Income Multiplier	0.565	0.168	0.337	0.166

SOURCE: AUTHORS' CALCULATION FOR 2018 IO TABLE

construction sectors and the closely linked professional technical services sector. Among the four sectors we find output and employment multipliers that are high relative to the rest of the economy, particularly in construction related to infrastructure and other civil engineering projects. Because income multipliers here are relatively modest, it is clear that the bulk of output and employment effects are channelled through significant backward linkages. As we will see, construction sectors have significant linkages with local manufacturing and technical services, leading to indirect output and employment effects in these sectors for changes in final demand for construction. Accordingly, work stoppages on construction sites during the height of the pandemic in China resulted in acute ripple-out effects on intermediate demand. These ripple effects are compounded (e.g. construction declines lead to manufacturing declines which lead to further declines) to generate the steep jumps in unemployment characteristic of international experience with the pandemic.

A significant portion of the present stimulus is directed toward public health expenditures. The health services and related sectors constitute strategic sectors for managing the various public health challenges presented by the pandemic including the containment and treatment of disease in addition

TABLE 5   Multipliers for health services and allied sectors (in 10 thousand yuan)

	Health services	Medical products	Medical equipment
Sector VA	¥ 163,270,017.00	¥ 80,278,968.07	¥ 9,857,574.89
%GTVA	1.80%	0.87%	0.11%
Type 1 Output Multiplier	2.612	2.832	3.166
Type 2 Output Multiplier	3.610	3.638	3.881
Employment Multiplier	4.586	10.469	8.253
Income Multiplier	0.347	0.367	0.165

SOURCE: AUTHORS' CALCULATION FOR 2018 IO TABLE

to vaccine development and disbursement. In Table 5 we show a set of multipliers for health services and related sectors. For the health services sector we find significant output multipliers of 2.61 and 3.61 coupled with a relatively modest but significant employment multiplier of 4.59. As will be shown in the next section, the health services sector has significant linkages with the medical products and medical equipment sectors, which in their turn exhibit high relative employment multipliers. However, all three health sectors present relatively low-income multipliers, *likely due to formal education requirements.*

The health services sector is well-integrated across regions. Although the majority of hospitals are located in cities, up to 99% of health centres and a large portion of town and village clinics are concentrated in rural areas, providing the majority of total health services in China. Healthcare based on TCM or integrated with western medicine is in wide use by rural residents, who account for the largest portion of TCM clients. Household surveys suggest a growing trend among urban residents and college-educated individuals to seek health services in TCM hospitals and clinics. Altogether, these facts indicate that the IK sector occupies a substantial portion of the health services sector.

While the provision of healthcare services and products provide direct community benefits, which are often necessary to support overall economic activity, government spending here will also generate robust direct, indirect, and induced effects on economy-wide output and employment.

4   Modelling of Employment Effects after Fiscal Stimulus

This section presents further details for an impact analysis of Chinese Counter-COVID-19 expenditures. We model the employment effects of direct government injection totalling one trillion yuan. These expenditures are distributed as follows: 100 billion yuan are spent in *railway, road, tunnel, and bridge construction* and 500 billion yuan are spent in the *other civil engineering construction* sector as part of infrastructure projects, 300 billion are spent in the health services sector to fund public health and welfare programs, and 100 billion are spent in the public administration for broad support in the accelerated disbursement and extension of unemployment insurance for both urban and migrant workers. This distribution of government spending by sector is roughly representative of the total fiscal package spent in 2020, excluding tax and fees cuts and direct spending in the financial sector. Domestic employment effects are derived in terms of absolute monetary value of induced labour requirements and in terms of physical jobs using standard sector wages[11] and adjusted for import exposure.

In terms of output effects, the estimated value of additional sectoral output generated in our model totalled 3.05 trillion yuan.[12] The additional modelled employment corresponding to this increase in output amounts to over 7.7 million new domestic jobs. This figure is well within reach of the Central Committee's goal of 9–10 million jobs[13] and it is likely that the remaining gap in desired employment can be generated on the basis of substantial nationwide tax cuts and subsidized expansion in credit availability targeting MSMEs.

These employment effects are explored in further detail in this section, starting with Table 6 which shows the employment effects on the top 10 sectors by VA. We find that the sectors likely to see the most job growth are in public administration followed by agricultural products, business services, and wholesale and retail trade. The large increases in employment for the public administration sector are not surprising given the effect of a direct increase of government consumption in these sectors. However, the indirect effects of the overall stimulus turn out to be quite large, with significant spill-over effects

---

11   Sector wages are calculated as the national average wage for urban units by sector in 2020, including both private and state-owned enterprises. Wage data are from the National Bureau of Statistics in China (2021).

12   Indicating an estimated output multiplier of around 3.05 for the modelled stimulus.

13   The goal of additional 9 million comes from the CPC's May 2020 Report on the Work of the Government (Keqiang, 2020). The 10 million figure refers to the amount of additional employment needed to have maintained the 2020 annual unemployment rate constant.

TABLE 6   Employment outcome for top 10 sectors by VA

	Real estate	Wholesale	Financial services	Public administration and social organization	Agricultural products
Rank	1	2	3	4	5
%GTVA	7.39%	5.40%	5.29%	4.66%	4.35%
Added Value of Labor Input Requirement (in 10 thousand yuan)	¥485,755.28	¥1,631,806.44	¥2,195,257.56	¥10,126,670.87	¥7,931,413.31
No. of Additional Domestic Workers	69,585	217,546	201,391	965,198	469,969

	Retail trade	Residential housing construction	Education	Business Services	Road cargo transportation services
Rank	6	7	8	9	10
%GTVA	4.11%	3.54%	3.42%	2.67%	2.26%
Added Value of Labor Input Requirement (in 10 thousand yuan)	¥1,647,979.99	¥0	¥181,369.61	¥2,018,420.44	¥545,563.94
No. of Additional Domestic Workers	220,503	0	23,417	256,680	68,940

SOURCE: AUTHORS' CALCULATION FOR 2018 IO TABLE

in the agricultural products, business and financial services, wholesale, and retail trade sectors. Employment gains of over 2.49 million jobs in the top 10 VA sectors amounts to 32.4% of the total increase in employment for the present stimulus.

One of the government's main priorities during the economic recovery in the first and second period of the crisis was the stabilization of employment. An important first step to stabilization is to prevent net employment losses at their source. As we saw, the most affected sectors in terms of output and employment were the consumer-facing industries in wholesale and retail trade, accommodation, and other allied service industries. Table 7 reports the modelled employment outcomes for pandemic-sensitive service industries that were disproportionately impacted by the COVID-19 shock. We find significant employment gains in the reported service sectors. Including the wholesale, retail, transportation, and business services sectors, the overall modelled employment gains for pandemic-sensitive service sectors totalled 985,254 domestic jobs. These results suggest that the present stimulus is generally well-targeted to stem net employment losses, but an important question becomes the speed of the realization of these gains. The actual realization of these gains will come to depend on the speed of recovery of domestic consumption expenditures.

An uneven recovery with the slow recovery of retail expenditures may translate into weak employment growth in the service sector. There is reason to be optimistic since domestic tourism and travel revenues are experiencing a relatively quick recovery in 2021, driving positive expectations for the growth retail expenditures throughout the year. However, structural factors are also at play. As a significant component of total consumption expenditures, the recovery of total consumption expenditures will depend in part on the restoration of disposable income on the part of China's large rural and migrant population. *Accordingly, it is important for China to focus stimulate domestic demand through rising labour incomes and reducing inequality.*

Critical to employment stabilization in the early phases of the recovery was the restoration of production in the manufacturing sectors. Many of these jobs were restored once production restrictions were lifted and social distancing measures relaxed. However, maintaining a resilient front to stabilize employment will continue to lean on steady growth in manufacturing to support overall recovery. Table 8 shows that the greatest employment gains in manufacturing are found in the electricity and heat production, coal mining and processing, and steel rolled products, and metal products sectors. This result is due to the high number of linkages between these sectors and the construction sector. The various materials required for medium to long-term infrastructure

TABLE 7   Employment outcomes for services

	Meals and food services	Accommodation and hotels	Resident services
%GTVA	1.27%	0.47%	0.95%
Added Value of Labor Input Requirement (in 10 thousand yuan)	¥ 361,287.31	¥ 448,233.90	¥ 142,144.81
No. of Additional Domestic Workers	74,207	71,959	26,524

SOURCE: AUTHORS' CALCULATION FOR 2018 IO TABLE

projects are sourced from local manufacturing industries, generating a sustained employment effect, even after adjusting for import exposure. Thus, public investment and subsidies for infrastructure projects are likely to support well-paying domestic employment for many low-skilled and medium-skilled workers in manufacturing, providing up to 5% of total employment gains.

Much of this increase in employment will be disproportionately generated in manufacturing-intensive regions on the coast, in provinces like Guangdong, Zhejiang, and Shenzhen, as opposed to China's less developed interior provinces.

Since we modelled a total 600 billion yuan increase in government spending in construction sectors, we expect both large direct effects and significant indirect effects as intermediate demand from construction activity ripples outward in connected or related sectors. Observing Table 9 we indeed find large direct gains of over 260,000 additional domestic workers in *the railway, road, tunnel, and bridge construction* sector and 1.3 million additional domestic workers in the *other civil engineering construction* sector. Additionally, we find significant gains in the professional technical services and building renovation and construction services sectors. Employment gains in construction and allied-industries account for a 26% of total employment gains and thus provide one of the main pillars of employment growth for the present stimulus.

Another major source of employment growth in the present model comes from strategic spending in the health services and related sectors. Direct government expenditures in support of public health programs are targeted at improving basic capacity for pandemic control, treatment, and the distribution of essential goods and emergency aid. Improving capacity in this sector

TABLE 8 Employment outcome for top 10 manufacturing sectors by VA

	Electricity and heat production and supply	Steel rolled products	Coal mining and processing products	Metal products	Petroleum and natural gas mining products
Rank	1	2	3	4	5
%GTVA	2.21%	1.55%	1.32%	1.28%	0.98%
Added Value of Labor Input Requirement (in 10 thousand yuan)	¥ 700,615.44	¥ 626,251.31	¥ 755,745.34	¥ 618,990.22	¥ 432,679.45
No. of Additional Domestic Workers	81,927	88,379	92,227	88,112	25,587

	Whole cars	Refined petroleum and nuclear fuel processed products	Electronic components	Waste resources and waste materials recycling processed products	Auto parts and accessories
Rank	6	7	8	9	10
%GTVA	0.96%	0.93%	0.78%	0.78%	0.77%
Added Value of Labor Input Requirement (in 10 thousand yuan)	¥ 2,807.28	¥ 92,518.94	¥ 206,063.77	¥ 261,676.97	¥ 130,505.87
No. of Additional Domestic Workers	361	12,292	12,068	32,077	17,559

SOURCE: AUTHORS' CALCULATION FOR 2018 IO TABLE

TABLE 9   Employment outcome for construction and allied-industries

	Professional technical services	Railway, road, tunnel and bridge engineering construction	Building decoration, decoration and other construction services	Other civil engineering construction
%GTVA	1.45%	1.24%	0.73%	0.66%
Added Value of Labor Input Requirement (in 10 thousand yuan)	¥ 2,502,008.96	¥ 16.84	¥ 647,439.08	¥ 9,988,287.36
No. of Additional Workers	237,618	264,081	102,768	1,305,331

SOURCE: AUTHORS' CALCULATION FOR 2018 IO TABLE

TABLE 10   Employment outcomes for health services and related sectors

	Health services	Medical products	Medical equipment
%GTVA	1.80%	0.87%	0.11%
Added Value of Labor Input Requirement (in 10 thousand yuan)	¥ 9,745,694.85	¥ 1,485,298.29	¥ 157,007.34
No. of Additional Domestic Workers	1,099,191	191,042	13,280

SOURCE: AUTHORS' CALCULATION FOR 2018 IO TABLE

will require major lab or inputs from both high-skilled and low-skilled workers including additional doctors and nurses, social workers, counsellors, in addition to caretakers and medical aides. In addition, there are notable gains in the high value-added medical products sector (note that this sector has high relative import exposure). Table 9 indicates gains of over 1.3 million domestic and regionally local jobs in health services and related sectors over the short to medium term (around 16.9% of total employment gains). It is quite possible also that this boost in capacity will become permanent as part of the government's ongoing healthcare reforms (Meng et al., 2019), and to prevent future outbreaks.

Additionally, with China's aging population (Flaherty et al., 2007), health-care will gradually occupy larger shares of total value-added over time and are certain to become important sources of future employment (Table 10). Many of these jobs will need to be generated across China, with particular need in rural areas where the majority of health centres and village clinics are located, including many practicing TCM or TCM/western integrated practices.

5   Summary and Policy Recommendations in an Imperfect Crisis-Infested World of 2020s

Our analysis highlights the salience of considering the economic and social shocks of pandemics and development from a SEICA perspective. Accordingly, the following conclusions and recommendations may be relevant for other economies in various stages of development, particularly those with sharply uneven development patterns and large populations of rural residents.

First, in light of uneven development and structural inequalities, we find that the current stimulus has not done enough to generate economic activity and strengthen the recovery of rural provinces. Although there are some employment gains expected to be spread across regions including in construction, agriculture, and public health, the bulk of employment effects of the stimulus favour employment growth in urban areas. This is mainly by design, since a large portion of employment losses during the height of the pandemic were indeed concentrated in these areas, impacting also employment opportunities for hundreds of millions of migrant workers. However, this view failed to recognize that rural areas suffered disproportionate economic impacts from the COVID-19 shock despite having much lower infection rates than urban areas.

Accounting for the disproportionate effects of the pandemic on less developed provinces (i.e. Gansu, Guizhou, Xinjiang and Yunnan) and rural areas, residents in these areas may be more vulnerable to acute food and resource shortages as a result of the travel restrictions and production stoppages. Maintaining commitments to the prevention and reduction of poverty and hunger in these areas will require continued attention paid to the situation of poor households and individuals facing emergency situations. The provision of relief packages and transfers have been limited in the present stimulus to emergency situations, which has plausibly excluded many rural residents and migrant workers whose cases have gone unmonitored and without access to government representation.

Second, given the overemphasis on supply-side matters of the stimulus, perhaps from the strategic perspective of export-led growth the government will also need to focus more attention on restoring broader domestic demand as a means of achieving sustainable recovery. In order to maintain momentum in the present recovery, policy makers should continue to facilitate job creation for less-skilled workers in both urban and rural areas through tax support for MSMEs and job training programs and improve market expectations by maintaining a resilient front against future outbreaks through vaccination drives and international cooperation. Additionally, rural residents may require augmented relief packages and direct transfers in the interest of ensuring the sustainable recovery of household expenditures.

Third, the present crisis calls for pro-labour policies intended to stimulate domestic demand via rising incomes. This strategy for China has its precedent in a previous recession. Just before the 2008 financial crisis, a team of economists from UNCTAD, of which one of the authors was a member, advised the Chinese government to focus more on domestic demand from wage-led growth strategy. In addition, Khan (2010) suggested a more sustainable development strategy with a focus on renewable energy use that seems to have been adopted by and large by the Chinese policymakers.

6   WCS and Chinese Ambiguities

There are indeed many paradoxes with respect to the actual nature of the Chinese economy. Is it capitalist or socialist or market socialist or something else? How can concrete analysis of the Chinese economy help us in understanding the actual nature of the Chinese economy? Where is China located in the Global Geopolitical-economic System? We need a guiding methodology that captures the complex social, economic and political ontologies dialectically. That is to say, such a complex systems approach must analyse various salient contradictions at different levels of analysis ranging from the local to the global arenas.

Using deductive, inductive, and abductive modes of reasoning I build up a theory from the bottom up to understand 21st century Chinese paradoxes and ambiguities. These paradoxes and ambiguities are not accidental but relate to tensions in the moral economy of PRC with a revolutionary non-capitalist past in the capitalist world of the early 21st century. I will examine these emerging issues both theoretically and empirically and begin a conversation between the theorists and practitioners. In this way in particular, our discussion of COVID-19 responses in PRC in light of the Crisis-prone nature of the rest of WCS is intended to begin the much-needed dialogue regarding the contemporary relevance of a complex multi-layered innovative economy like that of the PRC. Though much remains to be done, the chapters that analyse the contradictions in the WCS in light of the COVID crisis, together with my discussion of the Chinese case illustrate the paradoxical nature and experiences of Chinese development which nevertheless is demonstrably superior to the US-led WCS in handling crises. Needless to say, we need to identify the opportunities in and constraints to the Chinese quasi-socialist strategy over time in order to critically assess how capitalist or socialist it is. Most importantly, our analysis coupled with the rest of the book can already provide some guidance on how to tap the potential of non-capitalist complex economies for increasing human wellbeing, addressing in particular the constraints arising from the real stratifications in the Chinese and the Global Political Economy. My ultimate normative concern here involves–congruently with the intentions of the authors of this book–considerations of how to make further progress in the promotion of human well-being in light of enhancing human capabilities theory pioneered by Amartya Sen and developed by several others. In particular, I have developed over the last decade a specific intersectoral approach. I call my approach a Socially embedded Intersectoral Capabilities Approach or SEICA. It can be shown that the SEICA indicators ranging from health and education to political and social aspects of freedom concretely institutionalized can help assess the failures of WCS and the mixed successes of countries struggling to break away from WCS. Clearly, human well-being depends crucially on the nature of socio-economic-political system. Hence the normative theory must be located within an approximately true theory of the complex global political economy that is applicable scientifically. This will surely be the next big step to take by progressive 21st century social sciences.

7   Conclusions: Possible Global Futures–Socialism or Barbarism?

We have presented critically perhaps the most detailed analysis of China's response to the COVID crisis. Calculations based on the 2018 IO table for China identified the direct and indirect effects of counter COVID-19 government expenditures on overall employment in the Chinese economy. We find that the real estate sector is the largest in terms of sectoral value-added, followed by the wholesale trade, financial services, public administration, and agricultural products sectors. The largest value-added sectors among manufacturing industries are electricity and heat production, steel rolled products, coal mining products, metal products, and petroleum and natural gas mining products. While these sectors are undoubtedly important for supporting local economic activity and employment, it should be noted that among the most strategically important manufacturing sectors are those with the greatest exposure to imports. Critically dependent on imports are the following sectors in terms of import exposure: electronic components (341.3%), petroleum and natural gas mining products (201.2%), and automobiles (40.2%).

The calculated multipliers indicate that rural and low-income households are most likely to benefit from changes in final demand for wholesale and retail trade, agricultural products, construction, and accommodations sectors.

In terms of modelled employment effects, we find that the greatest source of added employment is found in construction, agriculture, the pandemic-sensitive service industries, and in the public health and social work sector. For construction and public health/social work in particular, these employment gains come largely from direct additional government expenditures in these sectors as part of counter COVID-19 economic and social welfare goals. Since infrastructure projects and healthcare spending are targeted across China, it is likely that direct employment gains in construction and public health will be distributed fairly evenly across regions. The increase in agricultural employment is highly significant given a growing need for the creation of job opportunities in rural areas and under-developed provinces. For growth in services and manufacturing, we should expect job growth for low- and middle-skilled workers, providing jobs for low-income urban residents as well as migrant workers.

Employment gains for construction, public health services, and public administration come largely from direct additional government expenditures in these sectors as part of counter COVID-19 economic and social welfare goals. Significant employment gains are found to come also from indirect increase in intermediate demand through backward linkages. Sectors that have seen the largest indirect employment gains are agriculture and the pandemic-sensitive service industries. Employment gains have also been seen across manufacturing sectors to a lesser extent on account of backward linkages tied to the construction sector. The increase in agricultural employment is significant given the growing need for the creation of job opportunities in rural areas and under-developed provinces. For growth in services and manufacturing, we should expect job growth for low- and middle-skilled workers, providing jobs for low-income urban residents as well as migrant workers.

Even after adjusting our modelled employment effects for import exposures, we were able to estimate that total domestic employment gains from the present stimulus would be significant and expected to meet the Central Committee's overall employment creation goals, with a large portion of these gains concentrated in construction and allied-manufacturing sectors.

The analyses in CRISIS, INEQUALITIES AND POVERTY, complemented by the present afterword show convincingly that the crisis-prone WCS will continue to inflict great harm on the most vulnerable people in society. Consider also the real presence of aggressive imperialism fostered in the advanced countries through the finance capital, and structural compulsions of the WCS. The dangers of global confrontation and war mongering particularly by the ruling classes in the US with segments of EU and Japan following are real. The choice between the two paths acknowledged even by a prescient bourgeois economist like Schumpeter is clear. Schumpeter (1954) had presciently pointed towards the dire possibility of global conflagration which now looks all too alarmingly real. Being somewhat of a pessimist, he was reluctant to see the prospects for a progressive peaceful socialism although he acknowledged the possibility of a non-capitalist future also. To be fair to him, the legacy of socialism in the 20th century has been ambiguous at best. The Chinese case since 1978 is particularly interesting from this standpoint. Clearly there are many ambiguities in the Chinese case also – not the least being the restoration of hierarchical management and stifling of grassroots democracy that existed during the Yenan period and at the post-1949 revolutionary moments. But it must be acknowledged that however imperfect or ambiguous, the non-capitalist elements of the complex social, economic and political entity called PRC have managed both the 2008–9 global financial crisis and the COVID crisis so far, much better than the US-led WCS. One can only hope that with further democratic socialist oriented reforms and future revolutions in these directions in parts of WCS, the world can avoid the dire conflagration feared by Schumpeter and Arrighi among others. Not only this hopeful negative result of avoidance, but the PRC has also shown that even in a WCS dominated by neoliberal ideology, it is possible to move towards a path of moderate prosperity by following an alternative – however imperfect – to neoliberalism, and one hopes, peace. The crucial question, of course, is if PRC can control the private capitalists and pro-capitalist state and party elements. Only if this crucial precondition is fulfilled will PRC be able to reduce various kinds of inequalities and practice a SEICA-inspired egalitarian capability enhancing policy regime. Moving forward, although by no means a sure prospect, China in the 21st century may even lead a new genuinely socialist bloc in our time. If PRC fails to do this, other revolutionary actors in other parts of the world must carry the torch of egalitarian and democratic socialist movement forward. Rosa Luxemburg was right: we have to choose in our lifetime between socialism or barbarism.

References

Aaberge, R. and A. Brandolini (2015), "Multidimensional Poverty and Inequality", in A. B. Atkinson and F. Bourguignon. (eds.), *Handbook of Income Distribution*, Vol. 2A. Amsterdam: North-Holland. pp. 141–214.

Acemoğlu, D. (1998), "Why Do New Technologies Complement Skills? Directed Technical Change and Wage Inequality", *Quarterly Journal of Economics*, 113 (4): pp. 1055–1089.

Adams-Prassl, A., Boneva, T., Golin, M., and Rauh, C. "Inequality in the Impact of the Coronavirus hock: Evidence from Real Time Surveys", *Journal of Public Economics*, 189:104245, 2020.

Alacevich, M. and A. Soci (2019), *Breve storia della disuguaglianza*, Bari: Editori Laterza.

Alvaredo, F., A. B. Atkinson, T. Piketty and E. Saez (2013), "The Top 1 Percent in International and Historical Perspective", *Journal of Economic Perspectives*, 27 (3): pp. 3–20.

Amiel, Y., and F. A. Cowell (1999), *Thinking about Inequality: Personal Judgment and Income Distributions*. Israel and London School of Economics: Ruppin Institute.

Andrasfay, T., and Goldman, N. (2021) "Reductions in 2020 US life expectancy due to COVID-19 and the disproportionate impact on the Black and Latino populations", *Proceedings of the National Academy of Sciences of the United States of America*, 118:e2014746118. Available at (accessed on 5th November 2021): https://www.pnas.org/content/118/5/e2014746118.

Arrighi, G. (1994), *The Long Twentieth Century: Money, Power and the Origins of Our Times*. London: Verso.

Arrighi, G. (2007), *Adam Smith in Beijing: Lineages of the Twenty-First Century*. London and New York: Verso.

Arrighi, G. and B. J. Silver (1999), *Chaos and Governance in the Modern World System*. Minneapolis, MN: University of Minnesota Press.

Arrighi, G., P. Hui, H. Hung and M. Selden (2003), "Historical Capitalism, East and West." In G. Arrighi, T. Hamashita and M. Selden (eds.), *The Resurgence of East Asia. 500, 150 and 50 Year Perspectives*. London and New York: Routledge, pp. 259–333.

Atkinson, A. B., and A. Brandolini (2010) "On Analyzing the World Distribution of Income," *The World Bank Economic Review 24*: pp. 1–37.

Atkinson, A. B., and A. Brandolini (2011), "On the Identification of the 'Middle Class'", in J. C. Gornick and M. Jäntti (eds.), *Inequality and the Status of the Middle Class*, Stanford CA: Stanford University Press, pp. 77–100.

Atkinson, A. B. and T. Piketty (eds.) (2007), *Top Incomes over the Twentieth Century: A Contrast Between Continental European and English Speaking Countries*, Oxford: Oxford University Press.

Atkinson, A. B. and T. Piketty (eds.) (2010), *Top Incomes: A Global Perspective*. Oxford: Oxford University Press.

Atkinson, A. B., L. Rainwater and T. M. Smeeding (1995), *Income Distribution in OECD Countries: Evidence from Luxembourg Income Study*, Paris: Organisation for Economic Co-operation and Development.

Aum, S., Lee, S. Y., and Shin, Y. *COVID-19 Doesn't Need Lockdowns to Destroy Jobs: The Effect of Local Outbreaks in Korea*. Working Paper no. 27264, National Bureau of Economic Research, Cambridge MA, 2020. Available at (consulted 20th October): https://www.nber.org/papers/w27264.

Azcona, G., Bhatt, A., Encarnacion, J., Plazaola-Castaño, J., Seck, P. Staab, S., and Turquet, L.(2020) From Insights to Action: Gender Equality in the Wake of COVID-19. Technical Report, UN Women, New York NY, 2020. Available at (consulted 20th October): https://www.unwomen.org/en/digital-library/publications/2020/09/gender-equality.

Baldini, M. and S. Toso (2009), *Diseguaglianza, povertà e politiche pubbliche*. Bologna: Il Mulino.

Bandyopadhyay, S., J. A. Bishop, and J. G. Rodriguez (2017), *Research on Economic Inequality: Poverty, Inequality and Welfare, Volume 25*. London: Emerald Publishers.

Banksy (2009), *Rickshaw*, Street Art. Courtesty of Pest Control Office.

Barclays Capital (2011) "Euro: Greek Top 40 and the 'Voluntary' Question", *Global Rates Strategy Report*, 17th June 2011, pp. 41–51.

Barro, R. J., Ursúa, J. F., and Weng, J. (2020) *The Coronavirus and the Great Influenza Pandemic: Lessons from the "Spanish Flu" for the Coronavirus's Potential Effects on Mortality and Economic Activity*. Working Paper no. 26866, National Bureau of Economic Research, Cambridge MA. Available at (consulted 20th October): https://www.nber.org/papers/w26866.

Barton, D., Chen, Y., & Jin, A. (2013). Mapping China's middle class. *McKinsey Quarterly*.

Becker, G. S. and B. R. Chiswick (1966), "Education and the Distribution of Earnings", *American Economic Review,* 56 (1–2): pp. 358–369.

Beland, L.-P., Brodeur, A., and Wright, T. *COVID-19, Stay-At-Home Orders and Employment: Evidence from CPS Data*. Discussion Paper no., 13282, IZA – Institute for Labor Economics, Bonn, 2020. Available at (consulted 6th November 2021): https://covid-19.iza.org/publications/dp13282/.

Berkhout, E., Galasso, N., Lawson, M., Morales, P. A. R., Taneja, A., and Pimentel, D. A. V (2021). *The Inequality Virus. Bringing Together a World Torn Apart by Coronavirus Through a Fair, Just and Sustainable Economy*. Oxfam Briefing Paper, Oxfam International. Available at (consulted 6th November 2021): https://www.oxfam.org/en/research/inequality-virus.

Birdsall, N. (2010), "The (Indispensable) Middle Class in Developing Countries", in R. Kanbur and M. Spence (eds.), *Equity and Growth in a Globalizing World*. Washington DC: World Bank Group, pp. 157–188.

Boniol, M., McIsaac, M., Xu, L., Wuliji, T., Diallo, K., and Campbell, J. (2019) *Gender Equity in the Health Workforce: Analysis of 104 Countries*. Health Workforce Working Paper no. 1, World Health Organization, Geneva, 2. Available at: https://apps.who .int/iris/bitstream/handle/10665/311314/WHO-HIS-HWF-Gender-WP1-2019.1-eng .pdf [accessed on 6 November 2021].

Bosmans, K., K. Decancq, and A. Decoster (2014), "The Relativity of Decreasing Inequality between Countries", *Economica 81*: pp. 276–292.

Bradley, J., Ruggieri, A., and Spencer, A. H. (2020) "Twin Peaks: COVID-19 and the Labor Market", *COVID Economics*, 29:164–192. Available at (consulted 20th October): https://cepr.org/sites/default/files/CovidEconomics29.pdf.

Brandolini, A. (1999), "The Distribution of Personal Income in Post-War Italy: Source Description, Data Quality and the Time Pattern of Income Inequality", *Temi di discussione*, No. 350. Rome: Banca d'Italia.

Bresson, F., and K. Labar (2007), *"Leftist", "Rightist" and Intermediate Decompositions of Poverty: Variations with an Application to China from 1990 to 2003*. Working Papers 76, ECINEQ, Society for the Study of Economic Inequality. Available at (consulted 20th October): http://www.ecineq.org/milano/WP/ECINEQ2007-76.pdf.

Braudel F. (1958), Histoire et Sciences sociales: La longue durée, Annales, Année 1958, 13 (4): pp. 725–753.

Brzeziński, M. (2013), *Income Polarization and Economic Growth*, National Bank of Poland Working Paper, No. 147, Warsaw. Available at (consulted 20th October): https://www.nbp.pl/publikacje/materialy_i_studia/147_en.pdf.

Cajner, T., Crane, L. D., Decker, R. A., Grigsby, J., Hamins-Puertolas, A., Hurst, E., Kurz, C. and Yildirmaz, A. *The U.S. Labor Market during the Beginning of the Pandemic Recession*. Working Paper no. 27159, National Bureau of Economic Research, Cambridge MA, 2020. Available at (consulted 20th October): https://www.nber.org/ papers/w27159.

Calderón, C. and A. Chong (2009), "Labor Market Institutions and Income Inequality: An Empirical Exploration", *Public Choice*, 138 (1): pp. 65–81.

Capaldo J, (2014). *The Trans-Atlantic Trade and Investment Partnership: European Disintegration, Unemployment and Instability*, GDAE Working Papers 14–03, GDAE, Tufts University. Available at (consulted 19th October 2021): https://sites.tufts.edu/ gdae/files/2019/10/14-03CapaldoTTIP.pdf.

Card, D. and J. E. Dinardo (2002), *Skill Biased Technological Change and Rising Wage Inequality: Some Problems and Puzzles*, National Bureau of Economic Research, Working Paper, No. 8769, Cambridge MA.

Celse, J. (2017) "An Experimental Investigation of the Impact of Absolute and Relative inequalities on Individual Satisfaction", *Journal of Happiness Studies 18*: pp. 939–958.

Chakravarty, S. R. (2009), *Inequality, Polarization and Poverty: Advances in Distributional Analysis*, New York, NY: Springer-Verlag.

Chakravarty, S. R. (2015), *Inequality, Polarization and Conflict: An Analytical Study*, New York NY: Springer-Verlag.

Chatterjee, M. (2014), *Multidimensional Poverty*, Oxford Poverty & Human Development Initiative (OPHI) Oxford Department of International Development. Available at (consulted 19th October 2021): https://www.ophi.org.uk/wp-content/uploads/MD -poverty.

Chen, J., Liu, E., Luo, J., & Song, Z. (2020). "The Economic Impact of COVID-19 in China: Evidence from City-to-City Truck Flows" Available at (consulted 20th October): https://scholar.princeton.edu/sites/default/files/ernestliu/files/truck_f low_and_covid19-42.pdf.

Cheng, E. (2021). "China says retail sales grew 17.7% in April, missing expectations". *CNBC*, May 16th .

Cho, S. J., and Winters, J. V. (2020) *The Distributional Impacts of Early Employment Losses from COVID-19*. Discussion Paper no. 13266, Bonn: IZA – Institute for Labor Economics. Available at (consulted 20th October): https://covid-19.iza.org/publi cations/dp13266/.

Clementi, F. and F. Schettino (2015), "Declining Inequality in Brazil in the 2000s: What is Hidden Behind?", *Journal of International Development*, 27 (7): pp 929–952.

Clementi, F., A. Dabalen, V. Molini and F. Schettino (2017), "When the Centre Cannot Hold: Patterns of Polarization in Nigeria", *Review of Income and Wealth*, 63 (4): pp. 608–632.

Clementi, F., V. Molini and F. Schettino (2018), "All That Glitters is not Gold: Polarization Amid Poverty Reduction in Ghana", *World Development*, vol. 102: pp. 275–291.

Clementi, F., M. Fabiani, and V. Molini (2019a). "The Devil is in the Detail: Growth, Polarization, and Poverty Reduction in Africa in the Last Two Decades", *Journal of African Economies,* 28 (4): 408–434.

Clementi, F., H. A. Khan, V. Molini, F. Schettino, and K. Soudi (2019b). *Polarization and Its Discontents: Morocco Before and After the Arab Spring*. Policy Research Working Paper 9049, Washington, DC:World Bank. Available at (consulted 20th October): https://openknowledge.worldbank.org/handle/10986/32658.

Clementi, F., A. Dabalen, V. Molini and F. Schettino, (2020a). "We forgot the middle class! Inequality underestimation in a changing Sub-Saharan Africa," *The Journal of Economic Inequality*, 18(1): 45–70.

Clementi, F., M. Fabiani and V. Molini (2020b), "How Polarized is Sub-Saharan Africa? A Look at the Regional Distribution of Consumption Expenditure in the 2000s", *Oxford Economic Papers*. 73 (2): pp. 796–819,.

Conti, P. L., M. G. Pittau and R. Zelli (2006), "Metodi non parametrici nell'analisi della distribuzione del reddito: problemi empirici ed aspetti metodologici", *Rivista di Politica Economica*, 96 (3): pp. 195–242.

Cowell, F. A. and E. Flachaire (2015), "Statistical Methods for Distributional Analysis", in A. B. Atkinson and F. Bourguignon. (eds.), *Handbook of Income Distribution*, vol. 2A, Amsterdam: North-Holland, pp. 359–465,.

Cowell, F. A. (2016), "Inequality and Poverty Measures." In M. D. Adler and M. Fleurbaey (eds.) *Oxford Handbook of Well-Being and Public Policy*, Oxford: Oxford University Press, pp. 82–125.

Cugat, G., and F. Narita (2020) *How COVID-19 Will Increase Inequality in Emerging Markets and Developing Economies.* IMF Blog, October 29th. Available at (consulted 20th October): https://blogs.imf.org/2020/10/29/how-covid-19-will-increase-inequality-in-emerging-markets.

Dabla-Norris, E., K. Kochhar, N. Suphaphiphat, F. Ricka and E. Tsounta (2015), *Causes and Consequences of Income Inequality: A Global Perspective*, Staff Discussion Note, no. 13, Washington DC: International Monetary Fund.

Dagum, C. (1987), "Gini Ratio", in J. Eatwell, M. Milgate and P. Newman (eds.), *The New Palgrave Dictionary of Economics*, vol. II, London: Macmillan, pp. 529–532.

D'Angelo P. and M. Virdis (2013), *Operazione Blue Moon – Eroina di Stato* [documentary film], Mattite Spezzate and Blue Film in collaboration with Rai Storia.

De Sena P and S D'Acunto (2020) *La corte di Karlsruhe, il mito della "neutralità" della politica monetaria e i nodi del processo di integrazione europea*, SIDIblog – blog della Società italiana di diritto internazionale e del diritto dell'Unione europea. Available at (consulted 20th October): http://www.sidiblog.org/2020/05/14/la-corte-di-karlsruhe-il-mito-della-neutralita-della-politica-monetaria-e-i-nodi-del-processo-di-integrazione-europea/.

Deutsch, J., A. Fusco and J. Silber (2013), "The BIP Trilogy (Bipolarization, Inequality and Polarization): One Saga but Three Different Stories", *Economics: The Open-Access, Open-Assessment E-Journal*, 7 (22): pp. 1–33.

De Vries, Jan (2008). *The industrious revolution: consumer behavior and the household economy, 1650 to the present.* New York: Cambridge University Press.

Doerr, S., and Gambacorta, L. (2020) *COVID-19 and Regional Employment in Europe.* Bulletin no. 16, Basel: Bank of International Settlements. Available at (consulted 6th November 2021): https://www.bis.org/publ/bisbull16.htm.

Duclos, J.-Y. and A. M. Taptué (2015), "Polarization", in A. B. Atkinson and F. Bourguignon. (eds.), *Handbook of Income Distribution*, vol. 2A, Amsterdam: Elsevier, pp. 301–358.

Easterly, W. (2001), "Middle Class Consensus and Economic Development", *Journal of Economic Growth*, 6 (4): pp. 317–336.

Engels, F. (2010 [1891]), Introduction to Karl Marx's *The Civil War in France. In Marx/Engels Collected Works*, vol. 27, London, Lawrence & Wishart, pp. 179–192.

Esteban, J.-M. and D. Ray (1994), "On the Measurement of Polarization", *Econometrica*, 62 (4): pp. 819–851.

Esteban, J.-M. and D. Ray (1999), "Conflict and Distribution", *Journal of Economic Theory*, 87 (2): pp. 379–415.

Esteban, J.-M. and D. Ray (2008), "Polarization, Fractionalization and Conflict", *Journal of Peace Research*, 45 (2): pp. 163–182.

Esteban, J.-M. and D. Ray (2011), "Linking Conflict to Inequality and Polarization", *The American Economic Review*, 101 (4): pp. 1345–1374.

Fan, C. C. (1997). Uneven Development and Beyond: Regional Development Theory in Post-Mao China. *Blackwell Publishers Ltd.*

Fares, M. and Dustine Volz (2017), 'It's made in Vietnam!' At inauguration, origin of red Trump hats shocks many, *Reuters*, January 21st. Available at (consulted 19th October 2021): https://www.reuters.com/article/us-usa-trump-inauguration-hats-idUSKB N1542YL.

Federal Reserve Bank of St. Louis (U.S. Office of Management and Budget and Federal Reserve Bank of St. Louis) (2021), *Federal Debt: Total Public Debt as Percent of Gross Domestic Product.* Available at (consulted 19th October): https://fred.stlouisfed.org/ series/GFDEGDQ188S.

Feenstra, R. and G. H. Hanson (1996), "Globalization, Outsourcing, and Wage Inequality", *American Economic Review*, 86 (2): pp. 240–245.

Feenstra, R. and G. H. Hanson (1999), "The Impact of Outsourcing and High-Technology Capital on Wages: Estimates for the United States, 1979–1990", *Quarterly Journal of Economics*, 114 (3): pp. 907–940.

Feenstra, R. and G. H. Hanson (2003), "Global Production Sharing and Rising Inequality: A Survey of Trade and Wage", in E. K. Choi and J. Harrigan (eds.), *Handbook of International Trade*, Malden, Massachusetts: Blackwell, pp. 146–185.

Fehr, E., and K. M. Schmidt (1999), "A Theory of Fairness, Competition, and Cooperation." *Quarterly Journal of Economics 114*: pp. 817–868.

Fiegehen, G. C., P. S. Lansley and A. D. Smith (1977), *Poverty and Progress in Britain 1953–1973*, Cambridge: Cambridge University Press.

Figini, P. and H. Görg (2011), "Does Foreign Direct Investment Affect Wage Inequality? An Empirical Investigation", *The World Economy*, 34 (9): pp. 1455–1475.

Fitch Ratings (2020), *Global QE Asset Purchases to Reach USD6 Trillion in 2020*, Non rating action commentary, 24th April. Available at (consulted 19th October 2021): https://www.fitchratings.com/research/sovereigns/global.

Flaherty, H. J, Liu, M. I, Ding, L., Dong, B., Ding, Q., Li, X., & Xiao, S. (2007). "China: The Aging Giant", *Journal of the American Geriatrics Society.* 55 (8): pp. 1295–1300.

Foster, J. E. and M. C. Wolfson (1992), *Polarization and the Decline of the Middle Class: Canada and the US*, Working Paper no. 31, Oxford: Oxford Poverty and Human Development Initiative, University of Oxford.

Foster, J. E. and M. C. Wolfson (2010), "Polarization and the Decline of the Middle Class: Canada and the US", *Journal of Economic Inequality*, 8: pp. 243–273.

Franzini, M. and M. Pianta (2009), "Mechanisms of Inequality: An Introduction", *International Review of Applied Economics*, 23 (3): pp. 233–237.

Franzini, M. and M. Pianta (2016), *Disuguaglianze. Quante sono, come combatterle*, Bari: Laterza.

Franzini, M. (2007), "Le disuguaglianze economiche: mercato, società e politica. Un'introduzione", *Meridiana*, vols. 59–60, pp. 9–31.

Frederiksen, A. and O. Poulsen (2010), *Increasing Income Inequality: Productivity, Bargaining And Skill-Upgrading*, Discussion Paper no. 4791, Bonn: IZA Institute of Labor Economics.

Freeman, R. (2010), "Does Inequality Increase Economic Output?", in D. Grusky (eds.), *Controversies about Inequality*, Stanford CA: Stanford University Press.

Fuceri, D. and P. Loungani (2013), "Who Let the Gini Out?", *Finance & Development*, 50 (4): pp. 25–27.

Furceri, D., Loungani, P., Ostry, J. D., and Pizzuto, P. (2020) "Will COVID-19 Affect Inequality? Evidence from Past Pandemics", *COVID Economics*, 12: pp.138–157.

Galasso, V. (2020) "COVID: Not a Great Equalizer", *CESifo Economic Studies*, 66: pp. 376–393.

Garrote Sanchez, D., Gomez Parra, N., Ozden, C., Rijkers, B., Viollaz, M., and Winkler, H. (2020) *Who on Earth Can Work from Home?* Policy Research Paper no. 9347, Washington DC: World Bank. Available at (consulted 20th October 2021): https://openknowledge.worldbank.org/handle/10986/34277.

Gini, C. (1912), *Variabilità e mutabilità*, Bologna: Tipografia di Paolo Cuppin.

Gunder, F. A. (1998), *Reorient: Global Economy in the Asian Age,* Berkley: University of California Press.

Gradín, C. & Wu, Binbin, (2020). "Income and consumption inequality in China: A comparative approach with India," *China Economic Review*, Elsevier, vol. 62 (C).

Hayami, Akira (2015), *Japan's Industrious Revolution: Economic and Social Transformations in the Early Modern Period.* Tokyo: Springer, pp. 95–97.

Hilferding, R. (1910), *Finance Capital: A Study of the Latest Phase of Capitalist Development,* available at: https://www.marxists.org/archive/hilferding/1910/finkap/index.htm.

Hill, R. V., and Narayan, A. (2020) *Covid-19 and Inequality: A Review of The Evidence on Likely Impact and Policy Options*, Technical Report, Centre for Disaster Protection, London. Available at: https://static1.squarespace.com/static/5c9d3c35ab1a62515124d7e9/t/5fe218df9507416a29d49d32/1608653024173/WP_3_22Dec.pdf [accessed on 5 November 2021].

Hobson, J. A. (1902), *Imperialism: A Study.* New York: James Pott & Co.

Hou, J., S. Gelb, and L. Calabrese, (2017) The Shift in Manufacturing Employment in China. Overseas Development Institute (ODI). *Supporting Economic Transformation (SET) Background Paper.*

Huang, T. and N. R. Lardy (2020). "China's fiscal stimulus is good news, but will it be enough?" *Peterson Institute for International Economics*, 26th May.

Hungerford, T. L. (2013), *Changes in Income Inequality among U.S. Tax Filers between 1991 and 2006: The Role of Wages, Capital Income, and Taxes*, January 23rd. Available at (consulted 20th October 2021): https://ssrn.com/abstract=2207372.

Hughes, D. W. (2018). *A Primer in Economic Multipliers and Impact Analysis Using Input-Output Models. UT Extension Institute of Agriculture*, University of Tennessee. Available at (consulted 20th November 2021): https://extension.tennessee.edu/publications/Documents/W644.pdf.

International Labour Organization (ILO) (2009) *World of Work Report 2009: The Global Jobs Crisis and Beyond / International Institute for Labour Studies.* Geneva: ILO.

International Labour Organization, Organisation for Economic Co-operation and Development (ILO/OECD) (2015), *The Labour Share in G20 Economies*, Report prepared for the G20 Employment Working Group Antalya, Turkey, 26th-27th February. Available at (consulted 20th October 2021): https://www.oecd.org/g20/topics/employment-and-social-policy/The-Labour-Share-in-G20-Economies.pdf.

International Labour Organization (ILO) (2020a), *ILO Monitor: COVID-19 and the world of work. Second edition – Updated estimates and analysis.* Available at: www.ilo.org.

International Labour Organization (ILO) (2020c), *World statistic: The enormous burden of poor working conditions.* Available at (consulted 18th Oct 2020): https://www.ilo.org/moscow/areas-of-work/occupational-safety-and-health/WCMS_249278/lang.

International Labour Organization (ILO) (2021) *World Employment and Social Outlook: Trends 2021*, International Labour Office, Geneva. Available at: https://www.ilo.org/global.

International Monetary Fund (IMF) (2008), *World Economic Outlook, October 2008: Financial Stress, Downturns, and Recoveries.* Available at (consulted 20th October): https://www.imf.org/en/Publications/WEO/Issues/2016/12/31/World-Economic-Outlook-October-2008-Financial-Stress-Downturns-and-Recoveries-22028.

International Monetary Fund (IMF) (2019) *World Economic Outlook, October 2019 Global Manufacturing Downturn, Rising Trade Barriers*, https://www.imf.org/en/Publications/WEO/Issues/2019/10/01/world-economic-outlook-october-2019.

International Monetary Fund (IMF) (2019) IMF Annual Report – Our Connected World. Available at (consulted 20th October): https://www.imf.org/external/pubs/ft/ar/2019/eng/assets/pdf/imf-annual-report-2019.pdf.

International Monetary Fund (IMF) (2020). World Economic Outlook, October 2020: A Long and Difficult Ascent. Washington DC: IMF Publication Services. Available at (last accessed 6th November 2021): https://www.imf.org/en/Publications/WEO/Issues/2020/09/30/world-economic-outlook-october-2020.

Isaacs, K. P., Choudhury, S., Li, Z., and Nicchitta. I. A. (2021) *The Growing Gap in Life Expectancy by Income: Recent Evidence and Implications for the Social Security Retirement Age*. Technical Report, Congressional Research Service, Washington DC. Available at (consulted 20th November 2021): https://crsreports.congress.gov/prod uct/pdf/R/R44846.

Jagger, M and K Richards (1971), "Sister Morphine", song from the album *Sticky Fingers*.

Jaumotte, F. and C. Osorio-Buitron (2015), "Power from the People", *Finance & Development*, 52 (1): pp. 29–31.

Jinping, X. (2017) *Jointly Shoulder Responsibility of Our Times, Promote Global Growth*, speech given to the opening session of the World Economic Forum Annual Meeting, Davos, 17th January. Available at (consulted 20th October 2021): https://america .cgtn.com/2017/01/17/full-text-of-xi-jinping-keynote-at-the-world-economic-forum.

Joyce, R., and Xu, X. (2020) *Sector Shutdowns During the Coronavirus Crisis: Which Workers are Most Exposed?* Briefing Note no. 278, London: Institute for Fiscal Studies. Available at (consulted 20th October 2021): https://ifs.org.uk/publications/14791.

JP Morgan (2013), "The Euro are adjustment: about halfway there", *Europe Economic Research*, 28th May. Available at (consulted 19th October 2021): https://www.eur ope-solidarity.eu/documents/ES1_euro-area-adjustment.pdf.

Judzik, D., H. A. Khan and L. Spagnlo (2016) "Social capabilities–based flexicurity for a learning economy", *Sage Economic and Labour Relations Review*, 27 (3).

Jung, Hong-Sang & Thorbecke, E. (2001), "The Impact of Public Education Expenditure on Human Capital, Growth, and Poverty in Tanzania and Zambia: A General Equilibrium Approach", *Journal of Policy Modeling* 25 (8): pp. 701–725.

Keqiang, Li (2020), *Report on The Work of The Government*. Delivered by Premier Li Keqiang at the Third Session of the 13th National People's Congress of the People's Republic of China on May 22nd. Available at (consulted 7th November 2021): http:// english.www.gov.cn/premier/news/202005/30/content_WS5ed197f3c6d0b3f0e 94990da.html.

Khan H.A. and Thorbecke E. (1988). *Macroeconomic Effects and Diffusion of Alternative Technologies within a Social Accounting Matrix Framework*, Aldershot: Gower.

Khan, H. A. (1983) *Technology, Energy, Distribution and Balance of Payments: A Macroeconomic Framework*, unpublished dissertation, Ithaca, New York: Cornell University.

Khan H.A. and Thorbecke E. (1989), 'Macroeconomic effects of technology choice: mul-tiplier and structural path analysis within a SAM framework,' *Journal of Policy Modelling*, vol. 11, no.1.

Khan, H. A. (1997a), *Technology, Energy and Development: The South Korean Transition*. Cheltenham, United Kingdom: Edward Elgar.

Khan, H. A. (1997b), "Ecology, Inequality and Poverty: The Case of Bangladesh", *Asian Development Review*, 15 (2).

Khan, H. A. (1998), *Technology, Development, and Democracy*, Cheltenham, UK: Edward Elgar.

Khan, H. A. (2004), *Innovation and Growth in East Asia: The Future of Miracles*, New York: Houndsmills and London: Macmillan/Palgrave.

Khan, H. A. (2006) "Value, Social Capabilities, Alienation: The Right to Revolt", *Econpapers*, link?.

Khan, H. A. (2007)" A Theory of Deep Democracy and Economic Justice in the Age of Postmodernism", *Econpapers*. Available at (consulted 20th October) http://econpap ers.repec.org/paper/tkyfseres/2007cf468.htm.

Khan, H. A. (2010). "China's Development Strategy and Energy Security", in Amelia Santos-Paulino and Guanghua Wan ed. *The Rise of China and India: Development Strategies and Lessons*, London: Palgrave/Macmillan.

Khan, H. A., (2021), "COVID-19 in South Africa: An Intersectional Perspective based on Socio-economic modelling and Indigenous Knowledge Base", *Econpapers*. Available at (consulted 20th October) https://econpapers.repec.org/paper/pramprapa/108 321.htm.

Khan, H. A., F. Schettino and A. Gabriele (2017) *Polarization and the Middle Class in China: a Non-Parametric Evaluation Using CHNS and CHIP Data*, MPRA Paper 86133, University Library of Munich, Germany.

Kolm, S. (1976), "Unequal Inequalities, I." *Journal of Economic Theory 12*: pp. 416–442.

Krugman, P. (2002) "For Richer", *New York Times Sunday Magazine*, 20th October.

Kuznets, S. (1971), *Economic Growth of Nations: Total Output and Production Structure*. Cambridge, MA: Harvard University Press.

Lakner, C. and B. Milanović (2016), "Global Income Distribution: From the Fall of the Berlin Wall to the Great Recession", World Bank Economic Review, 30 (2): pp. 203–232.

Lakner, C., Mahler D.C., Negre M. and E. B. Prydz (2020), "How Much Does Reducing Inequality Matter for Global Poverty?", GLOBAL POVERTY MONITORING TECHNICAL NOTE 13, The World Bank Group.

Lanza, G. (2015), *La misurazione della disuguaglianza economica. Approcci, metodi e strumenti*, Milano: Franco Angeli.

Lau, L. J. (2020). *On Twin Circulations*. Lecture presented at the Center for Industrial Development and Environmental Governance, Tsinghua University date?.

Leibbrandt, A., and R. López-Pérez (2012), "An Exploration of Third and Second Party Punishment in Ten Simple Games." *Journal of Economic Behavior & Organization 84*: pp. 753–766.

Lenin V. I. (1964 [1899]) The Development of Capitalism in Russia, *Collected Works*, 4th Edition, Moscow, 1964, *Volume 3*, pp. 21–608.

Lenin V I. (2010 [1917a]), *Imperialism the Highest Stage of Capitalism,* London: Penguin.

Lenin, V. I. (2019 [1917b]), *State and Revolution*, Northport, NY: WellRead Books.

Levy, F. and R. J. Murnane (1992), "U.S. Earnings Levels and Earnings Inequality: A Review of Recent Trends and Proposed Explanations", *Journal of Economic Literature*, 30 (3): pp. 1333–1381.

Lewis, W. A. (1955), *The Theory of Economic Growth*. London: Allen & Unwin.

Liu, K. (2021). "COVID-19 and the Chinese economy: impacts, policy responses and implications," *International Review of Applied Economics*, 35 (2).

Liu, K. (2019). "China's reserve requirements and their effects on economic output and assets markets during 2008–2018", *International Journal of Monetary Economics and Finance* 12 (3): pp. 212–232.

Longo, M. (2019), Draghi: quel cocktail inedito di misure non convenzionali (Draghi: an unusual cocktail of unconventional measures), *Il Sole 24 Ore*, 24th October 2019.

Lops, V. (2012), La bolla mondiale del debito. Ci sono ragioni per credere che Usa, Giappone e Ue rientreranno mai dai rispettivi buchi di bilancio? (The world debt bubble. Will the USA, Japan and the EU ever manage to get out of their debt traps?), *Il Sole 24 ore*, 9th November.

Lorenz, M. O. (1905), "Methods of Measuring the Concentration of Wealth", *Publications of the American Statistical Association*, 9 (70): pp. 209–219.

Lustig, N., and Tommasi, M. (2020) *Covid-19 and Social Protection of Poor and Vulnerable Groups in Latin America: A Conceptual Framework*. Policy Document Series no. 8, UNDP Latin America and the Caribbean. Available at (consulted 6th November 2021): https://www.latinamerica.undp.org/content/rblac/en/home/library/crisis.

Ma, C., Rogers, J., and Zhou, S. (2020) *Modern Pandemics: Recession and Recovery*. International Finance Discussion Papers no. 1295, Board of Governors of the Federal Reserve System, Washington DC. Available at (consulted 6th November 2021): https://doi.org/10.17016/IFDP.2020.1295.

Madgavkar, A., White, O., Krishnan, M., Mahajan, D., and Azcue, X. (2020) *Covid-19 and Gender Equality: Countering the Regressive Effects*. Technical Report, McKinsey Global Institute. Available at (consulted 6th November 2021): https://www.mckin sey.com/featured-insights/future-of-work/covid-19-and-gender-equality.

Madsen, J. B., Islam, Md. R., and Doucouliagos, H. (2018) "Inequality, Financial Development and Economic Growth in the OECD, 1870–2011", *European Economic Review*, 101: pp. 605–624.

Mahler, D. G., Yonan, N., Lakner, C., Castañeda Aguilar, R. A., and Wu, A. (2021) "Updated Estimates of the Impact of COVID-19 on Global Poverty: Turning the Corner on the Pandemic in 2021?" *World Bank Blog*, June 24th. Available at (consulted 6th November 2021): https://blogs.worldbank.org/opendata/updated-estima tes-impact-covid-19-global.

Malpass, D. (2020) *Reversing the Inequality Pandemic: Speech by World Bank Group President David Malpass*. Speech at Frankfurt School of Finance and Management,

October 8th. Available at (consulted 6th November 2021): https://nl4worldbank
.org/2020/10/08/reversing-the-inequality-pandemic.

Marx K. (1968 [1877]) Letter to the editor of the *Otecestvenniye Zapisky,* Nov. 1877, *Marx and Engels Correspondence*; International Publishers.

Marx, K. (2010 [1848]), Speech on the Question of Free Trade. In *Marx/Engels Collected Works*, vol. 6, London, Lawrence & Wishart Electric Book: pp. 463.465.

Marx, K. (2010 [1858]), "The Original Text of the Second and the Beginning of the Third Chapter of A Contribution to the Critique of Political Economy," in *Marx and Engels Collected Works* Vol. 29. Lawrence and Wishart Electric Book.

Marx, K. (2010 [1859]) A Contribution to the Critique of Political Economy: Part One, In *Marx/Engels Collected Works*, vol. 29, London, Lawrence & Wishart Electric Book.

Marx, K. (2010 [1861–3]) Theories of Surplus Value. In *Marx/Engels Collected Works*, vols. 30–34, London, Lawrence & Wishart.

Marx, K. (1990 [1867]), *Capital: A Critical Analysis of Capitalist Production, Volume 1.* Translation by Ben Fowkes, London: Penguin Books.

Marx, K. (1990 [1894]), *Capital: A Critical Analysis of Capitalist Production, Volume 3.* Translation by David Fernbach, London: Penguin Books.

Marx, K. and Engels, F. (2010 [1847]), Manifesto of the Communist Party. In *Marx/Engels Collected Works*, vol. 6, London, Lawrence & Wishart: pp. 477–520.

Marx, K. (2010 [1841]), The Difference Between the Democritean and Epicurean Philosophy of Nature. In *Marx/Engels Collected Works*, vol. 1, London, Lawrence & Wishart: pp. 25–109.

McKinsey & co. (2018), *Rising corporate debt: Peril or promise?*, Discussion Paper 18 June 2018.

Meng Q., A. Mills, L. Wang and Q. Han (2019) "What can we learn from China's health system reform?" *British Medical Journal*, 365.

Milanović, B. (2005), *Worlds Apart. Measuring International and Global Inequality*, Princeton: Princeton University Press.

Milanović, B. (2019), *Capitalism, Alone The Future of the System That Rules the World*, Harvard University Press.

Miller, R. (1984), *Analyzing Marx*. Princeton: Princeton University Press.

Miller, D. & Blair, P. D. (2009) *Input-Output Analysis: Foundations and Extension 2nd Edition*. Cambridge: Cambridge University Press.

Mincer J. (1958), "Investment in Human Capital and Personal Income Distribution", *Journal of Political Economy*, 66 (2): pp. 281–302.

Mongey, S., Pilossoph, L., and Weinberg, A. (2020) *Which Workers Bear the Burden of Social Distancing?* Working Paper no. 27085, Cambridge MA: National Bureau of Economic Research. Available at (consulted 6th November 2021): http://www.nber .org/papers/w27085.

Niño-Zarazúa, M., L. Roope, and F. Tarp (2017), "Global Inequality: Relatively Lower, Absolutely Higher." *Review of Income and Wealth 63*: pp. 661–684.

Nissanov, Z. and M.G. Pittau, (2015), "Measuring changes in the Russian middle class between 1992 and 2008: a nonparametric distributional analysis". *Empirical Economics*. 50. 10.1007/s00181-015-0929-8.

National Bureau of Statistics of China (2021). Statistical Communique of the People's Republic of China on the 2020 National Economic and Social Development.

Nolan, B., M. G. Richiardi and L. Valenzuela (2019), "The Drivers of Income Inequality in Rich Countries", *Journal of Economic Surveys*, 33 (4): pp. 1285–1324.

Organization for Economic Co-operation and Development (OECD) (2011), *Divided We Stand: Why Inequality Keeps Rising*, Paris: OECD Publishing.

Organization for Economic Co-operation and Development (OECD) (2012), *Inequality in Labor Income – What are its Drivers and How Can it be Reduced?*, OECD Economics Department, Policy Note, no. 8, Paris: OECD.

Organization for Economic Co-operation and Development (OECD) (2020), Health Data, https://www.oecd.org/health/.

Pala, G. (1981), *L'ultima crisi*, Milan: Franco Angeli.

Pala, G. (2019), *L'ombra senza corpo*, Naples: Edizioni La Città del Sole.

Palomino, J. C., Rodríguez, J. G., and Sebastian, R. (2020) "Wage Inequality and Poverty Effects of Lockdown and Social Distancing in Europe", *European Economic Review*, 129: 103564.

Peet, John (2012) "So much to do, so little time", *The Economist*, 17th November.

Pareto, V. (1964 [1897a]), *Cours d'économie politique*, Geneva: Droz.

Pareto, V. (1897b), "Aggiunta allo studio della curva delle entrate", *Giornale degli Economisti*, 14 (8), pp. 15–26.

Pareto V. (1896 [1964]), "La courbe de la répartition de la richesse", reprinted in Busino G. (ed.), *OEeuvres complètes de Vilfredo Pareto, Tome 3: Écrits sur la courbe de la répartition de la richesse*, Geneva: Droz, pp. 1–15.

Peirlinck, M., Linka, K., Costabal, F. S., & Kuhl, E. (2020). "Outbreak dynamics of COVID-19 in China and the United States", *Biomechanics and Modeling in Mechanobiology*. 19 (6).

Phillipon, T. and A. Reshef (2012), "Wages and Human Capital in the U.S. Finance Industry: 1909–2006", *Quarterly Journal of Economics*, 127 (4): pp. 1551–1609.

Piketty, T. (2014), *Capital in the Twenty-First Century*, Cambridge, MA: Belknap Press.

Piketty, T. (2020), *Capital and Ideology*, Harvard: Harvard University Press.

Pires, L. N., de Carvalho, L. B., & Rawet, E. L. (2020), "Multi-Dimensional Inequality and COVID-19 in Brazil", *Investigación Económica*, 80 (315): pp. 33–58.

Pouliakas, K., and J. Branka (2020), *EU Jobs at Highest Risk of COVID-19 Social Distancing: Will the Pandemic Exacerbate Labour Market Divide?* Working Paper no. 13281, Bonn: IZA – Institute for Labour Economics. Available at (consulted 6th November 2021): https://covid-19.iza.org/publications/dp13281/.

Pozzan R. (2014), "Il segreto sul piatto", *Report* [documentary series], produced by the Italian state broadcaster, aired 19th October.

Pulliam, S., K. Kelly and C. Mollenkamp (2010) "Hedge Funds Try 'Career Trade' Against Euro", *Wall Street Journal*, 26th February.

Ravallion, M. (2003), "The Debate on Globalization, Poverty and Inequality: Why Measurement Matters." *International Affairs, 79*: pp. 739–753.

Ravallion, M. (2005), "A Poverty-Inequality Trade Off?" *Journal of Economic Inequality, 3*: pp. 169–181.

Ravallion, M. (2015), "The Luxembourg Income Study", *Journal of Economic Inequality, 13*: pp. 527–547.

Ravallion, M. (2018), "Inequality and Globalization: A Review Essay." *Journal of Economic Literature, 56*: pp. 620–642.

Rickards, J. (2011) *Currency Wars: The Making of the Next Global Crisis*, London: Portfolio.

Sandmo, A. (2015), "The Principal Problem in Political Economy: Income Distribution in the History of Economic Thought", in A. B. Atkinson and F. Bourguignon (eds.), *Handbook of Income Distribution*, Amsterdam: North-Holland, vol. 2A: pp. 3–65.

Schettino, F (2002), "Dollarizzazione e imperialismo", *La Contraddizione*, 92, Rome.

Schettino F (2011), "L'irresistibile declino", *La Contraddizione*, 135, Rome.

Schettino F (2013), "Diluvio di liquidità", *La Contraddizione*, no.143, Rome.

Schettino F (2015), "Il bazooka, l'Europa e la bolla", *La Contraddizione*, 150, Rome.

Schettino F (2018), *La crisis irreseulta*, Editorial Academica Espanola.

Schettino, F. and F. Clementi (2020) *Crisi, disuguaglianze e povertà*, Naples: Edizioni La Città del Sole.

Schettino, F. and H. A. Khan (2020), "Income polarization in the USA: What happened to the middle class in the last few decades?", *Structural Change and Economic Dynamics*, 53 (C): pp. 149–161.

Schettino, F., A. Gabriele and H. A. Khan (2021), "Polarization and the middle class in China: A non-parametric evaluation using CHNS and CHIP data", *Structural Change and Economic Dynamics*, Elsevier, 57 (C): pp. 251–264.

Schumpeter, J. (1954), *Capitalism, Socialism, and Democracy*. London: George Allen and Unwin.

Scorsese, M. (2015), *The Wolf of Wall Street*, Paramount Pictures.

Sen A. (1972), *On Economic Inequality*, Oxford: Oxford University Press.

Sen A. (1985), *Commodities and Capabilities*, Amsterdam: North-Holland.

Shaikh, A. (2016). *Capitalism: Competition, Conflict, Crisis*, Oxford: Oxford University Press.

Shibata, I. (2021), "The Distributional Impact of Recessions: The Global Financial Crisis and the Covid-19 Pandemic Recession", *Journal of Economics and Business*, May-June 115: 105971.

Smith, A. (1776 [1961]), *An Inquiry into the Nature and Causes of the Wealth of Nations*. 2 Vols. London: Methuen.

Sraffa, P. (1926), "The Laws of Returns under Competitive Conditions", *The Economic Journal*, Vol. 36, No. 144 (Dec., 1926), pp. 535–550.

Streeten, P. (1984), "Basic Needs: Some Unsettled Questions", *World Development*, 12 (9): pp. 973–978.

Sugihara K. (1996), "The European Miracle and the East Asian Miracle. Towards a New Global Economic History." Sangyo to keizai XI, 12: 27–48.

Sugihara, K. (2003), "The East Asian Path of Economic Development: A Long-term Perspective", in G. Arrighi, T. Hamashita and M. Selden (eds.), *The Resurgence of East Asia. 500, 150 and 50 Year Perspectives*, London and New York: Routledge, pp. 78–123.

Sutter, K. M. & M. D. Sutherland (2021). "China's Economy: Current Trends and Issues", *Congressional Research Service*.

Švejnar J. and Thorbecke E. (1986), *Economic policies and agricultural performance: the case of Nepal 1960 – 1982*, Paris: Development Centre of the OECD.

Tang, F. (2021). "China's post-coronavirus consumer spending 'not enough' to drive growth, says prominent economist." *South China Morning Post*, 12th April.

Tarp, F. (2017), *Global Inequality: Trends and Issues Engagement on Strategies to Overcome Inequality in South Africa*; 1st-2nd June – Kievietskroon Country Lodge, Pretoria, South Africa. Available at: https://www.wider.unu.edu/sites/default/files/Events/PDF/Slides/Tarp_GlobalInequality.pdf.

Townsend, P. (1979), *Poverty in the United Kingdom*, London: Penguin.

Wade, R. H. (2004), "Is Globalization Reducing Poverty and Inequality?" *World Development 32*: pp. 567–589.

Wade, R. H. (2013), *Our Misleading Measure of Income and Wealth Inequality: The Standard Gini Coefficient*. Retrieved September 18, 2021, from TripleCrisis: http://triplecrisis.com/our-misleading-measure-of-income.

Wang, H., Zhang, M., Li, R. et al. (2021). "Tracking the effects of COVID-19 in rural China over time", *International Journal for Equity in Health* Vol. 20: 35.

Wang, H., Dill, S., Zhou, H., Ma, Y., Xue, H., Loyalka, P., Syliva, S., Boswell, M., Lin, J., & Rozelle, S. (2020). Off the Epicenter: COVID-19 Quarantine Controls and Employment, Education, and Health Impacts in Rural Communities. *Rural Education Action Program Working Paper*.

Wangping, J., Ke, H., Yang, S., Wenzhe, C., Shengshu, W., Shanshan, Y., Jianwei, W., Fuyin, K., Penggang, T., Jing, L., Miao, L., & Yao, H. (2020). "Extending SIR Prediction of the Epidemics Trend of COVID-19 in Italy and Compared with Hunan, China", *Frontiers in Medicine (Lausanne)*, Vol. 7: 169.

Watts, H. W. (1968), "An Economic Definition of Poverty", in D. P. Moynihan (ed.), *On Understanding Poverty*, New York: Basic Books, pp. 316–329.

Wilde, C. (2021). "The Infinity Loop". Cheung Kong Graduate School of Business Blog Post.

Wilkinson R. and K. Pickett (2009) *The Spirit Level: Why More Equal Societies Almost Always Do Better*, London: Allen Lane.

Willem te Velde, D. (2004) *"Foreign Direct Investment and Income Inequality in Latin America: Experiences and Policy Implications"*, London: Overseas Development Institute. Available at (consulted 20th October 2021): https://odi.org/en/publicati ons/foreign-direct-investment-income-inequality-and-poverty-experiences-and -policy-implications/.

Wolfson, M. C. (1994), "When Inequalities Diverge", *The American Economic Review*, 84 (2): pp. 353–358.

Wolfson, M. C. (1997), "Divergent Inequalities: Theory and Empirical Results", *Review of Income and Wealth*, 43 (4): pp. 401–421.

World Bank (2001), "The Concept of Poverty and Well-Being", in *Poverty Manual*, Chapter 1, Washington DC: World Bank Group.

World Bank (2018), *The World Bank Annual Report 2018*. Washington, DC: World Bank. © World Bank. https://openknowledge.worldbank.org/handle/10986/30326 License: CC BY-NC-ND 3.0 IGO.".

Yang, Z., Zeng, Z., Wang, K., Wong S., Liang, W., Zanin, M., Liu, P., Xudong, C., Gao, Z., Mai, Z., Liang, J., Liu, X., Li, S., Li, Y., Ye, F., Guan, W., Yang, Y., Li, F., Luo, S., Xie, Y., Liu, B., Wang, Z., Zhang, S., Wang, Y., Zhong, N., & He, J. (2020). "Modified SEIR and AI prediction of the epidemics trend of COVID-19 in China under public health interventions", *Journal of Thoracic Disease*, 12 (3): pp. 165–174.

Niño Zarazúa, M, Roope, L, Tarp, F (2017). "Global Inequality: Relatively Lower, Absolutely Higher", *Review of Income and Wealth*, 63(4): 661–684.

Zettelmeyer, J., Trebesch, C., Gulati, M., Monacelli, T., & Whelan, K. (2013). "The Greek debt restructuring: an autopsy". *Economic Policy*, 28(75): pp. 513–563.

Zhang, C. (2019). *How Much Do State-Owned Enterprises Contribute to China's GDP and Employment?* Washington DC: World Bank. Available at (consulted 7th November 2021): https://openknowledge.worldbank.org/handle/10986/32306.

Index